4—
5/22

San Francisco

BAJA CALIFORNIA

Cape St. Lucas

Socorro Island

Galapagos Islands   0°

PACIFIC OCEAN

Mocha Island

Clarence Island

OIL, ICE, and BONE

Arctic Whaler Nathaniel Ransom

OIL, ICE, and BONE

Arctic Whaler Nathaniel Ransom

HELEN HILLER FRINK

PETER E. RANDALL PUBLISHER
Portsmouth, New Hampshire
2015

ISBN 13: 978-1-931807-96-8
Library of Congress control number: 2014948877

Published by
Peter E. Randall Publisher LLC
Box 4726
Portsmouth, NH 03802
www.perpublisher.com

Book design: Grace Peirce, nhmuse.com

Contents

Discovery

By the time I was twelve years old, I was taller than my grand-mother, Nathaniel Ransom's oldest daughter, a tiny woman made of bone and wire and will. My father was her only child, and so she continued to live with him after he married, at forty-two, a widow with a seven-year-old daughter. Grudgingly she ceded to her daughter-in-law control of the cookstove, the pantry, and the clothesline. My mother bore four more children in seven years, a rambunctious brood brought to heel in part by Grandma. In her youth she taught elementary school, but when she married, she lost her classroom, for New Hampshire law assumed that wives would be supported by their husbands. In her seventies she gladly resumed teaching children, caring but seldom affectionate. We grandchildren picked up the wooden matches Daddy had used to light his pipe, and she dipped them into a bottle of Carter's blue ink, scratching out letters and numbers on stiff paper, holding them up until we learned them by heart. She read to us, she taught us to read, and rarely, she told stories.

Her summer bedroom was filled with oddities: opalescent abalone shells, a sandalwood fan laced together with narrow blue satin ribbon, a tiny lacquered chest of drawers, small wooden boxes inlaid with ivory, a little porcelain statue of a slender dog, an ivory-handled button hook. The straw matting that covered the floor prickled the back side of my thighs as I listened while she sat on her bed, with its high Golden Oak headboard. She told a story of one of her ancestors who became a mariner in northern seas. As I later remembered her tale, he and his shipmates came upon a vessel frozen into the ice and set out in a rowboat to go to its aid. But the rescuers too became trapped, doomed to freeze to death or perish of star-vation. At home, this ancestor's wife had the second sight. Suddenly she saw a vision of her husband, the frail rowboat, the towering icebergs, the fur-clad crewmates huddled together in frigid misery, and she knew that he was dead and that she would have to raise their children alone. This vision slept in my memory for the next fifty years.

My grandmother came from Mattapoisett, the same small coastal Massachusetts town that was home to my mother's father. In the way that families came together in the nineteenth century, the Ransoms and the Hillers knew each other as schoolmates and neighbors. The whaling stories I heard more often were those of my mother's grandfather, Captain Matthew Hiller. He first sailed as a fourteen-year-old greenhand aboard the whaling bark *Willis*. On his third voyage, his whaling ship, the *Altamaha*, was set afire by the Confederate raider *Alabama*. He told an even more thrilling yarn of being flung out of an overturned whaleboat, flailing to stay afloat as he was swept into the gaping maw of a whale, his pants cuff snagged by the whale's tooth. When I began researching his thread of family history, I read everything I could find about his hometown, Mattapoisett. There I happened upon an account of the great whaling disaster of 1871, when thirty-two whaleships were lost to Arctic ice. Immediately that catastrophe re-kindled the memory of my paternal Grandma's story, and I embarked on a detour that was to prove more intriguing than the original search for Matthew Hiller's history. The first account I stumbled upon was a *New York Times* article from November 1871 announcing the safe return to New Bedford of several officers and crew from the whaling vessels abandoned along the Alaskan coast. Among the names listed was Grandma's father: N. C. Ransom, third mate of the *John Wells*. Reading his name in the *New York Times* lent solid weight to Grandma's tale of her ancestor, lost in the frozen sea as he attempted to rescue other mariners.

Surprisingly, the identity of Grandma's unnamed ancestor who froze to death remained an enigma, for her father, Nathaniel Cushing Ransom, and his father before him died at home in their beds. In a sense, the detour led me astray, in the way that a wrong path can sometimes lead to serendipitous discoveries. What I learned in fact was that Grandma's father, whom she never spoke of, although she revered her mother, had kept journals of four whaling voyages made between 1860 and 1875. These journals came into the possession of the New Bedford Whaling Museum, where I read them for myself. The journals depict whaling not as the maniacal quest of *Moby Dick*, nor as the lucrative industry of historic coastal towns, but as daily, back-breaking toil in unimaginably harsh conditions in an alien and hostile part of the globe.

His is not a captain's story. In fifteen years of whaling, Nathaniel Ransom never rose above the rank of third mate. He was not a commanding presence. At nineteen, making his second voyage as harpooner, he was my size, five and a half feet tall. Fully grown with his boots on he measured five feet nine. By then—he was nearing thirty—whaling had aged him: he struggled with excruciating headaches, toothache, frequent colds, kidney disease, gastro-intestinal ailments caused by poor diet and dirty water, and with the chest pains that foretold the heart disease that killed him at sixty-one. In his twenties he played the accordion, but so poorly that it was "just an aggravation," and he sold his instrument to the king of a remote Pacific island. He sailed around the Cape of Good Hope, into the Indian Ocean, the Tasman Sea, and all the waters of the Pacific. He sailed the Atlantic, around Cape Horn, and north to the Okhotsk Sea, the Bering Sea, the Beaufort, and the Chukchi. He married, fathered children, left them behind in Mattapoisett, and went to sea, longing for his "darling wife" and "little family" while the ship carried him oceans away for years at a time. His factual detailing of each day's journey—the weather, winds, the chores aboard ship, and the whaling itself, which modern readers condemn as brutal slaughter—drew me in. Grandma's family album shows a photograph of him, thinning hair, a short beard, cheeks that dimpled when he smiled. In him I recognized his youngest son, my great-uncle Everett, a marine engineer who became a sort of grandfather to his sister's children. Nathaniel Ransom, this ancestor of a hundred years ago, grew familiar.

To give him voice, I have created a handful of conversations and scenes as they might have happened. Readers will discern those conversations and images springing from my imagination yet rooted in historical research and distinguish them from passages taken directly from his journals and from other logbooks. To preserve the flavor of the whaling era, most original spellings found in journals and logbooks have been retained. Every date and name is historically accurate. Locations differing from modern place-names have been identified as far as possible. It is my fondest hope that the creative passages woven over this factual network serve to bring Nathaniel Ransom to life as he lived and breathed.

Chapter I: A Man at Fourteen

Seaman on the Barnstable,
May 22, 1860–April 28, 1864

Shipping agent David Kempton looked down at the boy standing in front of his desk. Not yet five and a half feet, brown eyes, brown hair—the boy couldn't be more than fifteen. "So you want to go a-whaling, boy. How old are you?"

"Fourteen last November, sir. I can—"

"Write your name here, your town, your age," Kempton commanded, scowling. Captain Brownson would grouse a-plenty at taking on another greenhand. But seamen were scarce in this season. If the whaler docked at San Francisco, half the *Barnstable*'s crew would jump ship, eager to try panning for gold. Most New Bedford whalers put into Lahaina or Hilo or Honolulu instead, and shipped a bunch of "Kanakas," as they called the Sandwich Island natives. Or they scoured the New Bedford wharves for hands from Cape Verde or the Azores.

"Here you are, sir." The boy pushed the ledger toward him.

He wrote a legible, even hand, Kempton saw. "You're expecting a long lay then? Say one two-hundredth? Do you know what a lay is, boy?"

"Oh yes, sir. My brothers have told me. James—he's the oldest—he's home from the *General Scott*, and he was third mate. Captain Eldridge says he'll be first mate when she sails in September. Then Sidney—he's boatsteerer on the *Mary Wilder*, and Theodore's boatsteerer on the *Sun*. Joseph—he's next me—he's on the *Clara Bell*."

"I don't ship the whole family. Now, show me your hands."

The boy held out his calloused hands, a scrim of dirt beneath the fingernails, the slice of a splinter in the thumb of his right hand—used to farm labor then. Perhaps he'd do after all. He'd split and stow down the firewood the ship would take on before rounding the Cape of Good Hope. He could feed the livestock they'd bring on board in the Azores, and he'd know how to kill chickens when the time came.

Kempton peered through the spectacles perched on the end of his nose. "Read me the names above yours."

"Charles Smith, Pottsville, Pennsylvania. Enos Stanton, Azores."

Kempton pursed his lips and exhaled slowly. The boy could read and write well enough. Likely he was just out of the common school, and if he had finished eight grades at fourteen he had a sharp mind. "All right, you'll do." He reached across and gripped the boy's hand. A firm, brief clasp. "You sail Tuesday next, May twenty-second. Be sharp."

In an instant the boy was gone, loping down Johnny Cake Hill, the office door clanging behind him. Kempton laid his spectacles on the desk and rubbed his nose. He turned the office sign to "Closed" and put on his hat. Perhaps down at the wharves someone would know something about these Ransoms from Mattapoisett.

David Kempton owned thirteen-sixteenths of the *Barnstable*, having bought a controlling share in the whaling bark for twelve thousand dollars five years before. His ownership prodded him to hire on the ablest crewmen he could afford. Much would be left to the shrewd judgment of Captain Leonard Brownson, since Kempton would not be aboard when the ship reached the Azores or Cape Verde Islands. Some owners preferred white seamen, even as green foremast hands, for one-twentieth of New Bedford's inhabitants were non-white; some of them freed slaves, others seamen from the Azores, Cape Verde, or Pacific islands mingling with remnants of the Wampanoag Indians in a free-wheeling polyglot city, humming with industry, lubricated and glowing with whale oil.

"Yes, he was a cabin boy," my mother would say whenever anyone mentioned that her grandfather, Matthew Hiller, had gone whaling at fourteen. The cabin boy was a kind of servant to the ship's officers; sweeping, tidying up, washing the captain's laundry if he bothered with that sort of thing. The job seemed safe enough for a fourteen-year-old. Only Matthew Hiller was no cabin boy, nor was Nathaniel Ransom. Both youths began whaling as seamen, sent into the dank forecastle below decks with two dozen twenty- and thirty-year-old foremast hands. Young Nathaniel Ransom jumped at the mate's orders, scrambled up the rigging, pulled his oar in the whaleboat, and sliced blubber with the two-handled mincing knife. In 1860 child labor was a fact of existence—on farms, in factories, or at sea.

A man at fourteen, Nathaniel Ransom was the sixth of seven sons on a farm that required the labor of two or three at most to work alongside their father, James B. Ransom. James was a farmer and carpenter from Carver, Massachusetts, who had been left with Nathaniel's four older half-brothers—James Jr., Charles, Sidney, and Theodore—when his first wife died. Helpless to care alone for four boys ranging in age from two to nine, he married a widow, Eunice Hammond Cushing Snow, whose five children had all died in infancy. They settled in Mattapoisett, part of the town of Rochester, and together they had three more sons: Joseph, Nathaniel, and Andrew. James Ransom's move from Carver to the Mattapoisett neighborhood called Dextertown brought his family closer to the waterfront, where whaling would lure away every one of his seven sons.

Rochester, Marion, and Mattapoisett, these lands of Sippican, were first settled by the Wampanoag tribe, whose word for "place of rest" gave Mattapoisett its name. Nine miles east of New Bedford, Mattapoisett at mid-nineteenth century numbered seventeen hundred souls, many of them small farmers who plied other trades in the off season. Earlier industries, logging and salt-making, gave way to shipbuilding using native oak and pine. Between 1740 and 1870, some four hundred ships of varying sizes were built in the town, many fitted out as whaling vessels during the peak decades from the 1830s through the 1850s. The advantages of Mattapoisett's harbor and the expansion in shipbuilding spurred growth in the little community that led to its separation from old Rochester in 1857.

When news of the California Gold Rush reached Massachusetts, where a widespread economic depression left many unemployed, men from neighboring towns formed The Mattapoisett & Bridgewater Mining & Mechanical Expedition to try their luck in trades other than farming, ship's carpentry, and whaling. They purchased a whaling bark called *Oscar*, which set sail for California in May of 1849. Among the investors was James Ransom Sr., Nathaniel's father, who owned one sixty-fourth share. Shortly after leaving port, the *Oscar* was struck by a heavy storm that forced it over on its beam ends. The crew managed to right the ship and sailed on to California. A few of the travelers made money, a handful came straggling home after a few years.[1] The *Oscar* too sailed back into Mattapoisett's harbor, and after a couple months of repairs and refitting, sailed again in November of 1851, this time for the North Pacific. James Ransom's third son, thirteen-year-old Sidney, sailed as cabin boy, to be gone from home for almost three years.

In 1855 when Nathaniel Ransom was nine years old, he watched four of his older brothers wave farewell from the decks of whaling vessels that put out to sea between August and November of a single year. His oldest brother, James Jr., embarked as third mate of the *General Scott* in October of 1855, headed for the Indian Ocean. Already an officer in charge of a whaleboat and crew, he was just twenty-one. Charles, the second-eldest son, had begun as cabin boy on the maiden voyage of the *Arctic*, built in Mattapoisett in 1850. The *Arctic* brought home 2,594 barrels of whale

oil and over twenty-two tons of bone, profiting from what whalemen
liked to call a greasy voyage. Like James Jr., Charles rose quickly to third
mate, though he was just nineteen when he embarked aboard the *Japan* in
November of 1855. Sidney Ransom's experience as the *Oscar*'s cabin boy
earned him a promotion to seaman on his next voyage aboard another
Mattapoisett bark, the *Willis*, the same voyage on which Matthew Hiller
first sailed as greenhand. Departing in late May 1855, the *Willis* antici-
pated a three-year voyage hunting sperm whales. Two days out from the
coast of Africa the ship ran into a school of them and in three weeks had
filled every barrel on the ship, even emptying casks of hard bread and
molasses to make room for the valuable oil. A year and a half later the ship
returned with 589 barrels of sperm oil and sixty-three barrels of whale oil
aboard. Sperm oil sold for $1.84 per gallon in 1856, and Sidney Ransom's
one-eighty-fifth lay amounted to over five hundred dollars.[2] He was just
sixteen. No wonder Theodore Ransom was eager to follow his older
brothers to sea. At fourteen he sailed for the South Atlantic as greenhand
on the *Clara Bell*, a Mattapoisett vessel built at the Leonard Hammond
yard. With the departure of four brothers, only twelve-year-old Joseph,
Nathaniel, and five-year-old Andrew remained at home to help with the
farm chores.

After the older boys were gone, the Ransom house was far from
empty. Besides Nathaniel's parents and brothers, the household included
five others in 1855: seventy-three-year-old Eliza Sparrows, twenty-seven-year-old mariner William Robinson, thirty-seven-year-old Abby
Robinson, and Sarah W. Cushing, age fifteen, and twelve-year-old Mary
N. Cushing. The Cushing sisters were likely related to Eunice Cushing
Ransom, and the others were boarders. William Robinson and Sidney
Ransom had served together aboard the *Oscar*, Robinson as boatsteerer
and Sidney as cabin boy. Robinson remained in town for just a few months
between voyages, and rented quarters suited him and his wife Abby well
enough.

The Ransom brothers shared an attic bedroom under the eaves
whenever they came home from the sea. Nathaniel Ransom knew the hot
smell of the roof in summer, the interminable drip of one persistent leak
in November, the clouds of steamy breath in winter. He knew the jaunty
angle of Sid's cap when he sauntered home from a whaling voyage,
coins jingling in his pockets. Nathaniel wore his older brothers' cast-off
britches, the knees thickened with patching, but the pockets were always
empty. He listened rapt to James and Charles and Sidney and Theodore—
their harrowing tales of raging storms weathered at sea, the topsails flung

to tatters in the gale, the spray sweeping the decks of the ship. He knew there was more to it than they ever revealed: was it fear? A shiver rose along his backbone and up the nape of his neck. He was determined to go and see for himself.

By 1860, when he was fourteen Nathaniel Ransom knew how to fish and shoot. He was curious and keen-minded, yet few Massachusetts children continued their education beyond the eight years of a town's common schools, and Mattapoisett offered nothing more until its Barstow School opened in 1871. In May of 1860, half a year after John Brown's raid on Harper's Ferry, the coming War Between the States rumbled like distant thunder. During the *Barnstable*'s four-year voyage, Nathaniel turned eighteen, and the journey kept him at sea in relative safety compared to the likelihood of being lured or conscripted into military service.

His decision to follow his older brothers into whaling was further motivated by the lure of potential earnings higher than those gained in toiling on his father's farm, or in New Bedford's humming Wamsutta cotton factory, which prospered so handsomely that the company was erecting its third mill as Nathaniel Ransom turned toward the city's wharves in search of work. More than five hundred whaling vessels sailed from Buzzards Bay ports in the year of his first voyage, forcing shipping agents like David Kempton to recruit seamen from as far away as Pennsylvania or Vermont, farm boys who had never breathed salt air. The discovery of petroleum in Titusville, Pennsylvania, in 1859 soon threatened the market for the whale oil that lighted homes, offices, and factories throughout the country. As the demand for whale oil fell, the bone—more accurately, the baleen—from humpback whales, right whales, and the gigantic Arctic bowheads, substantially increased the value of the hunt. In the years before synthetic materials, whalebone (baleen) could be split, steamed, and shaped into strong and flexible umbrella ribs, buggy springs and whips, corsets, hoops for women's dresses, and a host of other items.

The proceeds from a whaling voyage were divided—with approximately one-third going to the expenses of fitting out and supplying the ship, including pilot's fees and wharfage, one-third to its owners, and one-third to the captain and crew—allotted according to experience and seniority. Nathaniel's oldest brother James, returning as third mate of the *General Scott* in December of 1859, earned a "short lay," one-fiftieth of the catch. When he signed on again in September 1861, promoted this time to first mate, he could expect a lay of one-twenty-fifth, or twice as much. Inexperienced greenhands might be briefly duped into interpreting the larger denominator as a bigger share of the profits, though the reverse

was true. Deducted from a mariner's future earnings were charges for
bedding, for "liberty money" advanced to seamen when the ship was in
port, and the highly inflated costs for anything purchased from the ship's
slops chest, which contained clothing, boots, tobacco, knives, and other
tools. These doubtful prospects for gain were counterbalanced by the
chance for sudden riches such as Sidney's earnings from the *Willis*.

Besides the notorious sperm whale, New Bedford's whaling ships
captured and processed blubber from a wide variety of cetaceans: blackfish (pilot whales), California gray whales (which whalemen called devil-
fish, ripsacks, or mussel-diggers), the humpback and right whales that
furnished whalebone as well as oil, and blue whales that they called
sulphur-bottoms. In addition they killed dolphins they named grampuses
and cowfish, as well as sea turtles, porpoises, seals, and walrus, and tried
out their blubber for oil.[3]

In December, 1859, twenty-seven-year-old James Ransom returned
to New Bedford as third mate on the sperm whaler *General Scott*. One of
the greenhands he commanded, William Quinton, became a boatsteerer
and fourth mate on the *Barnstable*, ready to depart a few months later,
and James urged him to look after Nathaniel. James brought the youngest
of the Ransom brothers, ten-year-old Andrew, to wave goodbye from the
dock as fourteen-year-old Nathaniel left New Bedford harbor in May of
1860.

Three of Nathaniel's older brothers were then away at sea. Sidney
had risen to the rank of boatsteerer aboard the *Mary Wilder*, returning
home a month after Nathaniel's departure. His third voyage carried him
around Cape Horn to the northwestern coast of Peru. The crew found
profitable sperm whaling among the Galapagos Islands, where they also
captured several huge tortoises. Many shipmates became ill from eating
bad terrapin meat, but recovered after a few days. One late August night
they watched fire from a volcano on Albermarle Island (called Isla Isabela
today). This time Sidney earned a larger lay, or share, in the 953 barrels of
precious sperm oil brought back to New Bedford a month after Nathaniel
left port.

Theodore Ransom spent less than nine months at home on dry
land over a period of six years. He too became a boatsteerer, on a small
sperm whaler called the *Sun*, returning in July, 1860. He and Sidney spent
a few summer months together, but before winter reached Mattapoisett,
Theodore was off again, this time as third mate of the *Matilda Sears*. The
bark, considerably larger than the *Sun*, cruised for sperm whales among
the Galapagos and along the coast of Peru. Theodore left the ship before

it returned to its home port, for he and Sidney enlisted together in the Union Navy. Joseph Ransom, closest in age to Nathaniel, left home in late June 1858 on a sperm-whaling voyage that lasted six years, long enough to keep him at sea throughout nearly all of the Civil War.

For his part, Nathaniel Ransom was to make four whaling voyages over the next fifteen years, sailing east, south, north, and west; routes that zigzagged around every continent. Whaling ships like the *Barnstable* hunted humpbacks and right whales in the Atlantic and Indian Oceans, and chased the most valuable sperm whale around Japan, Australia, and New Zealand. As spring warmed, the ships ventured north into the Okhotsk Sea between the Kamchatka peninsula and the island of Sakhalin. Or they threaded their way through the Bering Strait into the Arctic Ocean. In early fall they lumbered south again to the Sandwich Islands (now Hawaii), laden with oil and whalebone. After off-loading their valuable cargo to be sent home on other vessels, and re-stocking in Hilo or Honolulu, they sailed south to Baja, California, along the western coast of Mexico, and down to Clarence Island at the southern tip of Chile pursuing gray whales and humpbacks. Voyages lasted three or four years as captains competed for a greasy voyage, bringing a lucrative catch back to their hailing port.

The bark *Barnstable* left New Bedford's harbor on May 22, 1860, bound first for the Indian and Pacific Oceans. The vessel measured 119 feet in length and was rated at 373 tons, a measure of its cargo space, with one ton (the space occupied by a tun, an ancient term for cask) equaling a hundred cubic feet. The *Barnstable* carried only a skeleton crew: three mates (the fourth, eighteen-year-old William Quinton also serving as boatsteerer or harpooner), three other boatsteerers, one cooper, and sixteen seamen— among them Charles Smith, from Pottsville, Pennsylvania, Enos Stanton from the Azores, and Nathaniel Ransom, the youngest of the crew. Yankee whalers were known for their ability to man a large vessel efficiently, and Captain Brownson could recruit experienced mariners in the Azores or the Cape Verde islands, sparing the ship's owners the expense of feeding them until they were needed for whaling.

As soon as he left New Bedford, Ransom began keeping a journal, a lifelong habit while he was aboard ship. The journal itself, now in the research library of the New Bedford Whaling Museum, consists of inexpensive foolscap, but its cover and first two pages are missing. In other places several pages are too faded to be legible. Further information about his life aboard ship, his whereabouts, and the whale hunt comes from New Bedford's *Whalemen's Shipping List and Merchants' Transcript* published between 1843 and 1914, and from logbooks and private journals kept by other whalemen. Aboard the *Barnstable* another seaman, young Samuel Colony from Dover, New Hampshire, also penned a private journal. The official logbook of the *Barnstable*, kept by the ship's mates, details locations, winds and weather, sails, the catch, other ships in sight, and altercations among the officers and men. The mates who kept the log used whale stamps to indicate their success. A whale's tail means that a whale was struck but escaped, often by sounding, or diving swiftly out of sight. An upside down image of the entire whale signifies that the whale was killed but sank and was lost. An intact whale means it was successfully killed and captured.

Each day without fail Nathaniel Ransom recorded the weather, the wind's strength and its direction, and the ship's course in his journal. Entries for his first voyage aboard the *Barnstable* give little or no information on the ship's location, although the official logbook faithfully reports latitude and longitude. Like other logkeepers, he took a keen interest in the catch of other ships; whenever possible he tallied their months away from port, and their take of oil and bone, seeking to estimate his own vessel's profitability. While all seamen longed for news of home, which he frequently received in later years, his journal aboard the *Barnstable* notes only that "all hands got letters" in port in Hawaii. His early writing seldom indicates which chores he did himself and which occurrences aboard ship simply transpired around him. Nevertheless, the most intriguing aspect of reading his journals is the search for the man himself, or rather the boy who turned his back on home at fourteen and set forth on a four-year journey into the unknown.

Cruising on Desolation Ground

After sailing out of New Bedford harbor, the *Barnstable* crossed the Atlantic using the prevailing westerly winds—sometimes "blowing a living gale"—to drive the ship eastward.[4] When the weather abated and the greenhands had recovered from seasickness, Captain Brownson ordered the whaleboats lowered so that all hands could practice pulling at the long oars. Whaling began in earnest in late June northwest of the Azores as the crew took two small blackfish, easy to spot by their distinctive dorsal fin just behind the head. Blackfish (the whalemen's term for pilot whales) were familiar to all coastal inhabitants near Cape Cod as schools of them often swam close to shore, where men herded them onto the beach by slapping their oars loudly against the water. Once beached or run aground, blackfish could easily be speared, and their blubber tried out on shore. In deeper oceans, schools of them frequented sperm whaling grounds, breaching or jumping out of the water to travel faster or in play. A ship might sail into the middle of the school, confusing the blackfish so that they could be easily harpooned. A harpoon blow often killed them, or a few cutting strokes from the lance. Measuring ten to twenty-five feet and weighing just a few tons, they could be hoisted whole onto the deck, and their blubber, only a few inches thick, stripped off lengthwise. They yielded a few barrels of oil apiece, but it was easy to refine, and could be added in small amounts to higher priced sperm oil without being detected. Since they were fairly easy to strike and posed little danger to whale-boats, whaling masters pursued them to practice a green crew. The men spent the next few days cutting and trying out blackfish blubber, "a hard old fourth of July" Nathaniel Ransom complained. As they sailed around Africa's Cape of Good Hope into the Indian Ocean, Captain Brownson kept the foremast hands busy "grinding blackfish irons cleaning out the fore hatch." Blackfish irons—the journals never use the terms harpoon or harpooner—were shorter and lighter than those used to strike whales. In the Indian Ocean the *Barnstable*'s crew hunted dolphins, porpoises, and grampuses or cowfish. Southeast of the Cape of Good Hope someone caught a sea turtle, a source of fresh meat as well as oil. Whalemen prized turtle meat, high in protein, and sometimes kept large tortoises turned on their backs in the ship's hold, where they could survive as long as a year without food or water.

After failed attempts at catching right whales on June 29 and July 8, the crew succeeded in capturing one on July 28 as they sailed south and east of Africa. In the 1600s schools of right whales as well as black-fish often swam close to Cape Cod and Nantucket, where Native Americans and early settlers found them so plentiful that they could harpoon a whale and tow it back to land to cut up and melt down its blubber, sometimes as thick as two feet. Due to their blunt shape and lack of fins, right whales swam slowly, and so much of their body weight was comprised of blubber that they remained afloat when killed, significant advantages to their hunters. One whale's blubber could yield as much as eighty barrels of oil, fifteen of them from its twenty-foot long lower lip and another six barrels from its huge tongue.

Right whales, rotund as an oil cask, measured perhaps sixty feet in length, weighing about a hundred tons when mature. Some whalemen distinguished between northern and southern right whales and between those found in the Atlantic and Pacific. By the early 1860s, right whales had become scarce in the northern Pacific, where Captain Barzillai Folger had first reported hunting them in 1837. Callosities, bony outgrowths rough as a coral reef, often protrude around the lips and "forehead" of the whale, teeming with whole colonies of whale "lice," actually tiny crustaceans that feed on the whale's dead skin. The whales follow floating beds of krill or plankton. While southern right whales favored warm waters to give birth or nurse their young, the northern right whales remained in colder waters year round. Their system of echolocation, using calls at a frequency too low for humans to hear, enables them to create a map of their migration routes, sometimes thousands of miles long. Although whalemen had no way of hearing whales' sounds, they knew from observation that they communicated. Because their eyes are located far to the side of the head, they are unable to see straight in front or behind, defending themselves by swinging their twenty-foot wide tail flukes from side to side. As the whaleboat approached a wounded right whale, the boatheader, one of the ship's officers, stabbed at its tapering back, attempting to sever the large vein and spinal cord, immobilizing the flukes. Right whales fought viciously for their lives, sometimes escaping with harpoons protruding from their backs and fathoms of line trailing behind them.

Whalers dubbed these whales "right" to signify that they yielded a double profit of both oil and bone, and figured on extracting eight-to-ten pounds of bone per barrel of oil. Whalebone did not refer to the hard skeletal frame, but rather to the baleen, those flexible keratin strips that these whales use to strain their food of miniscule crustaceans. When heated, this baleen, essentially the same material as human fingernails or horses' hooves, could be molded or shaped into a host of useful items: stiffening for caps, collars, hats; cushions for billiard tables; shoe-horns; fishing rods; boot shanks; buggy springs; and tool handles. The hairy inner edges of baleen strips provided stuffing for buggy seats and bristles for brushes.

At the end of July the *Barnstable*'s crew spotted the carcass of a sperm whale, the remains of the prey they were hunting, killed and stripped of its blubber by another vessel. In August, three months out and short of provisions, the ship sailed west, then north back around the Cape of Good Hope to Faial in the Azores, where Captain Brownson "shipped a cabin boy & one foremast hand." A few weeks later he stopped briefly at Palmertown in the Canary Islands (off the coast of Morocco) for fresh water, then continued south to Brava, one of the Cape Verde Islands. There he bought flour, bread, pigs, and hens. He let go two men, and hired on four more crewmen. As blackfish and porpoises swam nearby, the lookout spotted a blue whale, too far away to chase.

Near the equator, headed west and south once more, the crew amused themselves fishing off the ship during a lull in heavy rain squalls: "Thousands of skipjacks in sight caught 6 of them." Catching skipjacks, a species of large tuna, was good fun; baiting a hook with a scrap of salt pork or beef, Nathaniel Ransom lay out on the bowsprit and jigged his line up and down until the fish struck. The boy quickly mastered the technique and next day caught seventeen. It was no trouble at all to persuade the cook to fry up the fresh fish for supper.

As the *Barnstable* approached Brazil, the first and second mates, Daniel Aiken and Edwin Osgood, disappointed by the meager whale catch, asked for their discharge, and were left ashore in late October in Pernambuco (today Recife) on Brazil's east coast. Because the port was a common trading hub for whaling ships, they could expect to hire on as officers or crew of another vessel with rosier prospects. The departure of four men, including two senior officers, meant a major change in personnel, but whaling vessels seldom returned to their home port with the same crew that had set sail.

Shortly after the stop in Pernambuco, the *Barnstable* came upon a school of small sperm whales, females, and young calves: "[October 29] Saw the ship *Contest* with her boats lowered for whales she took 4 whales we lowered & took the same; PM cutting in," Nathaniel Ransom reported.

The sperm whale, made famous by Herman Melville's *Moby Dick*, was the largest of the toothed whales and the most elusive catch. "Harem schools" of females swam in front of a single mature bull whale who guarded the rear as they roamed between breeding and feeding grounds. A lookout in the ship's crow's nest could spot a sperm whale spouting three-to-five miles away because its single blow hole was far forward on its head; the spout of any other species of whale was much further back. A male sperm whale could measure up to eighty feet long and weigh as many tons, though the female was only two-thirds as long and one-third as heavy. While sperm whales swam slowly, they could plunge suddenly as much as a half mile to the ocean's depths and remain up to an hour underwater. A skin as much as a foot thick protected the layer of blubber from the whalemen's toggle irons and lances. Whalemen feared a bull sperm whale as a vicious fighter that could turn to attack the whaleboat or even the mother ship itself. Likely its fighting behavior derived from competing for the floating harem of females with their calves. Given that the *Barnstable*'s four whales yielded just eighty barrels of sperm oil, they were probably small females or calves, captured from a larger pod, a social grouping for mutual defense or care of the young. Because calves nurse for two years or more, mothers remain strongly attached to their young and aid one another in defending calves in their pod, even risking their own lives to circle the whaleboat that has taken one. This protective behavior made it possible for the *Barnstable*'s crew to take four of the small sperm whales in a single day.

The lower portion of the sperm whale's head cavity contained the "junk," a bloodless honeycomb of tough white fibers saturated with oil. Sperm oil remained stable at high temperature and lubricated the steam engines, looms, and spinneries spreading through New England with the tide of the Industrial Revolution. Lowell, Massachusetts required two hundred twenty barrels of sperm oil—the yield from three good-sized whales—to lubricate the machinery of a single cotton mill for just one year, but New Bedford merchants found a market closer by in the city's own Wamsutta textile factories.[5] In lamps it cast a clear, bright light valued for illuminating lighthouses and bridges, and it remained stable even in the cold of a January night in New Bedford. The upper portion of the head (known as the case) contained a waxy mass of pleasantly fragrant spermaceti. Liquid while inside the whale's head, the spermaceti congealed quickly once extracted, forming crystal-like shapes. Men bailed it carefully from the case, which might hold as much as five hundred gallons, attempting to salvage any precious bits that dribbled away. The task of kneading the waxy globules to restore them to a liquid state left the skin soft and pleasantly sweet-smelling, one of the few relatively agreeable chores in whaling. In the process men picked out the stringy oil-soaked integument whose fibers would otherwise char in the trypots and darken the precious oil. Spermaceti produced clean-burning candles with a pure white, nearly smokeless light and was used in the production of ointments and cosmetics. Spermaceti's function in whale anatomy was not fully understood. Melville speculated that this viscous mass absorbed shock, enabling the sperm whale to ram heavy objects without injuring itself. Modern zoologists understand that the structure of the sperm whale's head chamber and spermaceti amplify its system of echolocation, or the clicking sounds that function like sonar to find its prey. Nineteenth-century whalemen, unable to detect its low frequency loud clicking sounds, believed nonetheless in the sperm whale's ability to warn others of the whaleboat's approach. They also salvaged the whale's three or four dozen cone-shaped teeth, prized for handles and for carving or scrimshawing into button hooks, knife handles, piecrust crimpers, brooches, and other decorative objects.

The value of sperm oil and spermaceti had led predictably to over-fishing, and already by 1860 these whales had become scarce. The eighty barrels of precious sperm oil produced in the fall in the South Atlantic remained stowed in the *Barnstable*'s hold for the next three and a half years as the ship sailed the world's oceans without ever taking another sperm whale. At the end of November men could see finbacks, right whales, grampuses, and killer whales. Near the Crozet Islands in the South Indian Ocean, inhabited only by seals and penguins, Captain Brownson turned east once more in search of sperm whales, humpbacks, and right whales, but with meager success: "Raised school of large sperm whales lowered all the boats but did not see them again," Nathaniel Ransom wrote in early December as the *Barnstable* sailed midway between South America and Africa. Captain Brownson decided to hunt around Kerguelen Island, near Antarctica, a region named Desolation Ground for its remoteness from civilization.

And there the *Barnstable* arrived on Christmas Day: "Stiff breeze from the westward course southeast by south, weather cloudy. PM all sail set arrived on Desolation cruising ground took in sail hove to under close reefed main topsail fore topmast staysail; porpoises in sight struck one lost him. Sea Pie for dinner." The cook prepared this special treat in honor of Christmas. The name apparently derives from the French "six pâtes," meaning six layers of dough, for roasted meat from the ship's stores and fried onions were layered between sheets of pastry and then baked. The dish gave seamen a rare delicacy, and Captain Brownson brought some candy to the foremast hands in the forecastle. Nevertheless twenty-one-year-old Samuel Colony called it "a hard old Christmas in the Indian Ocean" unspeakably far from his New Hampshire home and family.

On Desolation Ground, right whales near the ship escaped the whalemen's harpoons. Bored and idle, they dangled a fishing line with a piece of pork over the ship's rail and caught an albatross for the curiosity of seeing one. Its wingspan of eleven feet powered the bird on long flights above the sea, or it plunged from great height to seize fish from the waves. Sometimes the seabird—men called it a gooney bird—would perch on the vessel's yard arm to survey broad expanses of ocean. On deck the crew mocked its clumsy gait as the ship's motion made it nearly seasick and unable to take flight. Occasionally men roasted the bird and ate its oily flesh that tasted of fish. Old timers teased the greenhands, telling them that eating gooney bird would make them waterproof.

By late January, the *Barnstable*'s crew had only taken another porpoise as they left Desolation Ground headed toward Australia, a frequent stop for New Bedford ships. Anchored south of Perth at Bunbury, the ship took on pigs, cattle, and a parrot. Nathaniel Ransom saw four whalers. "Boats came aboard from each. Sent one boat ashore for letters. One man got his rist jammed between the [anchor] cable and the boat. Stowing down oil, getting water, scrubbing off side of ship. Breaking out the captain's furniture . . . gentlemen and ladies aboard trading sent a raft ashore for water."

These February days offered a welcome chance to exchange news of home with crews from Massachusetts ports who frequented shipping agents' offices at Bunbury. Nathaniel wrote: "One watch ashore on liberty. *Elisha Dunbar* got in. A boat's crew came down to Bunbury from the ship *Plover* . . . Liberty men from the *Java* & *Progress* aboard." The *Plover* and the *Elisha Dunbar* hailed from Mattapoisett. The *Elisha Dunbar* could boast of a lucrative catch; its thirty-month voyage produced 530 barrels of sperm oil. Even better, the *Java*, departing and returning about the same time as the *Barnstable*, produced 1,292 barrels of precious sperm oil. Nathaniel Ransom also recognized other whaling vessels nearby: the *Lagoda* and the *Champion*. The less fortunate *Barnstable* headed for New Zealand at the end of February, carrying one passenger and "chasing sperm whales and peeling onions to pickle," a good job for a Mattapoisett farm boy who had turned fifteen in November.

As a common seaman, Nathaniel Ransom slept in the forecastle or fo'csle, a cramped, dingy, evil-smelling cave toward the bow of the vessel. Two tiers of bunks rounded the ship's hull below decks, space for a man to sleep, with his sea chest nearby. Men received a straw-filled bed tick as part of their outfit before embarking on the voyage, and often paid dearly for this layer of dusty bug-infested mattress. Aft of the forecastle in steerage slept those who outranked the common crew by virtue of their specific duties aboard ship: the four boatsteerers (whose task was to harpoon the whale while standing in the bow of the whaleboat), a cook, a carpenter, a blacksmith, a steward, and a cooper. Four mates shared cabins for two or four men, and the captain enjoyed the luxury of a private cabin. Quartered together in the fo'csle, Nathaniel Ransom made friends with Charles Smith from Pennsylvania. Somehow the pair stayed in contact years later. On November 18, 1866, he recorded that "C. Smyth, once a shipmate of mine" came aboard ship to visit him in Honolulu. The two greenhands, the boy from Mattapoisett and the twenty-four-year old from the coal country of Pennsylvania, learned the ropes together aboard ship. Two other young seamen made friends in the dank forecastle as well. Samuel Colony also wrote every day in his "Private Journal of a Whaling Voyage to the Atlantic, Pacific, and Indian Ocean."

Unfortunately, his eyesight failed, and after a year he turned over the journal to a crewmate, seventeen-year-old Gilman Clark from Bristol, Rhode Island, who continued daily entries.

Often assigned to working in the rigging, these young foremast hands faced a bewildering forest of masts, sails, and lines. The bark *Barnstable* carried three masts: the foremast and mainmast square-rigged (their three sails perpendicular to the center line of the vessel) and the rear mast (mizzenmast), fore and aft rigged, its sails parallel to the ship's center line. This type of bark rigging, most common on whaling ships, allowed them to be maintained by a skeleton crew while the officers and captain were cruising for whales. In configurations varying with wind speed and direction, the deck hands learned to set mainsails, topsails, top gallant and royal sails, staysails, jibs, and spankers. The journal entry "All sail set," meant that the three masts carried as much as 30,000 square feet of sail. Laid flat, the canvas sails would have covered two-thirds of an acre. With a good wind filling its sails, a whaling vessel traveled at nine knots, covering as much as two hundred miles a day. In foul weather, mariners reefed or double-reefed the sails to reduce their exposure to wind. To do so, they scaled the rigging and wrapped the heavy canvas sails around the horizontal yard arm. In a violent gale, the ship "hove to under close-reefed sails." Agility and courage were needed to climb the rigging in fair weather, for the uppermost royal sails stretched more than a hundred feet above the deck of the ship. In a gale, or the "strong breeze" often noted in the journals, working in the rigging placed life and limb in jeopardy, for while the ship pitched and rolled, the top of a mast swept a much larger arc. On a later voyage aboard the *Sea Breeze* Nathaniel Ransom watched aghast as "One man fell from the main top sail yard and struck in the reef tackle, came down on deck uninjured." The weather—blowing almost a gale—made survival in these circumstances miraculous.

Frequently the sails or lines needed repair. The ship's stores included yards of spare canvas and a wooden case containing oil-soaked wool to keep the sailmaker's needles from rusting. The needles, six inches long, varied in size, each with a triangular point to pierce the stout canvas. The sailmaker slipped a leather glove over his palm to push the needles through the fabric. Nathaniel Ransom quickly became adept at sewing, a skill he also applied to mending his own clothing.

When there was little else to do aboard ship, he worked at making "senate," or sennit, a rope braided from multiple strands of frayed lines. The recycled rope was wrapped around the rigging to buffer or strengthen it. Old ends of rope too short for other uses were tied onto a handle to make a rough mop for swabbing the decks. Frayed rope strands could be salvaged for oakum, thickened with tar and packed between the planks of the ship's hull to prevent seepage. Making spun yarn was another method of re-using old rope. First a man picked apart old rope, then twisted strands anew, using a device like a spinning wheel to wind them tightly together. As shipboard tasks went, making spun yarn was a good sitting-down job, and seamen liked to prolong the task as much as possible, telling stories as they did so; hence our expression "to spin a yarn." Names such as "John Spunyarn" (the equivalent of John Doe) appear in crew lists to identify Kanakas, or Pacific Islander seamen whose names the Yankee sailors could not pronounce or spell.

Much labor was required to move around cargo stowed in the hold, or "hole" as Nathaniel Ransom called it, a dark, dank space twenty feet below deck, redolent with the odors of bilge water, damp wood and whale oil. Furthest down were the "ground tier casks," filled with salt beef, pork, or fresh water. Many also contained "shooks" or barrel staves. To save space, barrels full of staves were stored in the hold and then "broken out" or hauled above decks to be assembled with their hoops and lids as needed to contain whale oil. "Setting up shooks" was the specialized trade of the cooper engaged for every whaling voyage. While oil was measured by the barrel (thirty-one and one-half gallons), it was stored in casks of varying sizes and shapes, some specially made to fit closely against the curved walls of the ship's hull. Whaling vessels might hold as many as three thousand barrels of oil, nearly ninety-five thousand gallons.

The ship's provisions included potatoes, molasses, flour, vinegar, salt beef and salt pork, dry hardened bread, onions, and little else. Later voyages mention oil, pickles, mackerel, coffee, and salt codfish in the larder. Tea made from boiled water disguised the foul taste of months of storage in wooden casks. Rice, beans, turnips, sugar cane, butter, raisins, pumpkins, and bananas appear occasionally in the journals, but the ship's stores included very little fruit or vegetables, which would have added variety as well as nutrition to the seamen's diet. In any whaling port, the ship took on barrels of potatoes. Sweet potatoes were dried aboard ship. "Irish" potatoes lay in an open, shaded pen on deck, dusted with lime to retard spoilage; but they rotted after a few months at sea, and Nathaniel Ransom often picked them over, tossing the rotten ones into the waves.

The whaling vessels also kept livestock aboard for fresh meat: cattle, sheep, pigs, and chickens. Since he had grown up on a farm, Nathaniel Ransom looked after these animals, though he only mentions bringing them aboard and butchering them a few weeks later. He leaves the reader to imagine loading a "bullock" aboard a whaleboat, rowing it out to a vessel anchored in deeper water, and then hoisting the animal aboard. If the strong gales and squally waters of the Arctic made seamen uneasy, the cattle, sheep, and pigs must have milled unsteadily in their pen on deck, struggling to keep their footing, and bellowing forlornly into the wind. Captains stopped at tiny tropical islands to trade for coconuts, which the crew cracked open to feed to the pigs. With no mud to wallow in, hogs kept fairly clean on the deck, and whalemen sometimes made pets of them. Because the ship lacked space to carry hay or grain, the livestock was usually slaughtered three or four weeks after being brought aboard. It is no wonder that seamen went ashore hunting or set out in whaleboats to fish whenever they had the chance. Among the animals brought aboard to enrich the common fare, Nathaniel Ransom mentions codfish, skipjacks and albacore tuna, turtles, ducks, rabbits, clams, and Arctic reindeer. Aside from the ingredients named here, shipboard fare is rarely described.

Its presentation aboard ship did nothing to make food more appetizing. The foremast hands lodged in the forecastle ate from a large wooden tub, called a kid. Each man supplied his own eating utensils and sheath knife and helped himself to the kid's contents as best he could. This method of containing or "serving" meals minimized spillage in rough seas. The main meal usually consisted of boiled salt meat in a kind of gravy, potatoes, and hardened bread that had been dried before storing to ensure that it did not mold. Sundays men received a pudding made of boiled flour and molasses, called duff, embellished with raisins on holidays. The chief attributes of this diet were that it was filling and supplied plenty of salt, supposedly useful in preventing seasickness.

The first year of the *Barnstable's* voyage fell far short of any hopes for profit. Its eighty barrels of sperm oil, finer than porpoise and black-fish oil, was worth only three to four thousand dollars. Based on prices quoted in the *Whalemen's Shipping List*, its cargo could scarcely pay for the ship's fitting (likely around $30,000), provisions, and repairs. Here the lay system's ingenuity becomes visible: with each whaleman allocated a fraction of the voyage's catch, if the hunt produced little, the crew earned almost nothing. The ship's owners risked very little.

In fact, New Bedford's whale oil industry had reached its peak profits in the early 1850s, years before Nathaniel Ransom shipped aboard the *Barnstable* as a greenhand. The *Whalemen's Shipping List* of July 2, 1861, counted fifty whalers lying idle at New Bedford's wharves. The editors lamented that whale oil that cost sixty cents per gallon to produce sold for only forty. Over-fishing had not only reduced the whale catch, it also increased the supply of oil and depressed prices. The newspaper reported that thousands of casks of whale oil stowed away while their owners awaited better prices now lay stored in sheds and covered in seaweed to prevent the casks from drying out, shrinking, and leaking oil.

The *Barnstable* sailed across the Tasman Sea in mid-March 1861 where it was "blowing a hurricane," but the ship escaped serious damage. Porpoises and humpbacks swam near New Zealand's coast, and on April 8 Nathaniel Ransom "saw sperm whales going slowly to windward; blowing not quite so hard; lowered for them, one boatsteerer darted." Cape Verdean boatsteerer James de Lomba had signed on as steward and now seized his opportunity for promotion and higher pay as a harpooner. Luck failed him; he missed the large whale, and the men had no chance to go after three others making to windward.

North to the Arctic

After this disappointment, Captain Brownson turned the *Barnstable* toward the Arctic, a whaling ground he knew well. Arctic whaling, the riskiest form of the hunt, was only around a dozen years old. A half-dozen American whalers first ventured into the Okhotsk Sea between the Kamchatka Peninsula and Sakhalin Island in the early 1840s hunting right whales. They quickly discovered the gigantic bowhead, first called the polar whale, whose baleen was the longest and broadest of any whale. By 1846, 292 vessels competed there, maneuvering in close quarters in Shantar Bay and the northeast gulf of the Okhotsk Sea. In 1848 Captain Thomas Welcome Royce (or Roys), master of the *Superior* of Sag Harbor, New York, first ventured further north through the Bering Strait, quickly filling the hold of his ship with casks of oil from the plentiful bowhead whales. Returning to Honolulu in May of 1849, he freely announced his discovery. Whaling masters, despite their taste for competition, preferred the companionship of other vessels as they hunted the fog-bound, frigid northern waters. Now they eagerly prepared to follow the path opened by Royce's explorations. Two hundred seventy-eight whaleships passed through the Bering Strait in 1852 pursuing the immense bowheads.

News of Royce's success quickly reached the Ransom household and Mattapoisett, whose ship builders and whalemen hastened to follow his route through the Bering Strait. Charles was the first of the Ransoms to hunt bowheads as a fourteen-year-old greenhand aboard the *Arctic* in

1850. Its catch of eighty barrels of sperm oil seemed paltry in comparison to the yield from bowheads: 2,594 barrels of oil and twenty-two and one-half tons of bone. At the end of his three-year voyage, the eighteen-year-old greenhand had earned about $350. After a year and a half on land, Charles sailed again, as third mate of the *Japan* from neighboring Fairhaven, bound once more for the north Pacific. The *Japan* returned in four years with 157 barrels of sperm, and 2,710 of whale oil, and 28,349 pounds of bone. But Charles was already dead, at twenty-one of a spinal complaint and necrosis, likely the result of a shipboard injury.

In May, 1859 Captain Leonard Brownson had returned from a hugely profitable voyage as master of the *Baltic*, producing 197 barrels of sperm oil, 3,065 barrels of whale oil, and nearly seventeen tons of whalebone in three Arctic seasons. Now in early 1861, as he steered the *Barnstable* past Samoa and toward the Arctic, Brownson busied his disgruntled crew—Nathaniel Ransom among them—"making a sheathing for the tryworks cover cleaning the trypots . . . making a beer cask . . . tarring down some of the rigging [and] trypots cover, making spunyarn & sennet; breaking out sugar & pickled onions."

In late May, finbacks and grampuses and a blue whale appeared. The crew shot just "one finback killed him he sunk."

"So ends the first year; Lat. 43:24; Long. 165:20," wrote the ship's official logkeeper on May 22, 1861, his disappointment nearly audible. The *Barnstable* had captured very little since leaving New Bedford exactly twelve months before.

May 27 found the *Barnstable* in the Bering Sea just east of the Kamchatka Peninsula, where the lookout spotted a whale. Quickly Captain Brownson shouted to lower the boats, but the oarsmen never got close enough to ascertain whether they had seen a right whale or a bowhead. Humpbacks appeared, spouted, and vanished over the next few days as the ship moved north and east. As May turned to June, illuminated by the long Arctic days, prospects improved. Near Siberia's Cape Navarin (Mys Navarin, 62°15′ N, 179°08′ E), just south of the Anadyr Gulf, Nathaniel Ransom saw his first bowhead.[6] "Tuesday June 4. AM saw one bowhead puffing pigs [harbor porpoises] in sight raised land saw a large seal; repairing the guns breaking out powder & shot." Unable to capture a bowhead, the crew shot seventeen seals, enough to fire up the tryworks to boil down their blubber. Nearby, bulky walrus lolled on the ice, and the whalemen pointed out other whaling vessels from New Bedford and Nantucket.

Captain Brownson frequently enjoyed a "gam" with ships nearby.

Maneuvering cautiously, two vessels approached within hailing distance, and using a brass speaking trumpet, one captain "spoke" the other ship's officers. If a longer conversation was feasible, the captain and officers might board the nearby ship to exchange news of home and prospects for the whale hunt. Off Siberia in early summer, Brownson gammed the *Braganza*, with 1,800 barrels of whale oil, and the *Montreal*, which had made 3,500 barrels of oil in three and a half years at sea. In comparison Brownson could report only a meager catch. Surely the summer bowhead season would bring better success.

"The Bone Was in Its Glory."

Like his competitors, Captain Brownson was only marking time in killing seals, for he was after the bowhead whale, a formidable prey. At least twice as long as a whaleboat, its massive size impressed men due to its stout, bulky shape rather than its length. Protected by an inch-thick black skin and insulated by blubber as much as twenty inches thick, it preferred water about thirty-two degrees. Like the right whale, the toothless bowhead fed on krill or brit, and when blooms of the tiny creatures spread a yellow color over the ocean's surface, whalemen took it as a sign that they had entered rich feeding grounds. Because bowheads' blubber was the thickest of any whale species, the yield of oil exceeded that from any other cetacean. Captain Simeon Hawes boasted of making 375 barrels from a single whale, although doubters cautioned that the cooling tank beside his trypots may have held oil from more than one whale as it was measured while being run into casks below decks.[7] By the 1860s, the average was closer to one hundred barrels for a bull whale and 140 for a female. As the bowhead's mouth gaped open, men glimpsed the upper jaw hung with as many as six hundred slabs of baleen. Whalers estimated that for every barrel of oil from an Arctic bowhead, they could extract seventeen pounds of baleen, and fourteen pounds from a bowhead in the Okhotsk Sea. The largest of these cartilage-like strips, as long as sixteen feet, hung from the center of the upper jaw, fringed with a brushy edge toward the whale's throat, and smooth at the outer edge. The whale gulped gallons of sea water teeming with krill, then used its bulky tongue to force water out through the massive screen of baleen strips, whose brushy inner edge strained and trapped the tiny animals, to be swallowed at once. A bowhead as long as seventy feet might weigh one ton per foot, its head comprising a third of its body, with the baleen weighing as much as 1,600 pounds, substantially more than the yield from a right whale.

Its price fluctuated with supply and demand, and with the dictates of women's fashion. Herman Melville, writing in 1851, opined that baleen had little value; it was in Queen Anne's time (1702–1714) that "the bone was in its glory" for stiffening hoop skirts. However, by the 1840s women's fashions called for corsets and for a capacious series of hoops called crinolines. Awkward as these hoop skirts appear today, they offered a woman two advantages: in cold weather her nether regions could be clothed in multiple layers of petticoats or warm pantaloons, and in summer heat the hoops lifted the skirt fabric away from her legs. Thanks to the whim of style, the price of baleen continued as fickle as fashion itself. At the beginning of the *Barnstable*'s voyage in 1860, a pound of whalebone sold for eighty cents. Four years later when the ship returned to New Bedford, the price had more than doubled, then averaging $1.80. In these economic circumstances, signing on board as a whaleman under the lay system and indeed the entire whale fishery represented a huge gamble in terms of both economics and human lives.

The transition from sperm whaling to chasing bowheads meant exchanging one peril for another. Unlike the pugnacious bull sperm whales, the toothless bowheads were unsuspecting and non-combative. A bowhead cow—larger than a bull—would often abandon her calf when pursued by a whaleboat, while sperm, humpback, and right whales usually sought to protect their young. Regular migration patterns also made bowheads vulnerable to the whalemen's pursuit. On the other hand, whale hunters left the sperm whale's warmer habitat for frigid Arctic seas, where sleet and snow immobilized the icy rigging, leaving a ship to drift between moving pack ice and the heavier ground ice on the ocean's bottom nearer shore. Clothed in furs and clumsy skins, a man thrown overboard from a whaleboat might freeze to death before he drowned.

By the time Nathaniel Ransom began whaling, over-fishing had driven the right whales and bowheads away from waters south of the 60th parallel, where whalers in earlier decades had found them plentiful. Further north the *Barnstable* found bowheads in large numbers in early summer as they followed fields of yellow brit toward the Bering Strait, eluding whaleboats as they swam:

> June 19: Saw one bowhead, lowered for him, saw no more of him.

> June 21: Saw some bowheads, lowered for them. Killed one, got under the ice, lost him, boats came aboard.

> June 25: Saw several bowheads; lowered for them. First mate

struck one at 10 o'clock. Got him alongside at noon. Waist boat
got stove.

These cryptic notes barely hint at the slim chance for capture, for bowheads
could travel two hundred feet under ice and break through a thickness of
two feet to surface for air far from the whaleboat pursuing them. Getting
the whale alongside only began the arduous work of manufacturing whale
oil aboard ship. First came the process of cutting in. Along the starboard
side of the bark, seamen rigged a cutting stage of planks and rails overhanging the open water. The whale was hauled beside and beneath the
cutting stage so that the ocean continued to support its massive weight.
The dead whale lay with its head toward the ship's stern, and fluke chains
near the bow were passed around the "small" of the whale just ahead of
its tail. Its head, containing the valuable baleen, was also secured.

Motionless now, the immensity of the bowhead's hulking carcass
became fully apparent. William Morris Davis, in his *Nimrod of the
Sea*, describes the bowhead in precise detail intended to help his nineteenth-century readers visualize the whale's true dimensions:

Charles Scammon, Bowhead Whale. From *The Marine Mammals of the North-western
Coast of North America*, 1874. (Courtesy of the New Bedford Whaling Museum.)

The blubber, or "blanket," of such a whale would carpet a room twenty-two yards long, and nine yards wide, averaging half a yard in thickness. You good, loving housewives, think of such a blanket-piece for the dark, cold nights of winter! And you farmer boys, set up a saw-log, two feet in diameter and twenty feet in length, for the ridge-pole of the room we propose to build. Then raise it in the air fifteen feet, and support it with pieces of timber seventeen feet long, spread, say nine feet. This will make a room nine feet wide at the bottom, two feet wide at the peak, and twenty feet long, and will convey an idea of the upper jaw . . . [and] bone, which in a large whale will weigh three thousand pounds . . . The wall of bone is clasped by the white blubbery lips . . . which at the bottom are four feet thick, tapering to a blunt edge, where they fit into a rebate sunk in the upper jaw. The throat . . . is four feet thick, and is mainly blubber interpenetrated by fibrous, muscular flesh.

The lips and throat of a two-hundred-and-fifty-barrel whale should yield sixty barrels of oil, and, with the supporting jaw-bones . . . will weigh as much as twenty-five oxen of one thousand pounds each. Attached to the throat by a broad base is the enormous tongue, the size of which can be better conceived by the fact that twenty-five barrels of oil have been taken from one. Such a tongue would equal in weight ten oxen. The spread of lips, as the whale plows through the fields of "brit," is about thirty feet. Sometimes in feeding the whale turns on its side, so as to lay the longer axis of the cavity of the mouth horizontally. Keeping the lower lip closed, and the upper one thrown off, and standing perpendicularly, it scoops along just under the surface where the "brit" is always most densely packed. After thus sifting a track of the sea fifteen feet wide and a quarter of a mile in length, the water foaming through the slatted bone, and packing the mollusks upon the hair-sieve, the whale raises the lower jaw; but still keeping the lips apart, it forces the spongy tongue into the cavity of the sieve, driving the water with great force through the spaces between the bone. Then, closing the lips, it disposes of the catch, and repeats the operation until satiated . . .

The tail of such a whale is about twenty-five feet broad and six feet deep, and considerably more forked than that of the spermaceti [sperm whale]. The point of junction with the body is about four feet in diameter, the vertebra about fifteen inches; the remainder of the small being packed with rope-like tendons from the size of a finger to that of a man's leg. The great rounded joint

at the base of the skull gleams like an ivory sphere, nearly as
large round as a carriage-wheel. Through the greatest blood-ves-
sels, more than a foot in diameter, surges, at each pulsation of a
heart as large as a hogshead, a torrent of barrels of blood heated
to 104 degrees. The respiratory canal is over twelve inches in
diameter, through which the rush of air is as noisy as the exhaust
pipe of a thousand horsepower steam-engine; and when the fatal
wound is given, torrents of clotted blood are sputtered into the
air or over the nauseated hunters.[8]

Once the leviathan was secured beneath the cutting stage, the next step,
cutting in, was entrusted to the captain and the ship's officers to ensure
that no valuable blubber was lost. Using sharp spades with handles
sixteen feet long, men teetered on the cutting stage above the whale's
carcass, the structure beneath their feet rolling and heaving with the
motion of the ship. Braced against the railing they plunged the edge of
a sharp cutting spade into the blubber, peeling it off around the whale's
body. A toggle and chain were attached to these huge blanket pieces, six
feet wide, over twenty feet long, and weighing several tons. At the bow
of the ship, men worked the windlass to hoist the blanket pieces aboard.
From time to time, the men on the cutting stage handed dull spades up
to the blacksmith, bent over his grindstone on deck to hone their edges
sharp.

Slithering across the greasy deck, men lowered the blanket pieces
to the blubber room below, where the crew cut the thick grayish-white
fat into smaller "horse pieces" a few feet square. These in turn were laid
over a plank or log for mincing. (Nathaniel Ransom spelled it "minsing.")
Cutting with a two-handled knife, men made a series of cross-hatches that
left the blubber attached to the black whale skin to increase the surface
area exposed to heat in the trypots. On deck men started the tryworks,
first igniting a fire of wood or coal in a brick hearth insulated from the
deck by a layer of sand or bricks. The "Bible pieces"—black-backed pieces
of blubber cut by the strokes of the mincing knife so that they resembled
leaves of a Bible fanned open—were now heated in the trypots, iron kettles
up to two hundred gallons in capacity surrounded by the fire. To obtain
oil of the best quality, the blubber had to be heated without boiling the oil,
and the pieces of blubber and skin had to be stirred to prevent sticking
to the surface of the iron pot. Pieces of skin that had given up all their oil
were then skimmed from the pot and used to fuel the fire. The process of
trying out—heating and melting the blubber—produced a black, greasy
smoke and a soot that settled on masts, rigging, and deck. Men breathed

the fishy odor of burning whale flesh as they stirred the trypots. The whale's enormous head containing the valuable whalebone had to be severed from the carcass and hoisted onto the deck. As the stench of dead and rotting krill poured from the bowhead's mouth and overspread the deck, the crew sawed and hacked strips of baleen from the jaw in sections, still attached to the gums, and stowed them below decks. Later, as the ship left the Arctic at the end of the season, the whalemen scraped away the partially rotted gum flesh, a process they called slushing. Finally, they washed the bone, dried it on deck, and bundled it into hundred-pound sheaves for shipment home from the Sandwich Islands.

The process of "minsing and boiling" the bowhead brought alongside the *Barnstable* on June 25 lasted from noon on Tuesday through Thursday. The Arctic summer gave twenty-four hours of light near the solstice, and whalemen worked around the clock whenever there were bowheads to strike, or blubber to mince and try out. They bailed hot oil from the trypots into a cooling tank on deck, and later ran it into casks for storage below decks. "Breaking out casks, stowing away oil, scraping decks, stowing away bone," Nathaniel Ransom listed his chores on Friday, June 28. To clean the ship, men scoured the deck with sand and old canvas. The final step in the process was to mix the ashes beneath the trypots with seawater to make a caustic solution akin to lye. It cut the greasy residue of blubber and oil coating the decks that whalemen called slubgullion. "All hands washing. Saw one bowhead. Killed a pig. Washed off decks," he recorded his Saturday labors.

On the Fourth of July the *Barnstable* reached Plover Bay (Provideniya, 64°22' N, 173°21' W), a settlement on the southern coast of the Chukchi Peninsula of northeastern Siberia. There, natives came aboard and bartered 440 pounds of walrus tusks, a bearskin, and two white fox skins for some of Captain Brownson's trade goods, metal tools, and brightly colored cloth. Through July the *Barnstable* cruised among other whaling vessels following the bowhead migration—northward and eastward along the Siberian coast through the Bering Strait, skirting the edge of the tongue of ice stretching down through the Chukchi Sea. The *Barnstable*'s bow boat took a bowhead on Sunday, July 21, but a few weeks later thick fog concealed their prey before the crew could even lower the whaleboats. Heavy weather "blowing a stiff breeze" hindered their hunt in mid-August, but they succeeded in taking bowheads on the 17th and 22nd and again on September 2.

After the solitary months of travel to the whaling grounds, Arctic whaling provided countless opportunities for sociability—with other seamen at least. Two dozen whalers, most from New Bedford and nearby ports, competed and collaborated within sight of each other's sails between May and October. Nathaniel Ransom reported the sight of a sail on the horizon with obvious pleasure. Seamen "spoke" the ship, communicating from one vessel to another about the season's catch, barrels of oil made, and the number of months away from port. In slack times or on Sundays the crew got a chance to go aboard the other vessel to exchange news. Because whaling vessels remained at sea for three or four years, they often carried newspapers and letters from home to deliver to ships in the Arctic that had left port a few seasons earlier. Even after two years, an issue of New Bedford's *Republican Standard* brought welcome news of familiar places and faces. Sometimes the gam brought sobering news from a neighboring ship. On a Sunday in early August 1861, Nathaniel Ransom's shipmates gammed the bark *Milo*: "Her 3rd mate died today at 9 o'clock AM and was buried at 4 o'clock PM. Gammed the *Milo* and *Florida*." A death aboard ship meant a lonely burial at sea, a graveyard desolate of any marker.

After taking nine bowheads, the *Barnstable* sailed south through the Bering Strait and passed Plover Bay on the Siberian coast on September 13. It was "blowing a heavy gale" which carried away the ship's topsail. Near St. Matthew's Island, inhabited only by Arctic foxes and a few polar bears, the crew took one right whale, smaller and less valuable than the bowheads. In heavy weather and thick fog, the ship traveled in company with the bark *Florida*, which had left New Bedford a year before the *Barnstable*. When the ships reached calmer waters in October, Captain Brownson went aboard the *Florida* and Captain Coddington Fish came aboard the *Barnstable*. Their voyage from the Arctic southward to the Sandwich Islands lasted about a month. After the rush of sudden pursuit of whales, the calmer weeks of travel again produced friction among the crew. Gilman Clark observed a quarrel between the captain and first mate about some water casks. "The mate said he would leave as soon as he got into port, but he dare not; you couldn't kick him out of the ship."

Hawaiian Ports: Bananas and Ladies

At nine at night on October 16, 1861, the *Barnstable* anchored in Hilo harbor, where it remained until November 4. The verdant tropical landscape with its smells of earth and ripening fruit struck all the whalemen's senses after months skirting the barren wastelands of Siberia. For the first time, greenhands tasted unfamiliar yams, taro, and coconut. Mouths watered at the mere sight of tropic fruits such as pineapples, melons, mangoes, and papayas. Bananas, readily available in the islands, would not reach New England until 1870. Those sold in supermarkets today are nearly all the Cavendish variety, which keeps only a short time unless refrigerated. The earlier Gros Michel bananas common in the Sandwich Islands in the 1860s had tougher skins and kept much longer in the hold of a ship. Ripe bananas provided a novel delight for men sated with potatoes and onions.

The first order of business in port was to get a raft of water and stow it down. Men roped empty casks together and towed them to shore with a whaleboat to fill them at a freshwater spring. Breakers could make the work of towing the full casks back to ship and hoisting them aboard far more difficult. One watch, half the crew, went ashore each day on liberty while the other scraped and painted the ship outside; repaired the waist boat, the whaleboat stored amidships; and "got off" or brought on board firewood and forty bags of potatoes. The *Barnstable* also off-loaded its cargo of whalebone, five and one-half tons of it. The voyage produced 660 barrels of whale oil; the average for the season was 780 barrels per ship. Forty-six whaling vessels arrived from the Arctic, and another thirty-four from the Okhotsk Sea. Nathaniel Ransom calculated his own comparisons in journal entries: the *Marengo* from New Bedford had made just two hundred barrels in twenty-six months while the *Montreal* claimed two thousand barrels in half that time. His own share of the profits from oil and bone made only about a hundred dollars, meager wages for a year and a half at sea. One captain writing to the *Whalemen's Shipping List and Merchants' Transcript* called Arctic whaling a lottery in which the captain's management and skill had nothing to do with the earnings of the voyage.

In port or at anchor the *Barnstable*'s crew visited those of a half-dozen other whaling vessels in the harbor. Hilo offered novel attractions for a fifteen-year-old from Mattapoisett: "Got off two boats of bannas [sic] brought off some ladies," Nathaniel Ransom wrote on October 30. Captain Brownson had gone ashore, leaving his officers aboard to handle discipline among the crew. Below that mention of ladies is a wide gap in the journal, leaving more space than usual for us to read between the lines. Sandwich Island women willing to come on board a whaling ship whose crew had spent seven months without eying a single female were no ladies. Numerous whaling narratives describe at greater lengths whalemen's encounters with women of the Pacific Islands, some swimming and playing nude in the waves near shore, some offering lithe naked bodies to strangers, some coerced into prostitution by brothers, fathers, and even husbands. Other whalers recount the cultural clash of Islanders' freer sexual mores with Nantucket and New Bedford Quaker ethics. Nathaniel Ransom's adolescent voice has nothing to say.

Captain Brownson's wife and three children lived in the Sandwich Islands, and he spent three weeks with them, relaxing in the port's cosmopolitan sociability. Several whaling captains moved their families to Hilo, Honolulu, or Lahaina, where they could spend a month or two each year together. If a captain's wife remained in New England, on the other hand, she might live with her husband for no more than two or three months every three or four *years*. After leaving Hilo, the *Barnstable* docked briefly in Honolulu before resuming its peregrinations southwestward toward the Tasman Sea and Desolation Ground.

"Two Years Out—Too Dry"

Nathaniel Ransom's second Christmas at sea found his ship on the New Zealand whaling ground, where finbacks and a right whale swam within sight. The crew lowered whaleboats to pursue the right whale but could not approach close enough to strike and came aboard once again. Captain Brownson ordered the seamen to take in sail, for it was breezing up. The new year, 1862, began amidst finbacks and porpoises, the only prey in sight. Nearing Antarctica, Nathanial Ransom sighted ice "burgs" on January 21 and 22. The ship turned north at the end of the month, trying out a little porpoise blubber, for they had caught nothing else. Near Pitcairn Island, west of Valparaiso, Chile, they "raised a small school of sperm whales, lowered three boats for them, got nothing, boats came aboard" (February 12, 1862). The crew made spun yarn and sennit and repaired sails during weeks of idleness in February and March. They captured a large turtle east of Tahiti and tried out its blubber, having nothing else to fill their empty oil casks.

From mid-March through mid-April the ship once again remained in Hilo where Captain Brownson lived ashore with his family. The mate in charge of the vessel kept its crew employed in repairing equipment, cleaning, and painting. Ordinary seamen, assigned to either the starboard or larboard watch, took turns at liberty ashore. Other shipmates touched a bit of home in Sandwich Island ports: "All hands got letters," Ransom noted in Honolulu, without specifying whether he too had word from his parents or brothers.

Beyond the comforts of family, Captain Brownson put into port to re-structure his crew. The poor catch and solitary months of busy-work aboard ship rankled his men. "Captain knocked the 3rd mate off duty" in mid-February. In Hilo, after Joseph Ribbit, Henry Reynolds, and one other man deserted, the Captain "shipped one white boatsteerer [harpooner] and 4 kanakas" (March 28, 1862). Yankee whalers considered these Pacific Islanders good hands, for they had paddled, swum, and fished since childhood. Uninterested in learning their surnames, agents and captains often simply listed them as Joe or Jim Kanaka. One writer who encountered Sandwich Islanders in 1845 described the men as "slender & of about middling height, not strong or spry except in the water . . . Both men & women although they greet one another with smiles & often laugh still there is a shade of melancholy & sadness on their brow & no joviality is among them."[9]

Two days after the four Kanakas and new boatsteerer joined the crew, five men ran away from the ship. Later in Honolulu, while two boats' crews were ashore on liberty, two other men ran away. After bringing wood, potatoes, four bullocks, eleven pigs, four sheep, and ducks and chickens aboard, the *Barnstable*'s crew off-loaded their five barrels of porpoise and turtle oil and caught the runaways before setting sail. Men's readiness to jump ship indicates how intolerable they found conditions on board. The close quarters, squalid conditions, lack of privacy and limited diet were compounded by back-breaking round-the-clock labor when the ship chased bowheads in the inhospitable Arctic waters. The Sandwich Islands attracted whaling masters because they were not part of the United States and runaways had no recourse to its laws. Aboard whaling vessels the captain functioned as the dictator of a floating prison.

During the month-long journey north into the Arctic, the *Barnstable*'s crew prepared for bowhead whaling. Men scraped the trypots, and they scraped and cleaned lances used to kill the whale, and the cutting spades used to peel off blubber. They made and rigged a cutting stage, made a rudder for one of the whaleboats, and moved the boats onto the cranes where they rested beneath the davits overhanging the rail of the ship. Disappointment over the poor catch fomented grumbling among the disgruntled crew. Lewis Swain, the third mate whom Captain Brownson demoted in February, wrote sardonically in the ship's log for May 22, 1862: "So ends two years with 700 barrels. Haven't seen a whale for 8 months. Sic Transit Gloria Mundi." Foremast hand Gilman Clark felt the same disappointment: "Two years out too dry with 85 barrels sperm and 600 whale [oil]. Hard luck."

Near Cape Navarin, south of the Anadyr Gulf, the crew "[s]aw a stinker took him alongside and cut him in." The dead whale, likely harpooned by another ship's whaleboat, had escaped only to die later. It putrefied until so filled with gas that the corpse rose to the surface and floated. The overpowering stench and vomitus revulsion caused by cutting in rotting whale blubber and baleen can only be imagined.

On the northern whaling ground off Cape Thaddeus (Mys Faddeya, 62°39′ N, 179°38′ E), Swain lost a bowhead in a nearly fatal accident. Nathaniel Ransom's account for May 31, 1862 reads: "Latter part we lowered, 3rd mate struck a bowhead, the 2d mate in trying to get fast to him pulled onto his back and got stove into about 100 pieces and afterwards the 3rd mate in towing the whale cut the line hitch, by which we lost the whale and was lucky that we did not lose ourselves some of us." The bowhead's flukes, twenty feet in breadth, could batter a whaleboat to splinters in an instant.

The *Barnstable*'s logkeeper, likely the first mate, soon "[h]ad a few words with Mr. Swain for not looking after things. He told me not to put my hands on him and I told him that he should obey my orders or he could not remain on board of this ship and he said he would get out of her as quick as he could." Jumping ship between Siberia and Alaska was a far different matter from escaping in Honolulu. Next day the first mate, eager to be rid of Lewis Swain, went aboard the *Catherine* and arranged for Mr. Swain to leave the *Barnstable*. Swain "took his things and went on board to work his passage." His departure left the *Barnstable* shorthanded for the next two weeks. Then on June 19, Captain Brownson took the fifth mate of the *Coral* aboard and shipped him as third mate. Beyond the friction of coping with an insubordinate third mate, Brownson was relieved to rid his ship of an outlier who might attract a following of disgruntled shipmates; for in two years his first, second, and third mates had all left the ship, discouraged by the poor catch.

The *Barnstable*'s crew lowered again for bowheads on June second, third, fourth, and fifth, each time without success. Thick fog and ice impeded their progress north as they spoke the *Reindeer*, which had already taken five whales this season. Captain Brownson anchored at Plover Bay, where a Chukchi settlement offered opportunities to trade for supplies, furs, and warm clothing. The *Barnstable* gammed the *Florida* and sent one boat ashore a-ducking. "Esquimeaux" came aboard offering walrus tusks, fox skins, fur mittens and boots to trade for tobacco and tools. The ship remained there during the latter half of June, waiting for ice to clear so that they could follow the bowheads further north. Unfavorable weather and ice delayed the beginning of the bowhead season until early July, a month later than in 1861. And by July half the season was gone, for bowheads had passed through Bering Strait and entered their summer feeding grounds in the Chukchi Sea, migrating east and northward toward Point Barrow.

Other ships reached the northern whaling grounds far ahead of the *Barnstable*. The *Florida*'s Captain Fish wrote New Bedford's *Whalemen's Shipping List* that he entered the Bering Strait on May first and found pleasant weather and whales as plentiful as porpoises. In July, the *Barnstable* finally traveled north of the Arctic Circle into the Chukchi Sea and reached sixty-eight degrees north latitude. The crew took four walruses on July 22 and a bowhead on July 24. Yet danger was never far away. On Sunday, August 10, the starboard boat struck a bowhead that pulled the boat and its crew underwater. The crews of other whaleboats rescued all hands and salvaged the whale. They towed the whale to the ship and worked until midnight cutting him in. Some mariners complained gloomily that whaling on a Sunday was a religious offense, sure to be punished by perils such as the loss of a whaleboat and the near drowning of its crew.

By early September, the *Barnstable* had caught five more bowheads, making just 540 barrels of oil, 20 percent less than the previous year, and about five tons of whalebone. It was some consolation to know that the price of whale oil had risen from about forty cents a gallon to nearly sixty due to increased demand and disruptions in trade caused by the Civil War.

The ship left the Arctic safely and once again reached Hilo in late October, remaining in Sandwich Island ports until November 29. In Hilo, Captain Brownson hired on three new crewmen and a new second mate, for in late August he "had knocked the second mate off duty against his will" after the first officer "had a few words with him." In port, Nathaniel Ransom learned that other whalers had made more profitable catches during the 1862 summer bowhead season: the ship *Fanny* had made 1,600 barrels of whale oil and the *Charles W. Morgan* had made 2,000. Ransom and his shipmates stowed down thirty barrels of salt beef, loaded four barrels of Irish potatoes, dried thirty bushels of sweet potatoes and brought aboard firewood, pigs, and hens. Brownson shipped his whalebone home from Honolulu, unloaded only a few barrels of whale oil, and carried the rest of his cargo southward.

Cruising off the Californian and Mexican coasts in January 1863, the *Barnstable* failed to catch any sperm whales; the Pacific sperm whaling grounds, where Sidney and Theodore Ransom had hunted a few years earlier, had about played out. Instead, Captain Brownson hunted a less valuable prey, the Pacific gray whales that breed and give birth in the warmer waters of sheltered bays. Southward along the coast Brownson sailed during the winter months, training his three new seamen taken aboard in the Sandwich Islands. Like the whalers themselves, the Pacific gray whales migrated south in winter and north in summer into the Bering, Chukchi, and Beaufort Seas, traveling in pods as large as forty whales and as far as six thousand miles. During the *Barnstable*'s winter cruise between the Arctic seasons, the crew caught five California gray whales. Nathaniel Ransom called them devil-fish or ripsacks because the females fought fiercely to protect their calves. Able to elude whalemen by remaining underwater up to an hour, their habit of feeding on the ocean bottom also earned them the name "mussel-diggers." Whalers spotted them by finding cloudy water where the ground-feeders had been digging. Usually the mother ship anchored in deeper water while the whaleboats approached the gray whales and their young in shallower bays. Hunters drove them further inshore to hinder their escape, targeting the calves first and hoping to strike their mothers soon after. Females sometimes covered a calf with one fin or shoved it ahead to escape the whaleboat. Bull whales swam further out to sea, further from the hunters' weapons. Of all the toothless baleen whales, the Pacific gray, forty-five feet long and weighing sixteen to eighteen tons, was the least desirable catch. A large female's reddish blubber, six to ten inches thick, might make sixty barrels of dark oil, considered inferior to oil from humpback, right, or bowhead whales. Her baleen, nearly white in color, was short, about fifteen inches long, with a heavy, brushy fringe along the inner edge of each strip. The *Barnstable* captured one devil-fish on January 9 that had to be towed nine hours to the ship and made just forty barrels of oil. The barnacles and whale lice (parasitic amphipods) made it appear ugly as well as vicious and unprofitable. Nevertheless, the Pacific gray's seasonal migrations offered whalers an opportunity to profit from the winter season.

Trouble broke out aboard the *Barnstable* again as discontent fomented among the crew. Back in Honolulu to unload oil in late March "the mate had a row with a man for not coming when they was called. He struck one man over the head with a broom and called him a son of a B," Gilman Clark wrote. His friend Samuel Colony who had given Clark his journal was discharged due to poor eyesight, left to make his own way home. A few days later "the steward got into a fight ashore and got his shoulder put out of joint." Matters turned more violent on April 6 when "the 4th mate had a row with the men about going ashore and one man lifted an axe to him when he lifted a club hammer and struck him over the eye cutting a severe gash" (Gilman Clark). As a result, all hands were called up before the American consul in Honolulu the next day. Ironically, the injured fourth mate William Quinton (James Ransom's friend) may have been the only one of the original officers still aboard the *Barnstable*. Its first and second mates had left the ship in Pernambuco after the first six months, and third mate Lewis Swain left the ship in the Arctic. No judgment against the axe-wielding crewman appears in the logbook; generally the consul only stepped in to settle violence or insurrection that the captain was not able to handle alone. Unruly seamen could be summarily discharged and left ashore to seek passage home on another vessel. Sometimes these outcasts became beachcombers, shiftless men without work left to fend for themselves in the Pacific islands. Captains distrusted them and were seldom willing to take them on as crew again. Sometimes the *Honolulu Friend*, the port's weekly newspaper, reported their names and reputation to warn against hiring them.

The *Barnstable* shipped home 202 barrels of oil from its winter cruise in the south and hired three Oahu natives before leaving Honolulu, April 19, 1863. After a brief stop on Kauai for potatoes and firewood, Captain Brownson sailed for his third season in the Arctic.

Hugging the coast of Siberia the ship made its way into the Anadyr Sea past Cape Thaddeus. The crew spotted several bowheads in early June and lowered boats to chase five of them off Plover Bay on June 30, but found no chance to strike. The logkeeper saw no cause for celebration on July 4, as there was plenty of ice in sight. Furthermore he felt ill: "Myself the Mate taken sick with the bowel complaint." Even worse, two weeks later another officer noted "the mate Mr. Trask got his hand cut by a bom lance exploding at the muzel of the gun." The mariners took a single bowhead in mid-July, but were otherwise unsuccessful. Heavy weather struck on August 19 when the *Barnstable* shipped a sea that carried away the bow boat, stove five of the stanchions for livestock, and washed all the crew on deck into the lee scuppers. As the failed season ended, the ship headed south in mid-September.

The size of the 1863 Arctic whaling fleet had fallen to just twenty-six vessels, which averaged a catch of 1,104 barrels of whale oil and eight and a half tons of whalebone. In comparison, the *Barnstable* fared poorly. Its Arctic bowhead season produced just 663 barrels of oil, and the captain shipped home seven tons of whalebone aboard the *Reindeer*. In port in Hilo, a discouraged Captain Brownson brought his wife and family aboard for the journey home to Massachusetts. Meanwhile Nathaniel Ransom and his crewmates loaded two hundred pounds of sugar and a sack of coffee into the *Barnstable*'s hold. Ashore in Honolulu Brownson hired a new second mate; the poor catch left officers and some crew thinking they could fare better aboard some other vessel. The New Bedford bark *Tamerlane* for instance, had taken thirteen whales in the summer season.

Seeking another source of income, Captain Brownson took aboard 780 barrels of oil from the *Tamerlane* to carry homeward late in 1863. The *Barnstable*'s logkeeper noted faithfully that the crew "wet the oil" each week, a precaution against leakage, for as the casks dried, they shrank, allowing oil to seep out between the staves. Below decks, Nathaniel Ransom lay sick and off duty in late December. Gilman Clark was assigned the chore of killing three hogs, but he kept one eye on the captain and mate squabbling, their hostilities exacerbated by the voyage's scanty catch. The ship sailed south, maintaining a lookout for whales as it edged the coast of Chile bound for Cape Horn. On February 7, in heavy rain and fog a severe gale stove the starboard boat. The mate reported more worrisome news: "At 9 AM oil got a light from one cask of the *Tamerlane*'s oil." Following a plume of smoke, the crew found the fire in the hold in time to put it out, but it had burned through part of the deck.

Gilman Clark saw that the mate's quarrel with the captain continued to fester as the ship cruised the Atlantic heading north and east around the bulge of Brazil: "The mate insulted the Captain's wife and girl the Captain ought to have put him in the scuppers any other master would." Brownson's inability to control his officers led Clark to sympathize, "Hard times if a Captain cannot be master of his own ship."

Even homeward bound, the whalers continued the hunt, taking a few porpoises in early February. Nathaniel Ransom recovered from his illness and returned to ship's duty. On April 4 he wrote, "Saw blackfish old man took them to be sperm whales lowered for them mate got one." But the chief order of business was to clean the ship before it reached port: "Washing bow boat breaking out molasses scrubbing bulwarks with sand & canvas." No wonder the *Barnstable* had "all sail set," for everyone was eager to reach New Bedford. To celebrate the end of whaling, Nathaniel Ransom and his shipmates "Hove the tryworks overboard. Stowed away the pots and cooler took the craft out of the boats cleaned it stowed it away." The cooler, a large metal tank that contained oil from the trypots until it had cooled sufficiently to be barreled, and the cast iron trypots were scoured clean, but the grease-soaked bricks made a hearty splash as they were flung over the side. Craft or whalecraft was the whalemen's term for the tools of the hunt: harpoons, lances, oars, paddles, line, line tubs, and other implements used in the whaleboats. Two days before arriving in port Nathaniel Ransom ended his journal, writing simply, "Almost home."

As the *Barnstable* sailed into New Bedford's harbor on April 28, 1864 the value of its cargo had increased considerably. The average price of sperm oil—the *Barnstable*'s had spent three years in the hold appreciating in value—was now $1.61 a gallon. Whale oil—the ship had produced 2,065 barrels—was now ninety-five and one-half cents a gallon. The 25,000 pounds of bone should sell for $1.62 a pound.[10] Nathaniel Ransom's "long lay," a share of one-two-hundredth of the cargo's value, meant that he earned five or six hundred dollars for nearly four years' hard labor at sea—after subtracting charges for liberty money while the ship was in port and the costs of items bought from the slops chest. Still, the earnings were no lower than what a youth might expect from farming or factory work.

The *Barnstable* had left home with a crew of twenty-five. Fourteen men left the ship or deserted, dissatisfied with their earnings or working conditions; eighteen other crew signed on, some of whom may have left the ship later. The high rate of turnover was not unusual among whaleship crews. What seems more remarkable is that Nathaniel Ransom did not flee the ship. Perhaps he was accustomed to hardship and toil before he set foot in the fo'csle. More likely his perseverance indicates his sturdy, uncomplaining character.

The bark itself was sold to New York for the merchant service. Captain Leonard Brownson, however, made one final voyage. This time he tried his luck sperm whaling in the Pacific. When he set sail from New Bedford aboard the *Spartan* in late November of 1864, Gilman Clark went with him as third mate. Eleven months later they returned with 553 barrels of sperm oil in the hold, a short voyage, and Brownson's last.

Eighteen-year-old Nathaniel Ransom for his part laid his journal aside once he reached land. He wrote nothing of walking home into the early spring after four years at sea. He never described the overpowering scent of pine trees, the feel of warm soil between his fingers, or the tender patter of spring rain on new leaves. Only the youngest of the Ransom brothers, thirteen-year-old Andrew, remained at home to greet him.

Six months later Joseph returned from whaling, for he had signed aboard the Mattapoisett bark *Clara Bell* just months after Theodore returned to port in that ship. Though the ship brought home 1,450 barrels of valuable sperm oil, the *Clara Bell* had lost an entire boat's crew (six men) in December 1863 when fast to a whale. Deadly risk and tempting

American Whaler. Lithograph by E. C. Kellogg, circa 1850. Print Number 143 (Frink family collection) bears handwritten inscription "Spartan" on verso. Captain Brownson made his last voyage in the sperm whaler Spartan (1864-1865).

profits went hand in hand. For his part Joseph could boast of augmenting his earnings with a special reward for sighting a large sperm whale that had made ninety-seven barrels of oil.[11]

Life on shore left Nathaniel Ransom restless. "He soon sailed from Plymouth in the schooner *Profit*, Captain Bartlett, on a cod-fishing trip to the Grand Banks."[12] Slab-sided planks of cod were salted and laid on racks to dry before being stored in barrels or shipped to Europe, where Catholics abstained from eating meat on Fridays and during Lent. Sugar plantation owners in the Caribbean bought dried cod as a cheap source of protein and salt and fed it to their African-born field workers in place of beef or more expensive meats. Thrifty Yankees freshened salt cod overnight and then parboiled it on the woodstove all morning. At Saturday noontime they forked pieces of cod atop boiled potatoes and mashed them together, cutting in minced onion and scraps of fried salt pork for a dinner some called Cape Cod turkey.

Nathaniel Ransom returned from cod-fishing in September 1864 and went to school in Middleboro for a few months. Then in February of 1865, near the end of the Civil War, he sailed from New Bedford in the bark *Commerce* under Captain Robinson to Mobile, Alabama. The city of thirty thousand was a heavily fortified port and a center of ship building for the Confederacy. Admiral David Farragut and the Union Navy blockaded Mobile, battling clouds of mosquitos that carried yellow fever. The city capitulated to Union forces on April 12, 1865, three days after General Lee's surrender at the Appomattox courthouse. Nathaniel Ransom, aboard the *Commerce*, was in the Mobile harbor at this final battle of the Civil War. He then sailed homeward via the port of Boston.

Casting about for his next venture, the young man was drawn to the Mattapoisett wharves where he might find work. There he glimpsed a slender, dark-haired girl carrying a dinner pail. Nathaniel recognized Sarah Dexter, a neighbor and once a schoolmate, who had come to bring her father his noonday meal. He watched as Ephraim Dexter knelt on the rounded hull of an overturned vessel, pounding strands of oakum—tarred rope—between the planks. The iron-banded head of his long-handled wooden mallet rang out as he struck the caulking iron, a flat blade curved to follow the oakum between the planks of the curved hull. As a young man Ephraim Dexter had made two whaling voyages and was once shipwrecked. Settled on land, he took up his father's trade of ship's caulker. On his skill depended the seaworthiness of vessels like the *Oscar* and the *Willis*. Holding his caulker's mallet aloft, he paused for a moment and caught Nathaniel Ransom's eye. Then he laid down his mallet, clambered down from his perch, and went to fetch his dinner pail.

Chapter II: "Who wouldn't sell a farm to go whaling?"

Harpooner on the Sea Breeze,
October 18, 1865–November 31, 1868

Sarah Amanda Dexter wore her dark hair parted in the middle and pulled the braids neatly back, fastening them around her head. Her gray eyes gazed steadily at Nathaniel beneath dark, straight eyebrows. The Dexters settled in Mattapoisett before the Revolution and became a large clan, although Sarah's household was small. Her father, Ephraim Dexter, worked at Mattapoisett's shipyards as a carpenter and a ship's caulker. He and his wife, Laura Snow, had lost a son, Oscar, who lived less than two years. Sarah grew up with a younger sister, Phebe, and a brother, Philander. When she was ten years old and Philander eight, the family moved into a new cedar-shingled house with white trim that Ephraim Dexter built on Mattapoisett's Pine Island Road near the Ransom farm, where children could walk to the ocean. An old tintype photograph taken when Sarah was about twelve shows her seated amidst her wide skirts, her hand lovingly resting on her brother's shoulder. Philander, wearing a sailor suit, stands solemnly beside her, their cheeks tinted a rosy hue. In May 1860, Philander died at the age of ten. Four-year-old Phebe died just two months later. When Nathaniel Ransom came courting, only Sarah remained with her grieving parents. During the months ashore before his second whaling voyage, he wooed her and won her heart.

Change swirled around the young couple in Mattapoisett as the Civil War drew to a close. Nathaniel Ransom and his brothers, home from the South, discussed their prospects for making a living from the sea. James, the eldest brother, had married at the age of twenty-eight, shortly before his second voyage aboard the sperm whaler *General Scott*, this time as first mate. His eighteen-year-old bride, Almeida, soon gave birth to a daughter and named her Etta. The child was four by the time she first saw her father. His ship returned in the summer of 1865 with all of its original crew, a rare occurrence for a whaling vessel. Although the voyage produced a meager catch of sperm and whale oil, its crew escaped the reach of Union army conscription. James and his young family settled in New Bedford, where he left the sea and turned his hand to carpentry.

Sidney and Theodore Ransom had enlisted together in the Union Navy in the fall of 1861 and served for three years. Sidney sweated aboard the gunboat *Sagamore* patrolling the tepid waters of Florida, Alabama, and Mississippi as the ship burned the rebels' cotton bales and captured several Confederate vessels. Theodore learned gunnery at the Brooklyn Navy Yard in New York. He became acting master's mate of the steamships *Circassian*, *Winona*, and *Arkansas* supplying Union warships in the West Gulf Blockading Squadron in 1863. He was discharged and returned home after his three-year enlistment in the navy expired in October 1864. The Ransom brothers wrote loving letters home to their father and to one another, sending news of distant climates and faraway ports. In May of 1863, Sidney assured his father that his steam-powered gunboat, the *Sagamore*, and Theodore's *Winona* looked just alike, for they exchanged postcards of their vessels. Sidney spent five weeks in southern Florida in early spring, pronouncing it "a first rate place to stay if not for the mosquitos." James's wife Almeida sent Sidney an ambrotype photograph of his niece, little Etta. Sidney closed the letter to his father with genuine affection: "Give my love to Mother and all the folks. Take good care of little Etta." Sidney was discharged in December 1864 and returned home into a New England winter.

Theodore, meanwhile, met a young Creole woman in New Orleans, and had fallen deeply in love by the time he returned from his naval service. The parents of Jeanne d'Arc Guartney opposed her marriage to a non-Catholic. The young couple married nevertheless, and Theodore brought his bride back to Massachusetts. Although the pair never had children, Theodore's nieces and nephews grew fond of their Aunt Josie. Theodore and Josie settled in Somerville, nearer Boston, where he became a traveling merchant. Like James and Sidney, Theodore never returned to whaling.

Joseph Ransom had barely disembarked from the *Clara Bell* in the fall of 1864 when he enlisted in the Union Army's 35th US Colored Infantry Volunteers. He seemed more distant from his family than any of the Ransom brothers, and seldom wrote to them. "I don't think Joseph has used me just right," Sidney complained to their father as he battled mosquitos aboard the *Sagamore* in the Florida swamps. Joseph came home shortly before the end of the war, and he married Mary Sampson Faunce in New Bedford at the beginning of March 1865. They remained in Mattapoisett, where Joseph found nothing better than work as a day laborer, for returning Union soldiers seeking jobs crowded the towns and cities.

The War had taken its toll on New England's whaling fleet as Confederate raiders like the *Alabama* destroyed forty-six vessels, among them the *Elisha Dunbar* and Matthew Hiller's *Altamaha* from Mattapoisett. Two of the whaling barks familiar to Nathaniel Ransom and his *Barnstable* shipmates, the *Catherine* and the *Milo*, were captured and sunk in the Arctic by the Confederate raider *Shenandoah*. Its captain, James Waddell, resisted news of General Robert E. Lee's defeat and continued burning and sinking Union whaleships until the end of June 1865. Another thirty-nine aging whalers were weighted with granite blocks and sunk to blockade the Confederacy's harbors of Charleston and Savannah. These two "stone fleets" and the predations by Confederate warships reduced the size of the whaling fleet at the end of the Civil War to about a hundred vessels, from a pre-war total of nearly twice that number.

The Civil War also changed whaling technology and economics as the winds of battle swept across the American landscape. Both Theodore and Sidney had manned vessels powered by steam-driven propellers as well as sails; steamers transported passengers between New Bedford and New York. Yet owners of New Bedford's whaling fleet, unwilling to invest precious dollars in the industry's uncertain future, preferred to re-fit older sailing ships instead of outfitting new steam vessels for the risky whale hunt. Not until 1880 would auxiliary steam power make inroads into Arctic whaling, although it offered ships the critical advantage of maneuvering quickly between moving pack ice and nearby land.

Young men who enlisted or were conscripted into Union forces had decreased the supply of manpower ready to sign on for a whaling voyage, forcing New Bedford's ship owners and their agents to rely increasingly on recruits from the Azores, Cape Verde and Canary Islands, or Kanakas from the Pacific islands. Now at war's end the labor market swelled with the ranks of soldiers back from battle. Mariners found the east coast whaling fleet shrinking as shipping agents moved their business to California or the Sandwich Islands to avoid the costly return voyage to New Bedford or smaller nearby harbors. Mattapoisett's *Clara Bell* for instance, Theodore and Joseph Ransom's first whaling ship, now called San Francisco its hailing port. From San Francisco captains could communicate by telegraph, completed in 1866, with shipping agents in New Bedford for instructions about how and when to most profitably transport the season's cargo back east or hold it on board waiting for oil and whalebone prices to rise. Soon completion of the trans-continental railroad in 1869 would also make San Francisco the most economical choice for refitting ships and hiring on seamen without the costly voyage back to New Bedford. Already a railroad across the narrow Isthmus of Panama enabled whalers to ship cargo back to New England ports without carrying it around Cape Horn.

Whalers turned increasingly to the icy North Pacific as the sperm whale fishery played out, prowling as the *Barnstable* had done along the Kamchatka Peninsula north to Siberia's East Cape for bowhead and right whales. Countless discussions arose disputing whether North Atlantic right whales and the northern Pacific bowheads were really two distinct species. Whalemen generally argued that they were indeed different, in behavior as well as location, although decades later harpoons and tools recovered from whale carcasses proved that these species migrated from one coast of Arctic North America to the other. As petroleum oil gained a larger share of the market for lighting and lubrication, it diminished the value of whale oil. At the same time, increased demand for whale-bone, particularly in women's corsets and hoop skirts, raised prices so that the Arctic bowhead became the most valuable prey in the seas. The inevitable result—over-fishing—forced whaling vessels to venture further north, arriving earlier and staying later to pursue the gigantic whales. One estimate suggests that the Yankee bowhead hunt which began about 1846 (and intensified rapidly after Captain Royce's passage through the Bering Strait in 1848) killed about 18,650 of the enormous cetaceans. Half were taken by 1863, and two-thirds by 1867.[1] Bowheads caught in the later years of the hunt were smaller and younger, averaging forty-five or fifty feet, and a whale that made a hundred barrels of oil was a lucky catch. Because bowheads reached sexual maturity after twenty years, the population regenerated itself only gradually. Although the easy catches of the first two decades of Arctic whaling seriously depleted the stock of bowheads, neither ship owners nor captains, astute at assessing the movement of drifting ice or the spout of a distant humpback, could yet foresee an eventual collapse of New Bedford's whaling industry. After all, the whaling business had already weathered slack times and heavy seas. Cape Cod and Nantucket shore whaling for blackfish and right whales had faded with grandfather's memories. Who could forecast the effects of the Civil War's reduction in the whaling fleet or the improved weaponry the war made available to whalemen? After the Gold Rush lured young miners to claims and camps in California, the American West opened to wagon trains of settlers and homesteaders. The limitless expanses of the northern Pacific, where whaling fortunes might still be made, beckoned as the last unconquered frontier. Heeding the lure of whaling, Nathaniel

Ransom's youngest brother, fifteen-year-old Andrew, shipped out from New Bedford aboard the *Hunter* at the end of August in 1865.

Nathaniel Ransom himself was nearly twenty and had seen the world when he decided to venture around Cape Horn a second time. Sarah Dexter gave him her picture and promised to write to him faithfully, letters he treasured wherever they reached him, months after she had sent them. But the young couple spent the next four years apart, for six months after returning from the surrender of Mobile, Nathaniel signed on aboard the whaling bark *Sea Breeze*, bound for the Okhotsk Sea.

His love for Sarah prompted him to seek earnings sufficient to establish a household for the two of them. Ironically, the surest way to build their future together seemed to be leaving her behind for another Arctic whaling voyage. At any rate he would escape the plodding toil of farming and the noise-wracked confinement of New Bedford's factories. Before he boarded the *Sea Breeze* on October 18, 1865, the New Bedford Port Society Seamen's Register measured him as 5 feet 6 inches tall, with light complexion and brown hair. In adulthood he remained slight of build, possibly a result of the hard labor and poor nutrition in adolescence. This time he touted his experience and keen sense of aim and signed on as one of four boatsteerers (harpooners), earning a one-hundredth lay of oil and one-eighty-fifth for whalebone. The agent for owner Jonathan Bourne handed him a hundred dollar cash advance and charged him ten dollars for his ship's outfit, including a straw mattress and blanket.

As he had done at fourteen, the young man carried a simple blank book aboard ship. The second "Private Journal of Nathaniel C. Ransom, Mattapoisett, Massachusetts" is headed "Atlantic Pacific & Arctic Ocean again." Cardboard bound and written on inexpensive foolscap, its first pages are obscured by penmanship practice by some other hand. Beginning on the day of departure he entered the *Sea Breeze*'s name and that of Captain James Hamilton at the top of each left page, and recorded the ship's location at the top of the facing page. Some pages were written in pencil, or ink which faded and obliterated the writing. The writer used no punctuation at all, leaving the reader to guess how his run-on sentences fit together. In the style typical of whalers' logbooks, he seldom refers to himself in the first person, except when detailing the physical ailments that plagued him more frequently as he grew older.

What moved the young boatsteerer to write? The responsibility for recording each day's weather, wind, whales, and sails belonged to the *Sea Breeze*'s first mate, not to the youth who titled his account "Private Journal." The difference between such journals and actual ships' logs often remains unclear, so that museum collections refer to Ransom's book and others like it simply as logbooks. Some authors of these private accounts reflected on their own mortality, the fleeting passage of time, and the fragility of a mariner's life. Some wrote as if they planned to share the history of their voyages with loved ones who remained at home, minimizing the hazardous, unpleasant aspects of a voyage and describing exotic locales and unfamiliar races at greater length. Some preserved their own memories of distant places and hair-raising adventures for their older, quieter years. Whatever his own motivation, Ransom's daily entries become longer and increasingly revealing with each of his four journals.

The 472-ton bark *Sea Breeze* was considerably larger than the *Barnstable:* 123.3 feet long, 29 feet wide, with a depth of 16.4 feet, manned by a crew of thirty-two, most of them Yankees except for a second mate, Abram Coffee, listed as Indian, a German cooper, three Cape Verde seamen, and two Sandwich Islanders. Just as New Englanders settled amidst a network of neighbors and kinfolk when they moved westward, whalers embarking on a voyage favored the company of known companions. Abram Coffee hailed from Sag Harbor, New York, as did the *Sea Breeze's* first mate, Josiah Foster. Two Mattapoisett boys, Edward Cushing, age nineteen, and Joshua, seventeen, signed on together. The two youngest in a family of eight children, they may have been related to Ransom's mother, Eunice Cushing. Enos J. Stanton, the Azorean who had made his first voyage aboard the *Barnstable* with Nathaniel Ransom, now hired on as the *Sea Breeze's* steward. Whaling was still a young man's game; most of the crew ranged in age from seventeen to thirty-three.

Aft of the forecastle in steerage, Nathaniel Ransom now shared quarters with three other boatsteerers, the cook, carpenter, blacksmith, steward, and cooper. Promotion out of the forecastle and into steerage also meant that he no longer ate from the kid, the shared tub of food supplied to foremast hands. Instead the steward Enos Stanton served meals to the carpenter, blacksmith, and boatsteerers at a table after the captain and mates had eaten. On the other hand, the boatsteerer (*The Whalemen's Shipping List* and Ransom's journals never use the term harpooner) occupied a tenuous position, belonging neither to the ship's officers nor to its common crew. Boatsteerer Dean Wright, aboard the whaler *Benjamin Rush* in 1842, complained in his journal that a man who would ship as boatsteerer:

> [M]ust be either mad or drunk, or else or a saint . . . He is not respected at all, he has more work to do than all hands besides, and he has no privileges whatever but to bear blame for

everything which may go wrong in the ship. If the Captain finds
a smoothing plane dull he immediately says that a boatsteerer
has been planing his iron pole and dulled it. If there is two
quarts of tobacco juice found spit on the deck it is lain directly
to the poor boatsteerer . . . He needs to be a sailor, a whaler, a
mechanic, a saint, a bully, a man of no kind feeling whatever,
and very little sense. He ought to be a man . . . built of steel and
. . . cannot tire, and does not require sleep or bodily rest of any
kind; one who can content himself in any place which he can
call his own, or where he is not liable to be crowded out. And
he ought to be a man who can be an officer and still be a tar
. . . who can show himself worthy of confidence in all and not
have any placed in him, & be contented to be called a good man
and used like a dog—and do all this for the sake of advance-
ment of which he is not at all sure, when it is done. A Boatsteerer
is placed between two fires, being neither man nor officer, yet
required to be both. He is beneath the officers and not above the
men. He has to obey everybody and be obeyed by nobody, give
no ungentlemanly language to any person but take it from every
person, look cross at none but be frowned upon by all.[2]

Mariners who persisted in whaling generally rose from their first rank
as seaman to the next step up, boatsteerer, as did each of the seven
Ransom brothers. While Nathaniel's keen eyesight, good aim, and agility
had earned him the promotion to boatsteerer on his second voyage, his
success in the unenviable position described here says much about his
developing character.

Like the smaller *Barnstable*, the *Sea Breeze* was rigged as a bark,
its configuration of sails and lines by now familiar. It carried five whaleboats: two bow boats, two astern, and one waist boat hung above the
larboard (port side) deck opposite the cutting stage. Each of the ship's
four mates headed one whaleboat, with the captain as master of the fifth.
Each boatheader, the captain or one of the mates, chose his own crew and
boatsteerer. Nathaniel Ransom pulled the bow oar of the whaleboat as
it cruised or pursued a whale. The mate sat in the stern steering toward
the whale, commanding the crew who faced him to pull hard and fast on
the oars, their backs toward the whale. Men sat on opposing sides of the
boat, each working a single oar that varied in length with the breadth of
the boat: shorter oars toward the bow and stern, and a seventeen-foot oar
at the wide center of the whaleboat. Astern the mate grasped the long
steering oar. Often the crew raised the sail to speed toward the whale
using both wind and oars. Shaped to a prow at both ends, the whaleboat

could reverse direction in an instant to escape the furious charge of a whale or the sweep of his flukes. As they drew closer to their prey, the crew peaked their oars and used paddles to approach more quietly. The bow oarsman had the task of bringing the boat as nearly parallel to the whale as possible, behind his jaws and ahead of his swinging flukes. As they came onto the whale, the mate ordered Nathaniel Ransom to "Stand up and give it to him!" He rose in the bow of the thirty-foot whaleboat, left knee braced in a leather padded semi-circle cut into the bow cover, and grasped his iron. At the closest possible moment, he "darted" or threw his toggle iron fifteen to twenty feet into the body of the whale, aiming for its heart or lungs. If successful, the throw lodged the iron's two-part head in the body of the whale. As the wounded whale pulled away from the boat, one pointed half of the hinged iron head swung back, embedding the weapon more firmly in his flesh. The harpooner's task was not to kill the whale, but to wound and get "fast," meaning firmly hitched to the whale, as fathoms of hempen rope whirled rapidly out of the line tub when the injured whale plunged frantically ahead. As the whale thrashed about, dove to the ocean bottom, or towed the whaleboat rapidly to windward, the boatsteerer quickly moved astern, changing places with the mate, whose job was now to plunge a lance into the whale's lungs and churn it from side to side enlarging the wound until the whale choked to death on his own blood. The boatsteerer now steered as close as possible to the whale while his mates endeavored to make fast to him with other lines to prevent his escape. In the violent confusion of going on the whale, green-hands were apt to leap out of the boat or recoil in horror as the whale's bloody spouting showered down over them. Nathaniel Ransom's role as boatsteerer demanded strength, agility, and imperturbable daring. "It is the harpooneer that makes the voyage," Melville asserted.

Aboard the *Sea Breeze*, Ransom also learned to calculate latitude and longitude and recorded them scrupulously whenever he took the data himself. Latitude was measured at high noon using a sextant to determine the angle between the sun and the horizon. Determining longitude was more complex, and required using a sextant to measure the relative position of celestial bodies at a given time, then comparing that measurement to one taken at the vessel's home port for a certain hour. He became adept at calculating longitude, despite his brief formal schooling. The inclusion of latitude and longitude on some of the journal's pages enables the reader to locate precisely the ship's whereabouts as its whaling voyages traced a zigzag pattern back and forth across the Pacific.

Unlike the *Barnstable*, which meandered through the South Atlantic,

Indian, and South Pacific oceans before turning toward the Arctic, the *Sea Breeze* set a course for the Okhotsk Sea from the outset. Headed southeast from New Bedford, Nathaniel Ransom watched the *General Scott* sail just in sight astern, likewise bound for the North Pacific. His brother James had been its first mate on a voyage that ended the previous June, with a disappointing catch of sperm oil and little else to show for nearly five years at sea. The *Sea Breeze* "got the anchors on the bows stowed the chain below picked the boats crews & watches." The choosing of boats' crews meant that all seamen lined up on deck, ready to flex their muscles and boast of their whaling prowess as the officers mustered them like prospective buyers at a slave auction. The captain picked his boatsteerer, then the first mate made his choice, then second mate, and so forth. The round continued as each boatheader chose his second man, and so on until each whaleboat's crew was complete. Nathaniel Ransom apparently became the boatsteerer in the fourth mate's boat; perhaps he was younger and smaller than the boatsteerers chosen by the higher-ranking officers. The crews of whaleboats headed by the first and third mates became the larboard watch, larboard being the usual term for the port (left) side of the vessel. Crews under the command of the second and fourth mates comprised the starboard watch. The ship's schedule divided the day into four-hour watches; during the dog watch from 4 to 8 p.m. the entire crew remained on deck.

In contrast to Ransom's report of routine chores as the ship left port, its first mate, Josiah Foster of Sag Harbor, indulged in more somber reflections:

> From here we commence our voyage which causes many cares and anxieties and is attended with so many perils and dangers from beginning to end. And with sad and heavy hearts do we leave our native land[;] perhaps never more to meet this side of the other world causes a gloom and sadness to settle on our hearts not easily to be shaken off. But still hope, that benign angel, bids to look forward and still to hope that God in his Providence will return us all to our native land and our friends with a successful and satisfactory voyage to our owners and all concerned.[3]

The first mate may well have taken the gale that struck the *Sea Breeze* one day after leaving New Bedford as an ominous sign. Nathaniel Ransom saw "decks covered with water fore & aft above & below. Everything in the steerage got adrift; steerage half full of water all my things got wet through my books paper and matches all spoilt and my pictures badly injured. Latter part stove our waist boat all to pieces." The heavy weather that swamped his belongings was only one of the obstacles to keeping a journal aboard ship, where ink might freeze and salt spray, fog, or high seas erase the record of the past weeks or months or years. The privacy and quiet essential to contemplation and thoughtful writing were nowhere to be found above or below deck.

One of the pictures badly injured was a photograph of Sarah, his greatest treasure. He had also brought a Quaker work and other books aboard to while away the dreary hours in the long passage toward the Arctic, and a good supply of writing paper, to send letters home to Sarah as well as his family. He dried out these frail reminders of home as best he could, and spent the following Sunday "trying to amuse myself by looking at my pictures reading etc. but feeling rather lonesome at best." After the storm passed the greenhands were "getting over being sick" while Nathaniel set to work "drying onions & turnips . . . peeling onions getting them ready for pickling."

As rough weather continued he "was obliged to eat my big apple that Sarah gave me on account of its rolling, so ends this day of work." Work was the only way to banish melancholy thoughts of those he left behind: "all hands on deck all day lashing up spars repairing the waist boat getting the whaling craft ready coiling up tow lines & setting up some of my irons . . . grinding lances got up some new irons . . . getting my boat craft ready." But Sundays continued oppressively dreary: "I am lonesome enough so I shall have to read my Quaker [book] so ends these lonesome 24 hours." The crew "caught an albatross cooked him up for hands fore & aft," while Nathaniel savored the treats given him by loving friends back home: "I ate my last apple with one of the boatsteerers help one Mary Nye gave me." The cranberry sauce his mother had given him lasted until Thanksgiving Day on November 30.

"Luck to Discourage a Jew and Try the Patience of Job"

Like Leonard Brownson of the *Barnstable*, Captain James Albert Hamilton served as master of several whaling vessels, and began whaling in the Arctic in 1859. He returned to New Bedford in May of 1863 from a profitable voyage as captain of the *Charles W. Morgan*. An experienced whaling master, he now set about training the *Sea Breeze's* greenhands: "Picked the boats crews lowered the boats & practiced pulling all hands made out nicely so ends this days work." Soon they "raised a school of blackfish lowered for them starboard boat struck one no chance for the other boats to get fast 12 o'clock took him alongside hoisted him in on deck robbed him of his hide." Mincing and trying out the blubber took only a day, and boredom and discontent soon plagued Nathaniel Ransom again: "Morning tried out our blackfish oil making punch mats [thick rope padding to protect portions of the rigging] cleaning our blubber traps [gear] oh dear I wish we could catch a whale to pass away time but there is nothing but blackfish in sight today so ends these lonesome 24 hours . . . Patience and perseverance must be our motto."

His mood, "rather dull music," pervaded the 29th of November, his twentieth birthday. "Sarah wish I was where you could pull my ears & I certainly do but cannot very well just now," he lamented. Next day he imagined being home: "It is splendid weather but rather warm for Thanksgiving day so warm that I shan't go to L[ilburne] Hillers to the surprise party tonight but try to amuse myself by playing my fiddle. We ate up the last of Mother's cranberry sauce and I rigged out a porpoise iron. I guess that will do for Thanksgiving day." Lilburne, a Mattapoisett neighbor and schoolmate, was Matthew Hiller's younger brother. Playing the fiddle may be part of the same cheerful daydream as attending a party. Or did Nathaniel Ransom seat himself on an empty cask and saw away at the fiddle while his shipmates jigged and stomped on the deck?

A grimmer mood haunted the *Sea Breeze* as illness and mishap struck the crew. In early November fourth mate Stillman Smith was seriously injured: "working in the rigging parted the fore top sail halyards block came down struck the 4th mate on the back hurt him quite bad." As December began "Edward Cushing had a tooth pulled." Of course there was no one aboard who could properly treat a toothache; usually the captain performed necessary medical surgeries, and the outcome depended on his skill and the fortitude of the patient, anesthetized with rum, or nothing at all. An unnamed illness struck carpenter Roswell Darling, one boatsteerer, and one of the foremast hands. Nathaniel Ransom too felt "about sick . . . I have not been without a pain in my stomach not a day for the past 6 weeks." Unable to muster enough healthy men to lower a whaleboat, the Captain watched helplessly as sperm whales swam tantalizingly close: "Captain mate & 4th mate very sick and quite a number of others not very well we lay it to our bad water we have on board . . . Raised a school of something supposed to be sperm whales going quick to windward no use to lower for them. So ends this long Sunday." Hardier than most of his shipmates, he helped care for the captain, watching with him each day, and remaining on ship's duty, clinging to "patience and hope . . . December 6 Weather clear the sick folks a little better so much and so good today." A note of irony creeps into his musings: "Who wouldn't sell a farm to go whaling?" Next day found the first mate "very sick," and Captain Hamilton "gave orders to steer north in search of some ships" to seek help or safer drinking water. Too many crewmen were stricken to do more than observe the finbacks, killer whales and porpoises swimming near the ship. With the first mate, Josiah Foster, abed, another officer (likely the Indian second mate, Abram Coffee, from Sag Harbor) wrote in the logbook, "The Men is bad we have hardly a nuff to work the Ship now in each Wach." December 15 found the *Sea Breeze* "bound for the Falkland Islands after a fresh supply of water . . . Every officer on board sick with quite a number of others chief mate very sick not expected to live cooper a little better." Nathaniel Ransom "watched with the mate the Captain getting better." Two days later: "two more men sick officers remaining about the same I watched in the cabin as usual. Oh what a hospital I have got into." Walking among the sick men, some recovering, some writhing with fever, he saw that his own presence gave comfort. He might bring water or lay a freshly dampened cloth on a feverish forehead; he might raise a man's head so that he could drink. These gestures brought a nod of gratitude, a weak handclasp, and he saw that he was sturdier and braver than some.

Sarah's birthday on December 21 made him long for her: "Wouldn't I like to be where I could pinch Sarah's ears today. Came to an anchor off New Ireland one of the Falkland Islands sent a boat ashore got some fresh water. Also wild geese." After eating "a burnt goose for dinner" he "went up to the settlement a-gunning" and busied himself writing a letter to Sarah. Without identifying the 25th as Christmas Day, he reported that the "Captain gave orders to get the ship under weigh for Port Stanley as soon as the wind came fair. The cook most dead with several others. Our luck is enough to discourage a Jew and try the patience of Job so much today. Captain & 3rd mate very sick." He found better luck "goose hunting got 15 . . . 3 boats ashore for water. The Captain about crazy some say we are going to start for Port Stanley some for the Sandwich Islands and some for the Arctic Ocean. The sick getting better except the mate he remains about the same the third mate returned to ships duty." His thoughts meandered back to the previous year when he worked aboard the fishing schooner *Profit* bound for the Grand Banks: "I wish I was a cod fishing so much today."

At last on December 31, 1865, the *Sea Breeze* anchored off Port Stanley: "doctor came on board thought he could cure the sick in about two weeks we sent a boat ashore got a quarter of beef we furled our sails so ends the last day of this year." For the next two months the *Sea Breeze* lay at anchor in Port Stanley's harbor, its deck quiet, the crew felled by disease, its masts and spars bare of sail.

The *Sea Breeze*'s official logkeeper fretted as discord rumbled among the idle seamen: "four or five of the crew seamen very much dissatisfied and shows sines [sic] of refusing duty." Port Stanley offered few attractions to the men well enough to venture ashore. The town of a few thousand souls clung above rocky cliffs, buffeted by the icy chop of Atlantic waves as sea birds wheeled and swept beneath the overcast sky. Port Stanley at least included one decent hotel, a simple church and graveyard, a rough tavern or two, a courthouse, the offices of shipping agents and of the American consul, and some houses. First mate Josiah Foster left the ship in charge of third mate Edward Forman, writing that he "had to be brought on shore by the Doctor's and Captain's advice as the noise on board nearly and would of soon caused my death." The typhoid fever that ravaged the crew of the *Sea Breeze* was likely caused by bacteria breeding in dirty water casks. Men suffered from diarrhea, vomiting, high fever, delirium, and dehydration. In the poor sanitary conditions aboard ship, the illness was highly contagious and would prove fatal. Sickness devastated morale aboard ship; as officers burned and tossed in their bunks, seamen well enough to row ashore got drunk and amused themselves in Port Stanley. "Nearly all hands drunk . . . The fourth mate layed out with the delirium tremors caused by drinking so much liquor." In fact, the fourth mate's delirium may have been caused by typhoid fever. Nathaniel Ransom sought safer entertainment, filling his days by writing letters home and going on shore "to a theatre given by officers of the frigate *Narcissus*." Despondent over the loss of time and opportunity for profit, he envied the crews of other vessels entering the harbor with reports of whales taken and casks of oil filled:

> January 13 Doctor neglected coming on board. Mr. Cuffee our second mate fainted away shortly after he revived in a measure but not wholly. All efforts to bring him to proved fruitless and 5 minutes of 6 o'clock PM the poor man breathed his last and several others with myself washed him and layed him out.

Next day the crew well enough to walk:

> Took Mr. Cuffee's remains ashore to the meeting house. Minister preached his funeral sermon and from there we bore him to his grave. The fourth mate still crazy [delirious] the Captain & mate about the same.

Next day the first mate and fourth mate Stillman Smith were:

> [N]ot so well at 12 o'clock poor Mr. Smith breathed his last. Some of the men washed him & layed him out the Captain remaining about the same the Doctor on board the cook on duty again our 3rd mate on shore not very well so much for these serious 24 hours . . .

> January 16 Took Mr. Smith's remains ashore to the meeting house. Minister preached his funeral sermon and then we took him to his grave.

His shipmates buried thirty-year-old Stillman Smith far from his home in Gardiner, Maine.

The innocuous name of the *Sea Breeze* proved a fraudulent enticement, belied by the months-long travail of fever and dysentery that afflicted officers and seamen alike. Nathaniel Ransom lost the inborn fear of death. As he gazed on Abram Coffee and Stillman Smith it ebbed away unnoticed. The dead man's features remained recognizable, albeit distorted by disease. The man's spirit had fled, his voice gone still, but his earthly husk contained what he had heretofore been. Best get on with it then: wash the body, lay him onto a clean piece of sailcloth, and carry him to the Port Stanley burying ground. In later months the crew would at least count the dead mates Abram Coffee and Stillman Smith fortunate to have been buried in a Christian port in a marked grave.

With Captain Hamilton and his officers too ill to serve, the first mate of the smaller whaling bark *Union II* from Sag Harbor, Josiah Foster's hailing port, took command of the *Sea Breeze*. Nathaniel Ransom "went ashore to meeting" on Sundays and then "went to see the mate he looked quite lively" as he began to recover. Soon he brought Josiah Foster his clothing from the ship so that he too could attend church, giving thanks for his near escape from death. The *Sea Breeze* remained at Port Stanley until March third, two full months of idleness. The doctor continued daily visits to the sick who remained aboard, while Captain Hamilton lodged at the Eagle Hotel on shore. Crewmen went clamming, "took about 10 bushels of potatoes ashore sold them to the consul broke out some of the captain's tobacco latter part nearly all hands drunk the two men that ran away from the *Union* were caught . . . Two of our men were ordered to appear at the courthouse for raising a disturbance . . . They were ordered to pay $2.50 apiece or work 4 days for the consul." These shipmates fit the description of whalemen in Charles Boardman Hawes's 1924 book, *Whaling:*

> Though existence in a whaler was likely to be hell on earth, yet
> once out of his ship and safe ashore, the old-time whaleman
> shook off his troubles and danced a fling with no troublesome
> thought of who was to pay the piper . . . He spent with a free
> hand his every penny. He burst riotously into theatre, rum
> shop, and tavern; he hired a gig and drove hell-bent-for-election
> through the streets; he ogled the girls, he swapped jokes with the
> boys, he drank with all comers, and went on board as drunk as
> a lord and as proud as a king, ready all over again to buy with
> months of misery at sea a few pagan hours of paradise ashore.[4]

The men ordered to the Port Stanley courthouse for disturbing the peace and using threatening and abusive language chose work over the fine, for their whaling venture had produced no earnings at all, and time hung heavy on their hands. Unlike his shipmates, Nathaniel Ransom shunned those "golden hours of pagan paradise ashore" in favor of simply attending church there and sending a letter to Almeida, wife of his older brother James. To pass the idle days in port the crew entertained visitors aboard from other ships and even made some molasses candy.

After the months in Port Stanley it was a great relief to put to sea at last on March third. A week later in a thick fog with all sails set the *Sea Breeze* neared the tip of South America, bound round Cape Horn, a difficult passage that could take days or even weeks. Prevailing westerly winds swept across the Pacific, pushing west-bound ships constantly eastward. Narrow channels through the Magellan Strait or the passage between Cape Horn and the treacherous icebergs of Antarctica had to be navigated by quickly tacking ship to maneuver close to the wind. "Passed through the straits of land. Strong breeze from the eastward latter part. Wind hauled ahead. Shortened sail down to double reefed. Tonight weather clear. So much for this blessed 24 hours," Ransom wrote with relief. The end of March found the ship at latitude 31°55' S, off the coast of Chile north of Valparaiso. "Nice weather but no oil yet . . . I am feeling rather lonesome and the reason is because we have a head wind for I am in a hurry to get to the Sandwich Islands and from there on whaling ground." First mate Josiah Foster felt worse than lonesome, attributing his lingering illness to a "foul stench from below that made everyone sick." He found himself "far from well, nor ever shall be again . . . This poison has so affected my head and liver and nervous system that it seems I shall lose my reason."

Nathaniel Ransom took heart at the sight of "porpoises puffing pigs and skipjacks" in mid-April. "Afternoon raised a blackfish and cowfish in sight lowered for them. I struck a cowfish turned him up he was a dry skin so we cut him adrift and came on board. So much today and Sunday at that. Oh what a great beginning for a voyage." A cowfish usually reached a length of fifteen to twenty feet, but was more slender and grayer than a blackfish, with a beaked snout. The whalemen cut their dry skin adrift after seeing that it was an old porpoise that had grown thin and yielded little oil.

"Bound to the Lock up"

Three weeks later the *Sea Breeze* reached Honolulu and remained there May 7–12, 1866, while Captain Hamilton hired on a new second mate, Benjamin Whitney, and fourth mate, Charles Holt. Holt had left New Bedford a year before the *Sea Breeze,* sailing on the whaling bark *Minerva.* At six feet tall and twenty-four years old, he was ready to command a whaleboat crew. First mate Josiah Foster supervised the loading of provisions: 60 barrels of beef, 25 of pork, 20½ barrels of flour, one cask of molasses, shooks, hoops, heads, five pipes of bread—each pipe equaled four barrels—five pipes of rigging, and 106 barrels of water. The ship's blacksmith, William Brown from Philadelphia, went ashore in search of a better position on some other vessel. The German cooper, who had been put in irons below decks for three days for refusing to draw molasses for the crew, took his personal tools and left the ship. While captains could hire on seamen easily enough, locating craftsmen with these essential skills was far more difficult in the Sandwich Islands. After a few days, cooper John Evans returned to duty, but blacksmith William Brown did not.

In Honolulu Nathaniel Ransom found letters waiting for him, two from his father and two from Sarah. While all hands went into the town he remained on board, using the quiet moments to write to them both before going ashore. Adjusting his sea legs to Honolulu's straight level streets, he might have looked up to encounter Mark Twain, another spring visitor to the Sandwich Islands. Not yet the celebrated author of *Tom Sawyer* and *Huckleberry Finn,* Twain penned humorous descriptions of the island's culture and native people for newspapers on the mainland. He painted colorful pictures of the town's white cottages, lush green lawns, fragrant blossoming shrubs and mango trees, its streets of crushed coral, and hundreds and hundreds of feral cats. Among Honolulu's twelve to fifteen thousand inhabitants he admired the half-clad native girls and their easy grace on horseback, "with their gaudy riding habits streaming like banners behind them." These women rode astride as men did, rather than sidesaddle as proper ladies were expected to do. Their riding habit, Twain wrote, "is simply a long, broad scarf like a tavern tablecloth brilliantly colored, wrapped around the loins once, then apparently passed up between the limbs and each end thrown backward over the same, and floating and flapping behind on both sides beyond the horse's tail like a couple of fancy flags."[5]

Horseback riding on the beach in such girls' company appealed to Nathaniel Ransom, too. Ashore in Honolulu he met the *Sea Breeze*'s steward, Enos Stanton, his old shipmate on the four-year voyage of the *Barnstable*. After months aboard ship the pair itched for some novel exercise. They rented horses, galloping up and down the beach relishing every sensation of being on solid earth once again. Soon the two friends found themselves arrested:

> [B]ound to the lock up they said I had been riding too fast and so took me along with steward & put us both in the lock up. [Next day] Steward & myself went down to the courthouse where we were fined 25 cents apiece for fast riding as they call it not half so fast as I have seen them riding on horseback every day. We were put in the lockup again so much today. [Next] Morning steward & myself still in the negroes hands at noon the old man [Captain Hamilton] sent for us said he didn't know of our being in the lockup before but I know better.

Imprisonment brought more irritation than actual discomfort, for Twain described Honolulu's fortress-like prison as neat, clean, white, and so full of the fragrance of flowers that it might have been the King's palace. The ribbing that Nathaniel Ransom and steward Enos Stanton endured from their shipmates back on deck was a more humbling punishment than the two nights in jail. "Well we came on board ship and she was all ready to put to sea. We shaped our course for the Okhotsk Sea."

The Okhotsk Sea; "How Uncertain is Life"

Bounded on the west by the coast of Siberia and on the east by the Kamchatka Peninsula, the Okhotsk Sea lay further south and was somewhat less treacherous than the Bering Sea or Arctic Ocean. The lack of ice during the summer months robbed bowheads of the cover that protected them from whalemen. Captains here avoided the difficulty of navigating the narrow Bering Strait, often blocked by ice until bowheads had migrated north for the summer. Yet in the early years of the hunt so many vessels crowded into the Okhotsk Sea chasing bowheads and right whales that maneuvering along its crowded coastline presented other navigational difficulties. Here at last luck favored the *Sea Breeze's* whalemen. After seven months without any significant catch they captured four bowhead whales and three devil-fish in a single month between July 3 and August 3. Josiah Foster took satisfaction in recording that the crew had stowed down "per gages of cask 566 barrels of oil" by August 11.

Throughout the weeks of ceaseless labor the dangers of whaling remained ever present in Nathaniel Ransom's mind. On August 13 the *Sea Breeze* spoke the bark *Active*, which "had taken one whale since we spoke her last the whale upset the boat and one man was drowned. So much for this tedious day. I wish I was employed in some other better business than whaling." Josiah Foster concurred as he mourned the drowned mariner: "Poor man; how soon was his hopes blasted for this life, how soon was he taken from this to the Eternal world thus showing all of us how uncertain is life and all earthly hopes and prospects, blighted and gone in a moment. Such is life."

While Foster struggled to reconcile the death of a crew member with his own understanding of divine justice, Ransom instead reflected on bodily injury and suffering, pain that he too might experience whenever an accident struck. He recorded the next fatal incident aboard the *Sea Breeze*: "one man while loosing the mainsail fell from the main yard struck on the fore hatch with such force as to break it. He was picked up senseless. In examining him they found the pan bone of one knee broke and badly injured otherwise; he is not expected to live but a short time." Two days later, "Charles Cornell the man who fell from aloft breathed his last. He died very easy. He was washed and layed out so much this lonely day of our Lord." Josiah Foster entered the official record in his logbook, reflecting further on the enigma of divine justice: "At 1 o'clock we committed Charles Cornell's remains to the deep there to remain until the resurrection morn. Oh may we all realize this dispensation of thy Providence the uncertainty of life and oh God may we through thy grace and mercy and love be prepared to dwell with those in Heaven when called away from earth." During the dog watch when every member of the crew was on deck Cornell's clothes were sold at auction. Shipmates often bid high prices for the dead man's belongings so that more money could be sent to his family. Days before the clothing auction, however, Nathaniel Ransom "bought a shirt of the old man paid $1.20." Perhaps he wished he had instead taken advantage of the auction, although wearing a dead man's clothing during the voyage that ended his life could foster dark thoughts.

After the mournful rites of lowering the corpse into the sea, ordinary life continued. The captain and his new second mate, Benjamin Whitney, went ashore to pick huckleberries and blackberries. The following Sunday: "Splendid weather all day" Nathaniel Ransom found himself "blessed with the pleasure of having an awful cold in my head." As the *Sea Breeze* steered for Shantar Bay in the Okhotsk Sea, Captain Hamilton halted to gam the *Charles W. Morgan,* which he had commanded on its previous voyage.

September 11 brought another fatal accident at sea: "Saw a whale lowered for him Mate struck; the 3rd mate was second boat fast; his boatsteerer got entangled in the line and taken down. The line was cut as soon as possible but we never saw the poor fellow again." The boatsteerer— he himself was one—was always in danger. His aim, the strength of his thrust at the whale determined the catch—or the miss. As the fragile whaleboat moved onto the whale, its crew rowing silently, he had to ship his oar and stand at once. Bracing his knee into the half-round "clumsy cleat" without trembling, the whale so close the men smelled his spiracle, the swoop of his mighty flukes could pound the whaleboat and all aboard into the depths of the ocean. Each thrust a gamble, a chance more risky than any wager, and luck alone hauled the whalemen toward a successful strike or a lost whale and a stove boat. The boatsteerer needed to act as if everything was in his power, all the while luck—as swift and incalculable as lightning—wielded the only power. Death at sea was a most dreaded prospect, and now a familiar one aboard the *Sea Breeze,* which had lost four of its original crew, two to illness in the Falklands, and two to accidents in the Okhotsk Sea. "How uncertain is life and how soon we are gone," lamented Josiah Foster. Ransom preferred not to dwell on the accident; he concluded matter-of-factly: "Latter part finished cutting in the whale cleared up decks & coiled my line." His friend the steward, Enos Stanton, found opportunity in the accident, for he took the place of the boatsteerer who drowned.

Two other New Bedford whaleships, the *Ontario* and the *Helen Mar,* collided in late September in the Chukchi Sea far to the north. Thickening ice quickly surrounded the *Ontario,* too badly crippled to escape. Sensing acute danger, her crew refused duty and abandoned the bark with 1,400 barrels of oil in its hold. As the *Sea Breeze* ended the whaling season and turned southward Nathaniel Ransom resisted dwelling on such misfortunes: "Washing bone. Broke out a cask of fresh water and a barrel of flour. Course southeast by south. Got a pound of tobacco of the old man." Plugs of black tobacco bought from the slops chest commonly cost a dollar a pound. Despite the exorbitant price, nearly all whalemen smoked or chewed it, or both.

"Sunday October 24th: Nothing going on in the working line as this is the Lord's day but it is lonesome enough that is certain." The idle travel time between the Arctic whaling grounds and Sandwich Island ports seemed the most monotonous and solitary part of a whaling voyage. The ship might sail two hundred miles a day under favorable winds, or make hardly any headway against a heavy gale and high seas. Monotony reigned on deck, enlivened only by the ordinary work of cleaning tools, repairing sails, making spun yarn, breaking out provisions, or repairing and painting the whaleboats. Increasingly faithful to Quakerism, Sarah Dexter's heritage, Nathaniel Ransom chafed at labor imposed on Sundays. Usually whaling captains kept the Sabbath, unless there were whales in sight or cutting in and mincing and boiling underway. "Making preparations for Sunday exercises, reading, etc." he wrote later, an indication that Captain Hamilton generally observed Sundays as a day of rest.

The *Sea Breeze* returned to Honolulu for most of November 1866 to off-load and ship home its cargo of whale oil and bone and to re-stock provisions. There Nathaniel Ransom "received a letter from Father, 2 from Sarah, one from Lucie and one from Sidney." He had missed the March wedding of Lucy Smith to his older brother Sidney, who remained in Mattapoisett. Nathaniel treasured the precious letters from his own Sarah above all others. There in port "Other ship run into us carried away our flying jib but crippled her worse. Afternoon we bundled some of our bone . . . Took some of it aboard the *Isabella*. Evening I went aboard the *Lagoda*, saw Mr. Snow the master of her. Came ashore with him." Sarah Dexter's mother was born Laura Snow, and Nathaniel's own mother, Eunice Cushing, was the widow of Joseph Snow, a common surname in Mattapoisett. The *Lagoda*, the *Isabella*, and most of the other ships named in the journal hailed from New Bedford, Mattapoisett, or Fairhaven, and Ransom often knew members of their crews, nodes in the network of neighbors or relatives from places near his home. Benjamin F. Snow, only temporarily the *Lagoda*'s master, was its cooper and shipkeeper, having charge of the vessel when its officers were in port or pursuing a whale. If the captain lowered his own whaleboat, the shipkeeper had to command the vessel with a skeleton crew, a steward, cook, cabin boy, and a few others, maneuvering close to the whaleboats and signaling from the crow's nest the whereabouts of the whale.

A favorite topic of discussion among whalemen wherever they met was the comparison of the season's catch. Josiah Foster wrote to New

Bedford's *Whalemen's Shipping List and Merchants' Transcript* on November 24, 1866, that the *Sea Breeze* had made 645 barrels of whale oil and taken 8,850 pounds of whalebone in the Okhotsk Sea, slightly above average for the northern fleet. In comparison, Benjamin Snow could boast of a record catch: the *Lagoda* averaged a monthly yield of $4,364, a value of $200,755 between July 1864 and its return to New Bedford in May 1868, making what whalemen liked to call a greasy voyage. Jonathan Bourne, owner of both the *Sea Breeze* and the *Lagoda*, was fond of proclaiming, "Eternal vigilance is the price of success," an adage proven by his *Lagoda*, which made two of the ten most profitable voyages in the whaling history of New Bedford.

Going ashore with Benjamin Snow offered Nathaniel Ransom a chance to talk of home, to hear familiar names and places, and to forget for a few moments how many thousands of miles separated him from Mattapoisett harbor. In port, men could change their minds about staying on for the entire voyage, whose length in any case depended on how quickly the ship's hold was filled with oil. "Nov. 9th. 4th mate got his discharge shipped with the *Splendid* and sailed for home." Charles Holt,

The whaling bark *Lagoda* of New Bedford, Massachusetts. (Courtesy of the New Bedford Whaling Museum.)

the fourth mate who returned home, had been hired in mid-May when the *Sea Breeze* last docked in Honolulu and spent only the summer season aboard ship. Five other men also left the ship in port, and Josiah Foster was not sorry to see them go, for a couple of them had been surly and disobedient ever since the long stopover in Port Stanley. One of the troublemakers, William Gifford, had spent a day handcuffed and below decks in September for refusing to obey his orders. Nineteen-year-old Edward Cushing was among those who left the *Sea Breeze* as well. He returned safely to Mattapoisett, only to die there at the age of twenty-eight of typhoid fever—which he had escaped aboard ship.

Nathaniel Ransom however stayed with the vessel "breaking out and landing oil. Old man gave me $2 liberty money. I went ashore, cruised around awhile came on board again." And the next day: "Forenoon I went to meeting . . . and afternoon I wrote 2 letters. Bark *Courser* arrived in this port also the *Oregon*." He visited another Mattapoisett mariner, Edwin Winslow, third mate of the *Courser*. A few days later he returned to the *Courser* to see one of the boatsteerers, George Drumright from Boydstown, Pennsylvania. Soon Captain Hamilton hired on Drumright as his fourth mate (the third man to fill that post) based on advice Nathaniel Ransom had gleaned from Edwin Winslow. Hamilton also signed on another boatsteerer and several other crew members.

Aside from visits with former shipmates, neighbors, or friends, his excursions into the bustling port of Honolulu left Ransom disaffected and homesick:

> Fine weather all day, breaking out and landing oil. Evening I went up town a little while but soon got tired of it. Came aboard ship again. So much today . . . Stowed down a few ground tier casks. Afternoon washed off the deck. Evening I went ashore saw nothing very interesting. So ends this day. I have got a terrible cold besides . . . Filled the scuttle butt up with fresh water. Again stowed a few ground tier casks in the hole as usual.

The ground tier was the lowest layer in the hold of the ship where provisions and equipment such as barrels of shooks had to be stored precisely so that they could be brought up on deck (broken out) as they were needed.

"Sun. Nov. 18th E. Winslow came on board stopped a few minutes. Also C. Smyth once a shipmate of mine. Evening I wrote part of a letter to Sarah and one to David Cannon [a schoolmate in Mattapoisett]. Most all of our gang ashore. Two cows died in this harbor today." Charles Smith, his shipmate aboard the *Barnstable*, had likewise been promoted to boatsteerer, now aboard the *Islander*, which had left New Bedford just three weeks after the *Sea Breeze*. Meeting in Honolulu gave the two friends a chance to compare shipboard conditions, rates of pay, and the boatsteerer's position, balanced between seamen and officers. Now the newly hired boatsteerer, George Drumright, came aboard the *Sea Breeze* and later accompanied Nathaniel Ransom ashore. And next day the two men went aboard the *Courser* to say their farewells. They loaded provisions into the hold of the *Sea Breeze*, potatoes, "both sweet and Irish," and some pumpkins and sugar cane.

Chasing Humpbacks and Devil-Fish

Leaving Honolulu at the end of November, the *Sea Breeze* cruised south along the coast of California until late the following February. The only training for the new hands was catching a few porpoise—Nathaniel Ransom harpooned two of them—and a turtle, until humpbacks appeared in late December. Humpbacks' protruding lower jaw and stocky body, sometimes hung with crab-like parasites, gave them a particularly ugly appearance. Their spectacular breaching made them easy to spot as they fed along the west coast of South America and California, where the Arctic whaling fleet targeted them during the winter months unsuitable for whaling further north. Humpbacks, forty to fifty feet long, weighed around forty tons. They swam faster than other whales, making them harder to shoot with a harpoon gun or lance, and were apt to sink once wounded, but there was some advantage to killing them in shallow waters where they might be recovered. Their yellowish blubber, up to a foot thick, yielded forty to a hundred barrels of oil, its quality superior to that of the right whale. As many as five hundred strips of baleen, only a few feet long, added to the value of the catch. Marking December 21, 1866, as Sarah's birthday (she was nineteen), Nathaniel Ransom recorded the frustrations of chasing humpbacks:

> Fourth mate struck a humpback, got upset [capsized] and lost him. Afternoon the 2d mate struck another one, turned him up and the whale sunk. Two of our boats came aboard. Left the 2nd and 3rd mates to lay by him all night.

> Sat. 22 Three boats went off cruising awhile. Afternoon all 5 boats hooked on to the whale we sunk yesterday tried to haul him up but didn't make it out. Parted all the lines.

The sunken humpback carcass was marked with a buoy attached to the harpoon line. To raise a humpback from the ocean bottom, the boatheaders pulled the fastened rope over a spar that acted as a kind of windlass. Dead whales could decompose after a day or two, so that gases bloating the carcass added to their buoyancy. Crews of the five whaleboats needed to position themselves slightly away from the spot where the inflated whale carcass could surge to the surface, buoyed up by its own flotation gases with enough force to overturn the whaleboat. More often than not, however, the attempt to raise the dead whale fell short of success, and whaleboats returned to the hunt for live humpbacks.

> Sun. 23rd Fore part all 4 boats started off on a cruise as usual. Latter part the mate & second mate got one whale each; got one of them alongside 10 o'clock PM. Towed the other one all night, got him alongside tomorrow morning.

> Mon. 24th Two of our boats started off the rest went to work cutting in. Latter part finished cutting.

> Tues. Dec. 25th Splendid weather all day as usual. Fore part minsing and trying out oil. 4 boats started off as they commonly do. Latter part came aboard without any success today if it is Christmas.

The journal takes no notice of any holiday celebration nor respite from work.

In addition to chasing humpbacks, the *Sea Breeze* targeted sea turtles and California gray whales. Often both gray whales and humpbacks eluded their weapons: "Thurs. 27th Fore part 4 boats started off saw several devil-fish but didn't get a chance to strike any of them. Finished trying out our humpback oil. Old man went a-turtling got one." Huge sea turtles could live for several months in the hold of the ship. In shallow waters the crew sometimes tied them to a rope and put them overboard to swim beside the ship and freshen up. Their meat, sweet and tender, provided a welcome change of flavor from the usual fare aboard ship. In addition, their shell cavity contained as much as a gallon of truly fresh, potable water, and often a quantity of soft yellow fat, as good as butter. Aboard the *Sea Breeze*, turtle blubber went into the trypots to make oil.

The entry on December 29, 1866, reveals a wry sense of humor: "The boats went off cruising as they have done once or twice before." In fact, cruising for whales was an almost daily occurrence. This time it met with success:

> Afternoon the 4th mate struck a humpback cow & calf, turned

them up, towing them to the ship; about midnight got them alongside.

Sun 30th Fore part got the boats ready about noon & started off. Those who remained on board cutting in. Latter part finished cutting; some catching fish. John some better.

John Mather of New London, Connecticut, was another boatsteerer who became ill in mid-December. No one recovered quickly in the foul air and dark quarters below decks, where he lay ill for the next month.

"Dec. 31st Started the tryworks, the boats started off afternoon, came aboard. Minsing and trying out, getting the boat craft ready for use, sick man gaining." No mention is made of any New Year's celebration as 1867 began; the crew killed two whales, one sank, the other was cut in. Men continued to chase devil-fish and humpbacks in early January. Along the California coast the "old man went ashore clamming and gunning. Got a few ducks."

Captain Hamilton also adopted a more sophisticated weapon that would soon replace the toggle iron or harpoon that had been in use for decades: "About noon the old man started off on a cruise with the Greena gun but didn't set the world afire with it." William Greener's harpoon gun was a British invention about thirty years old. Weighing seventy-five pounds, the clumsy-looking weapon was mounted on the whaleboat's bow and swiveled to aim at the whale. A harpooner might dart his toggle iron twenty feet, a nearly futile attempt at striking the gray whales and humpbacks, now easily gallied (frightened) by the approach of a whale-boat. The Greener gun could shoot a shorter harpoon into a whale at a distance of ninety feet, four times as far as a boatsteerer could dart his iron. If the shot was successful, the crew hauled in the harpoon line, approaching the whale close enough to kill her with a bomb lance, a missile designed to explode after penetrating the whale's body. But the Greener gun was difficult to aim, particularly in rough seas, and the line attached to its harpoon altered its trajectory. Its recoil rocked the whaleboat and sometimes injured the gunner. Its position displaced the boatsteerer, since the captain or boatheader took charge of the Greener gun as well as the whaleboat's crew. Nathaniel Ransom's initial skepticism reflected a fear that the invention would lessen the value of his own skill as harpooner. However Captain Hamilton was not immediately successful: "Old man shot a whale with the Greener gun. The iron drawed the whale went off." Often the toggle iron or harpoon shot into the whale simply pulled out again, or drew away, allowing the whale to escape. Soon the captain met with better success:

> Old man struck a whale at midnight. We all found ourselves towing him to the ship.

> Monday January 4th boats started off about noon. The old man struck a whale with the Greener gun 2 o'clock commenced towing; midnight got the whale alongside tied him up until daylight.

> Laying in Maria Bay, California Tues. Jan. 15th [1867]. 3 boats went off on a cruise; mate stopped aboard at daylight – commenced cutting latter part boats came aboard. The 3rd mate missed a whale; the old man broke his boatsteerer to pay for it, a common occurrence among these old spouters.

To break the boatsteerer, likely Alexander Sawhill of Pittsburgh, meant to demote him to common crew, sending him into cramped quarters in the forecastle, while another man was promoted to his place as harpooner. The crews of merchant vessels derided whaling ships as "spouters." These were often older ships, re-fitted with bark rigging and reinforced hulls to withstand Arctic ice or ramming by wounded sperm whales. Smoke and soot from their trypots blackened sails and rigging, while whale oil and blubber greased the decks. For the whalemen themselves, it was easy to ignore the filth of a greasy voyage if it meant a lucrative catch and a quicker return home.

On a late January Sunday, Hamilton gave his crew a day of rest: "The boats remained on the craynes. Some employed in making repairs about the boats, others in sleeping & eating. So ends this day," wrote Nathaniel Ransom. Josiah Foster expressed his approval in more sanctimonious tones:

> Boats not off whaling which is very commendable in Captain Hamilton for there is nothing to be gained by a violation of God's law this is declared by God himself and daily ocular demonstration and experience of unprejudiced minds proves that in violating God's law there is nothing gained but in keeping his law much good is promised by Him who rules all things for man's good and for his own glory.

The daily business of whaling often contradicted the first officer's conviction that keeping God's law would bring much good. Next morning "four boats started off on a cruise. Old man struck a whale with the Greener gun iron drawed. The mate struck one, parted his line so we didn't get either of them," Nathaniel Ransom reported. The Greener gun caused other difficulties besides losing the iron darted into the whale: "4th mate struck a humpback; the gun kicked him so he couldn't work on him. We hung onto him until about midnight when the iron parted and I wasn't sorry."

Next day the crew took a whale and got him alongside the ship in a strong breeze. "In cutting in the whale a boatsteerer by the name of Matthews got his leg broke by the cutting falls parting" the ship's logkeeper wrote. The cutting falls, a system of ropes and pulleys, swung from the topmast to haul up blanket pieces of blubber from the cutting stage as men worked the windlass. Nathaniel Ransom knew the injured boatsteerer as John or Jack Mather from New London, and thought after a few days that he was getting better. The success in mending a broken leg depended on the captain's medical skills, or sometimes the carpenter made a splint and crutches.

Despite such setbacks, the *Sea Breeze* profited handsomely from the between seasons cruise in southern waters, taking fifteen whales, eight of them identified as humpbacks and three as gray whales, as well as a few porpoise and turtles. The first mate recorded a total of 535 barrels of oil stowed down at Maria Bay, although the crew lost four more whales in late February and early March. The ship was close enough to California that several whaleboats made a two-day trip north to San Francisco. Captain Hamilton hunted along the nearby shore: "Old man went a-clamming and gunning, got a rabitt [sic] and two bushel of clams." Nathaniel Ransom felt about sick enough to lay up: "I find myself dead with various complaints, headache, stiff neck and sore throughout my shoulders." The ship approached the southern tip of Baja California at Cape St. Lucas where a boat's crew from shore came "on board with nothing to trade. Afternoon old man came aboard, brought off bullock and some raisins. Put ship on a course for Sacorro [sic] Island. The cook and myself ½ dead with the same complaints as before mentioned." Entries for the following weeks describe an unnamed but persistent illness, perhaps contagious, since his berth was close to that of the cook and other boatsteerers: "I believe I am rather bad off. Evening I took a rum sweat." Drinking rum before bed, he bundled himself warmly into his berth to break the fever, but to little avail.

Throughout his illness, he continued his record of the ship's catch. On February 27, 1867, he wrote, "Cruising off Socorro Island [south of Cape St. Lucas]. Forenoon the boats started in shore. Afternoon the 4th mate struck a humpback, midnight got him alongside, went to work cutting him in. I believe that we that are sick are about the same." Next day he continued, "I am satisfied that I have got a fever."

The ship steered south until within sight of Clarence Island off the coast of Chile, where they took another humpback on March 10. They struck another that tangled their lines as darkness overtook them and they had to cut him loose. As the *Sea Breeze* changed course and headed north toward the Sandwich Islands, Nathaniel Ransom suffered a setback:

> March 14th It is Friday and I am writing up a few lines for yesterday on account of being unable to write them in the afternoon. I was taken with a severe pain in my bowels accompanied by a cramp in my hands and feet so I couldn't keep my hands open or my feet in their place. It lasted about one hour ½. The most severe pain that ever I had by far. The other sick gaining.

He remained below deck, hearing rainy weather: "A heavy rain I should judge by the way it pours down over my head." After three long weeks of misery "the sick returned to duty. I feel better, like myself again."

John, or Jack, Mather and Joshua Cushing did not recover. They were taken to the hospital in Honolulu, where the ship remained in port from March 31 to April 8, 1867. Captains who left sick or injured men behind in the Sandwich Islands had to cover their costs for three months lodging and medical care. It fell to the United States consul to arrange their passage home if the men did not recover well enough to resume work. Nathaniel Ransom paid Jack and Joshua a final visit just before leaving Honolulu. Hearing for the last time from the hospital that they were not any better, he pledged "I'll go back." Joshua Cushing, left in the Honolulu hospital, recovered and made his way home to Mattapoisett, where he and Ransom exchanged work and remained neighbors.

Captain Hamilton shipped 611 barrels of whale oil from Honolulu to New Bedford aboard the *Syrene.* At the shipping agent's office Nathaniel Ransom received letters from his parents, his brother Theodore, and from Sarah, letters he unfolded and read again and again. Returning to ship's duty he brought pumpkins, bananas, and a bullock on board, rowing back ashore to the shipping agent's office to mail letters home to Theodore, his cousin Mary Nye, his parents, and of course to Sarah Dexter.

The *Sea Breeze* stopped briefly in Waimea on the island of Maui, where potatoes were cheaper than in Honolulu, and then shaped its course for the Okhotsk Sea once more. Bored as usual by the long passage northward, Ransom repaired old sails and the starboard whaleboat. He doodled Sarah's name in his diary. At the end of April the ship reached the Okhotsk whaling ground amidst fog and snow. It felt "very cold on deck but quite comfortable in bed," thanks to two woodstoves, one in the forecastle and another near the after cabins. The crew saw finbacks and plenty of light ice, though thick fog hampered their whaling: "May 6th: Good breeze from the northward, the wind whalemen curse. Afternoon thick fog & a dead calm. The officers employed in playing top. So much today."

"A Good Season's Work"

Soon bowheads appeared in the Okhotsk Sea:

> Raised 2 or 3 bowheads, lowered for them, 2nd mate struck the whale, took his line, but after pulling we finally got another hold of him. Turned him up, took him alongside, robbed him of his hide. Afternoon boats started off for the ice again. Evening foggy, boats came aboard.

> Fri 9th May: 4th mate struck a whale, parted from him, lost him. Afternoon 2nd mate struck another one about 4 o'clock took him alongside, commenced cutting him in. So much & so good.

The subtle tone of satisfaction here masks the likelihood that he had harpooned the whales taken by the second mate's boat. Of the six bowheads caught by the *Sea Breeze* in the 1867 season, his skill took three. And the season had begun early in the Okhotsk Sea, sheltered between Siberia to the west and the Kamchatka peninsula to the east.

> Sat. 10th Started the works; cutting up & minsing blubber, cleared away the head. Afternoon raised one or two whales, lowered for them, chased them awhile, no chance to get fast. Boats came aboard.

> Sun. 11th Let the ship lay; minsing & trying out oil. Saw one whale to windward; still boiling, cooper setting up shooks.

> May 12th Making oil & stowing down, scraping & storing away bone. Two canoes of Esquimeaux aboard. Minsing, trying out oil; cooper setting up shooks. Saw a devil-fish; so much for this blessed day.

Working up toward the northeast gulf of the Okhotsk Sea the "Old man and 4th mate saw 4 bares & quite a number of finbacks but no bowheads. Latter part came aboard again. Cooper setting up shooks. Stowed away some of our bone." A string of days followed without taking a third bowhead. As the ship worked northeast as fast as the wind and ice would allow, the crew kept busy "making bow spun yarn & overhauling brace blocks; cooper setting up shooks." They killed the pigs aboard, having little fodder left and no way of housing them in the colder weather. They saw "mussel diggers" or gray whales, and whitefish, the small white Beluga found in northern waters. Whitefish blubber, only three or four inches thick, yielded just a few barrels of oil, so whalemen left them to the natives, who relished their fat and fed their lean meat to sled dogs.

To reach the west arm of the northeast gulf, Captain Hamilton sent two boats' crews "in shore to work up along the land," sometimes towing the ship with whaleboats, sometimes pulling it along by anchoring to the land or nearby ice and hauling the anchor chain in using the windlass. Either method made for arduous work. Lack of wind hindered progress, as did thickening ice around the ship, for summer had not yet reached the Okhotsk Sea.

Siberian natives came aboard when the *Sea Breeze* anchored in Ellis Island harbor in late May.[7] "Afternoon went ashore, brought off 3 natives, give them some rum and bread. Took them ashore again." Were the natives lured aboard in hopes they would join the crew? Captain Hamilton was not a man to offer simple hospitality to strangers, for both bread and rum functioned as currency. Sometimes captains allowed native women below decks when the randy crew became unruly, for it was easier to force the natives off the ship than to bring crewmen back on board after they had gone ashore looking for willing women.

Soon ice was thick enough for traders to return on foot:

> The natives came aboard on the ice with a deer. The old man got it of them for 3 bottles of rum. We killed it and dressed it off.

> Mon. 26th May, 1867. Laying in the west arm of the northeast Gulf. Before breakfast went in got a boatload of wood. After breakfast the old man & 3rd mate started off on a short cruise. Afternoon got back, found the mate aboard, reported having seen several whales during his cruise & that he came to the ship for provisions, had experienced rather bad weather so far.

The Okhotsk Sea varied in depth from about 3,000 to 5,000 feet, but was edged with shoals and uninhabited islands. Thick fog could make navigation particularly difficult, and when ships often lacked wind or space to maneuver safely, captains sent whaleboats out for several days in search of whales. Soon heavy ice surrounded the *Sea Breeze*:

> May 29th Thick fog the greater part of the day, the ship jammed hard in the ice but not quite ashore; she lacks but very little of being there. This evening we hauled up all of our chain, let her

have it. We have done all we can to save her & now if she goes ashore there is no one to blame.

Next day brought a reassuring prospect:

Good breeze from the eastward & fine weather . . . The ice begins to leave so I guess the ship won't go ashore this time.

Sat. May 31st 1867. This day commenced with a thick fog. Afternoon we went ducking—got two. The ship still jammed in the ice. Two bowheads passed by close to the ship.

June 1: Fine weather morning. The 4th mate's crew came aboard, told us they had a dead whale up in the head of the bay. The mate & 2nd mate were up there. The 3rd & 4th mates had their boats hauled up on the ice. We went to them on the ice, carried them provisions; midnight back again after a long time on the ice.

Since ice prevented the *Sea Breeze* from reaching the crew that had taken the whale, men had to cut off the blubber and bone on the ice where it lay and load it into their whaleboats. Dragging the boats behind them over ice or rowing through slushy water, they hauled as much cargo as possible back to the ship, heavy work even in fine weather and summer light. Through the following week, ice continued to hamper their efforts:

Morning the old man went ashore, traded for 5 deer and shot an old quail. Saw two ships outside of the ice. Two bowheads in sight afternoon. Two boats got to the ship all stove by the ice. Took them in on deck, went to work repairing them, drawed off the deer.

Wed. June 4, 1867 Laying in Ellis Island harbor, W[est] arm of the Gulf. Fine weather again today. We still have ice around us. We put the bow boat on the crayne & that is about all we have done today.

Thurs. 5th Strong breeze from the north eastward. After dinner we started off on one of the old man's wild notions under close reefed sail. We had hard work to carry any sail at all. About 6 o'clock got back to the ship again. Cooper setting up our shooks.

June 8th Morning raised whales, lowered for them. 2nd mate struck one; the whale took his line; we pulled after him for several hours & finally got another hold of him. Turned him up took him alongside got breakfast. 3 boats started off again for the ice. The rest of us cut him in. Evening two of the boats came aboard about 9 o'clock. We came to an anchor. So much for this day.

The ship's official logbook records the frustrations of hunting bowheads. On August 3, one whaleboat's crew struck a bowhead, but the iron broke, and the men came on board just after midnight. At 2 p.m., they saw the same whale and lowered for him and succeeded in taking him alongside. As the weather was very rough, the fluke chain parted before they could make the whale fast to the ship. The dead whale sank as the crew waited till the tide turned. Next day they again got the whale alongside, cut him in, and started the tryworks.

In late August, the *Sea Breeze* took on board four men formerly of the New Bedford whaling bark *Stella*, which had wrecked on Grampus Island. Mindful of their misfortune, as he steered through the Kuril Islands at the end of September, Josiah Foster expressed relief that his vessel had ended the 1867 season without loss of life: "so ends this season of whaling thankful for having a good season's work on board and thankful that our lives have been spared thus far and all well."

Having struggled to maintain his command over disgruntled seamen, Foster kept all hands employed in scraping and washing bone until the ship arrived in Honolulu on October 20. There two white seamen whom he had often named as troublemakers left the ship, as did John, Sam, Bob, and Jack Kanaka. Foster himself went ashore and got his discharge, claiming that Captain Hamilton had often found fault with him and tried to drive him out of the ship. Ever since his bout of typhoid nearly two years before, he had wrestled with an unruly and often defiant crew.

With his departure, another officer's hand continued the logbook, writing that "What we have left of the crew discharged onto *Ceylon* 384 barrels + of oil = 49 casks." The officers hired eight laborers from on shore to discharge another 1,115 barrels of whale oil, contained in 183 casks, onto the *Lagoda*. The *Sea Breeze*'s 1867 summer season had taken over twice as much whale oil (1,500 barrels) and bone (about eleven tons) as the average for the fourteen ships in the Okhotsk whaling fleet. While a ship might hold as much as three thousand barrels, ten of them filled with whale oil weighed a ton. In shipping his cargo home, Hamilton unburdened his ship by about 160 tons. The ship's carpenter went missing, but when Captain Hamilton came aboard on December 3, the *Sea Breeze* sailed out of Honolulu harbor headed south for another between-seasons cruise after California gray whales and humpbacks.

The logkeeper tallied the losses incurred in hunting them as the *Sea Breeze* sailed off the California and Mexican coasts. On Christmas Day, the vessel "came to an anchor in Maria Bay; raised two humpbacks lowered two boats; tried the Greener gun without success on account of being too close. Mr. Fisher [a newly hired officer] was hurt in the breast by the gun kicking." The crew's weaponry also included a yard-long bomb lance gun weighing some twenty-four pounds. Once fired from the shoulder, its successful shot triggered a bomb lance that penetrated the whale's skin and blubber and exploded on impact. Seldom did the bomb lance actually kill the whale; its purpose was to injure him and slow his speed and endurance in towing the whaleboat. Yet the bomb lance gun was no more fail-proof than the Greener gun's harpoon; at distances closer than thirty feet, the bomb lance might pass through the whale without striking any vital organs. The boatheader usually took charge of firing the bomb lance gun, whose kick, like that of the Greener gun, was enough to break a man's collarbone, or topple him backward into the whaleboat. Prudent officers secured the bomb lance gun to the boat by a rope so that it could be retrieved if its kick landed it in the water. Even if the nineteen-inch bomb lance struck the whale's vital organs, his capture was by no means assured.

On New Year's Day 1868, five of the *Sea Breeze*'s whaleboats lowered and struck two humpbacks. "One sunk with sixty fathoms of line and three irons and eight bomb lances. One boat got the other humpback & towed him to the ship." The bomb lances, the three harpoons, and the 120 yards of lost rope amounted to a considerable financial loss, evidence of the costs as well as the risks involved in chasing humpbacks. More equipment was lost two weeks later when the men "struck two devil-fish got one we lost one in the breakers and took 100 fathoms of line and four bomb lances. Next day struck a devil-fish with the Greener gun iron drawed." On February 7, the crew struck one devil-fish and it sank. "Two boats laid by him all night got him next day." February 10, Ransom recorded: "got another devil-fish alongside fluke chain parted, whale sunk; one boat laying by him. At 5 AM next day sent three boats after the whale parted the lines in trying to get him up and lost him." So it went, as the gray whales demonstrated their reputation as devil-fish. But they were plentiful in Bolinas Bay, and humpbacks swam abundantly near Socorro Island and Clarion Island.

The *Sea Breeze* returned to Honolulu in March and shipped home 360 barrels of oil, again aboard the *Syrene* of Boston. After replenishing provisions in Honolulu and Waimea, the ship traveled north through the Kuril Islands and reached the northeast gulf of the Okhotsk Sea. On May 5 the ship "raised ice, quite heavy snow squalls and very cold, ship covered with ice at 1 PM lowered two more boats saw no whales, snowing quite hard and a strong breeze; four men sick." Greenhands hired on in the

Sandwich Islands might well become sick at heart as well as in body at the first sight of an Arctic storm.

It was an inauspicious beginning to the *Sea Breeze*'s third Arctic summer season. The crew shot one finback but failed to kill him as the *Benjamin Cummings* and *Europa* hunted near Ellis Island harbor in mid-June. Third mate Hewitt, whom Captain Hamilton had hired on in Honolulu, took a small bowhead that had been killed some few days before by another ship; the whale had one iron and sixty fathoms of line attached, a bonus in equipment that compensated in some measure for the fact that it was a putrefying stinker. As Hewitt and Captain Hamilton worked at cutting in the whale, the crew snagged the cutting falls, and in the confusion the captain struck Hewitt on the head with a spade. A few days later near Grampus Island the crew took one bowhead. Next day a boatsteerer missed another. The harpooner's error brought a swift demotion back into the fo'csle. The logbook records, "the same boatsteerer missed two before he was taken out of the boat and sent forward. At 9 AM struck the whale, got him alongside and cut him in."

Off Crag Island in the northeast gulf the *Sea Breeze* took aboard a Spaniard and a "Chinaman" from the shore. The *Sea Breeze*'s logkeeper recounted that the Spaniard claimed to be owner of a trading vessel carrying $20,000 in gold and silver along with some Javanese slaves being transported to a cotton plantation, but that the Chinese man had killed the ship's captain and two officers. The crew demanded that the Spaniard navigate the vessel; he told them he didn't know how so they steered west for China and fetched up in the northeast gulf. "This man has lost ship, crew, cargo and money. He is to be pitied I suppose it was all he was worth in this world." The logbook says nothing further of the fate of these unusual passengers as the *Sea Breeze* continued pursuing bowheads. The strangers were likely taken ashore when the ship returned to the Sandwich Islands in the fall.

On July 23 and 25, the crew captured bowheads, but foggy and rugged weather hindered striking whales as the month came to an end. In early August they lost a splendid chance to strike a bull, cow, and calf on account of the irons getting foul of the whaleboat's sail. Weeks later the lookout could see plenty of whales; the crew missed one but took another. Then for five days strong winds and thick fog obliged them to call the boats on board, although whales swam nearby.

The logkeeper recorded two more deaths among the crew of the *Sea Breeze* near Grampus Island on August 27:

This day is a very sad one. At 5 AM saw whales and lowered.

Mr. Sylvia struck; it appears when he struck the whale the whale stove him in with his flukes. The boat filled and capsized. I was a short distance from him; before I could get there two men went down. One of them was Jethro Besse of Fairhaven. The other one was a Port[ugese] went by the name of Frank. We also lost the boat but saved the whale took him alongside and cut him in.

The toll of accidental deaths now stood at four. Joseph Sylvia, the boat-steerer, missed a whale the following week and was sent into the forecastle as punishment, with Azorean John Vero taking his place. In spite of these setbacks, by September 9 the crew had stowed down 1,109 barrels of oil. In "Dobrie town" (presumably a Russian settlement) Captain Hamilton bartered for potatoes and turnips, employing all hands in boating wood from shore, cutting it up, and stowing it down.

As September turned into October, the *Sea Breeze* cruised south-ward for right whales in the Okhotsk Sea, a nearly futile hunt, the logkeeper complained. Unsuccessful at approaching right whales on October 8 and 10, a boatsteerer "shot at a right whale with the Greener gun the iron did not go in on account of not being charged enough to give the iron force." Next day the crew "lowered for a right whale but did not fasten on account of the iron getting foul of the sail. October 12 have seen today three whales, lowered went alongside of one and the whale kicked the stern of the boat off and did not strike him. We have now got our hull boat the rest of them leak so it takes half of the time to keep them afloat." Poor luck at whaling exacerbated tensions among the crew. Second mate Joseph Fisher came to blows with the steward over the quality of a barrel of salt beef. As the captain tried to separate them, the steward bloodied Fisher's face, warning the captain, "keep away sir and let me get at the damned son of a bitch." Hamilton pushed the steward back into his state-room and ordered him to desist, but there was considerable blood on Fisher's face and he had gotten the worst of it.

After weathering a gale, the ship reached Honolulu at the end of November 1868. It would remain at sea for another two and one-half years, with plenty of space for more oil and bone in its hold; at 473 tons, it was the largest vessel Nathaniel Ransom served on. Now he was reluc-tant to remain with the ship while Sarah Dexter waited for his return.

On shore in Honolulu another man watched impatiently as the *Sea Breeze* approached the harbor.[8] The vessel's new first mate, a man with the magnificent name of Rodolphus Delano Wicks, had been waiting a month for the whaler to arrive. Wicks had embarked from New York City in September aboard the steamship *Alaska* and reached Honolulu on

October 21, traveling with Captain Charles W. Fisher, who was to assume command of the ship. The two men waited in port nearly a month for the *Sea Breeze* to arrive. Wicks lodged at the Sailors Home and filled his days with shooting ducks and pigeons. Like Nathaniel Ransom, he enjoyed riding; renting a horse he ventured out to Diamond Head and up Punch Bowl Hill. And like the *Sea Breeze*'s young boatsteerer, on Sundays he attended morning services at the Bethel and evening meeting at the Fort Street Church. He was no older than Ransom, and only a few inches taller, but sufficiently capable to rise to the rank of captain of the *Sea Breeze* three years later.

Captain Hamilton left the *Sea Breeze* in Honolulu, for his term as master ended; and he was weary of battling illness, the vicissitudes of bowhead whaling, and a discontented crew. The *Sea Breeze* shipped home 1,100 barrels of oil and sent home 141 bundles of bone weighing 13,529 pounds on board the *Ceylon* of Boston bound to New Bedford. The value of the catch rose after October news of a poor northern season caused a spike in the price of oil from sixty-five cents to $1.25 a gallon, and a surge in the price of whalebone, from sixty cents a pound to $1.42 and one-half cents.

As Wicks and Fisher took command of the *Sea Breeze*, they hired on twelve new crewmen. Among those who had decided to leave the ship was Nathaniel Ransom. Captain Hamilton took him to the shipping office to meet William Davis, captain of the whaling bark *Navy*. In his journal Ransom noted: "Nov. 30, 1868: This morning I got my discharge from the *Sea Breeze* and had to pay $61 for it." The payment summed up his charges for liberty money to go ashore, tobacco, and goods from the slops chest, and amounted to a substantial share of his earnings. He noted his next move cryptically: "Shipped as boatsteerer on the *Navy* Captain Davis the same time." Over the next six months, he would come to regret his decision.

Chapter III: "This Three or Four Years Lot of Trash"

Aboard the Navy,
December 1, 1868–June 12, 1869

Never one to divulge his private thoughts, Nathaniel Ransom left his decision to change course in Honolulu open to speculation. Throughout his voyage aboard the *Sea Breeze*, he came to trust Captain Hamilton, whom he had tended through the bout of typhoid in Port Stanley. Aware that the captain's term expired in November 1868, he also knew that the vessel would not soon return to New Bedford, and he was eager to return to Sarah Dexter.

The decision to sign on as boatsteerer aboard the *Navy* proved to be a costly mistake. First, he felt keenly the absence of familiar companions. During his first two voyages and in port he had visited old friends or other boatsteerers and former shipmates, but the majority of the *Navy*'s crew hailed from the Cape Verde Islands or the Azores. His thoughts haunted by the shipmates left behind, he felt "lonesome enough" as the *Navy* prepared to leave Honolulu. While Captain Hamilton enjoyed gamming other ships, aboard the *Navy* Ransom often lamented "no sail in sight."

While he filled his time in port writing letters home, Captain William Davis negotiated with other whaleships in port to carry their oil home as freight, for the *Navy*'s hold remained half empty after an unprofitable season. He took on board two thousand barrels of oil from the *Helen Snow*, the *Benjamin Cummings*, and the *Progress*, and wrote home to New Bedford that he planned to cruise—hunt in southern waters—and be home in August of 1869.

Captain Davis's wife, Susan Foster Davis, was most eager to reach home, for she had been living ashore in Honolulu while her husband's ship hunted in the Arctic. She hailed from northern Vermont's Caledonia County, and she was twenty-seven years younger than her husband. In 1863 she had given birth to their daughter in Vermont and named the girl Caroline Agnes after a beloved sister. She and her baby moved to coastal Massachusetts early in 1864, but little Caroline Agnes died before her first birthday. Lonely and grief-stricken, Susan joined Captain Davis aboard ship as the *Navy* sailed from New Bedford in November, 1865. Her diary of the homeward journey supplements Nathaniel Ransom's more laconic account of the *Navy*'s voyage, departing from Honolulu in early December 1868.

Several whaling captains' wives regularly sailed with their husbands. Among the Arctic whalers Nathaniel Ransom knew, Captain Jared Jernegan of the *Roman* had his wife and two children aboard. His daughter, nine-year-old Laura, kept a diary for part of her voyage.[1] Captain Thomas Williams likewise traveled with his wife and children aboard the *Florida II* (from San Francisco) and the *Monticello*. His wife gave birth during one journey, and her son became so accustomed to life at sea that he was at first reluctant to walk on land.[2] Some wives assisted their husbands in tending sick or injured seamen, but as a rule boundaries between the captain's wife and common seamen were rigid, though delineated only by the distance from forecastle to stateroom. Most captains' wives struggled with loneliness in the absence of female companionship, and all battled with dirt, idleness, and the necessary confinement to tight quarters. Often they tried to replicate on board ship their routines of housewifery ashore. Susan Davis for instance whiled away the hours knitting, embroidering sofa pillows, and sewing a nightdress and chemise for herself. She collected specimens of lava and coral to furnish her parlor at home, while her thoughts meandered among memories of loved ones a continent away.

In Sandwich Island ports, captains' wives (like Mrs. James Hamilton) enjoyed comfortable sociability, for food and domestic help were plentiful, and the Fuller House and the American House in Honolulu offered boarding places suitable to their tastes. The greatest discomforts they faced came from clinging to their tight corsets and multi-layered hooped skirts in the tropical heat, and from plagues of mosquitos. In Honolulu, Susan Davis made friends with Augusta Penniman, whose husband Edward commanded the whaling bark *Minerva*. The two women were the same age, and Augusta's son Eugene was just a few months older than Susan Davis's daughter Agnes would have been had she lived. On Oahu, the two women often rode horseback together. In contrast to the scantily clad native girls described by Mark Twain, the two captains' wives wore conventional riding habits and rode sidesaddle. They often visited a Protestant missionary, Reverend Samuel Damon, and his wife. Damon labored with his Hawaiian flock between 1842 and 1884, preaching strict temperance at the Bethel Union Church and Seamen's Chapel familiar to Nathaniel Ransom. The two captains' wives heard his sermons there or attended the Fort Street church. "Father Damon" also edited *The Honolulu Friend*, published every two weeks. Susan Davis and Augusta Penniman sometimes took tea and exchanged visits with other captains' wives, Helen Jernegan and Adeline Heppingstone; Captain Heppingstone's whaling vessel used Honolulu as its home port without returning to New Bedford.

Often whaling wives accompanied their husbands for the between seasons winter cruise along the California and Mexican coasts or into the South Pacific, returning to Honolulu when the whalers headed north into the Arctic in May. Although many women yearned for friends and family whom they would embrace again only after ocean journeys of thousands of miles, traveling part of the year aboard ship kept them closer to their husbands than the four-year separations faced by Nathaniel Ransom and Sarah Dexter.

Preparing to leave Honolulu aboard the *Navy* in early December, Susan Davis took comfort in attending a service at the Fort Street Church, where she might have seen Nathaniel Ransom in the congregation. The preacher chose Acts 27 as the basis of his sermon. The gospel recounts the voyage of the Apostle Paul from Alexandria to Italy; in the face of an ocean tempest and shipwreck on a Mediterranean island, his faith never wavers. Like Paul, she aspired to hold steadfast to her faith as a bulwark against the dangers of her homeward journey, which began on December 7, 1868. Her journal depicting life aboard a whaling bark differs broadly from the workaday experiences recorded by the *Navy*'s newly hired boatsteerer.

One day after leaving her temporary home in Honolulu, the *Navy* came to an anchor off Koloa, a minor port on the southern side of Kauai, the northernmost of the Sandwich Islands. Nathaniel Ransom and his shipmates "got off 5 cords of wood, took some blackfish oil ashore. Got chickens, sweet potatoes." The chickens became Mrs. Davis's property, though she complained that they ate nearly all the eggs they laid. The following Sunday men "Saw a sulphur-bottom. Nothing going on above decks." Sulphur-bottom was one term for the blue whale. Over a hundred feet long, a blue whale yielded eighty or ninety barrels of oil as well as baleen. The film of diatoms or tiny sea creatures attached to its underside gave the whale a yellowish or orange tinge the whalemen associated with sulfur. Because these whales swam rapidly, they were difficult to kill, but Captain Davis did not order any whaleboat to lower to attempt a capture.

Two days later Nathaniel Ransom found cause for serious concern: "The ship leaks badly." And soon he would add: "Pumped a dozen times as usual." A leaking ship was not uncommon on whaling voyages, and seamen were used to manning the pumps. However, the *Navy*'s leak was discovered after leaving Honolulu, and had not been caused by ice damage or running aground, as sometimes happened in the Arctic. A prudent captain should have found and repaired the leak while his vessel was in port. The leaking ship added to Susan Davis's uneasiness, too. She realized that the flow of water into the hold continued to increase even though the crew pumped every four hours for three days and two nights; "it does not look much like having a long voyage in her," she wrote.[3] Uncertainty about the cause of the leak heightened concern, for tiny teredo mollusks, so-called ship worms, could leave hull planking honeycombed with tunnels and ready to give way. In frigid Arctic waters, the ship worms posed little danger, but they thrived in tropic seas where their damage could cause a vessel to sink with scarcely any warning.

"Bugs, Worms, and Bedbugs"

Susan Davis's misery was compounded by bouts of insomnia, seasickness and headache. Even in the captain's stateroom, the old musty hay mattresses were sticky and dirty. On warm nights she could not rest well, and sleeplessness sapped her energy. "I had brandy on my stomach & so slept by cat naps," she confessed. Melancholy thoughts troubled her wakeful nights. "This is the 4th anniversary since I left country and friends," she mused a few weeks later. "One's life is soon gone and how soon one is forgotten; but a few years and their names are faded from memory. I feel that my kindred is passing away—only half our winters left and both parents gone. Soon we may be called and may we be in readiness when the summons shall come."

Her husband made a hammock, hoping that seasickness would fade if her bed swung with the motion of the ship. Confined to her cabin by illness, she fretted that the cabin boy's cleaning did not amount to much. "Everything is covered with bugs, worms, and bedbugs. Have hoped to keep clear of the last named but they are finding their way everywhere." Bugs had gotten into her fruitcake and she had to throw the whole thing away. Given these conditions in the captain's quarters, the steerage and forecastle must have been filthy indeed, although Nathaniel Ransom's journals take no notice of discomforts a mariner considered trifling.

Instead he worried that the ship wandered aimlessly with no clear

destination: "Saturday Dec. 19th Bound nowhere in particular I guess."
He had assumed the *Navy* would be whaling along the California and
Mexican coasts and then return to the northern Pacific in spring, as was
common practice among New Bedford whalers like the *Sea Breeze*. In
late December, he speculated: "Old man's bound to Japan I guess sperm
whaling." He kept busy catching skipjacks and breaking out water and
rice from the wet hold, pumped daily, though to little avail. The ship
passed Jarvis Island on December 24. "[N]ot a tree or anything green on
the island. Barely a sand bank. There is two or three houses on it, a guano
island owned by Williams of Honolulu," Susan Davis wrote. The coral
atoll, located about twenty-five miles south of the equator between the
Sandwich and the Cook Islands, lacked any fresh water source to sustain
human settlement. Its central lagoon had dried and filled with guano,
mined by American merchants for use as fertilizer, a profitable, though
malodorous business.

Next day Susan and Captain Davis celebrated Christmas, "had
quite a nice dinner for us but not like a home dinner. Extremely warm,
mosquitos plentiful, I cannot get anywhere but they tackle me." Nathaniel
Ransom wrote "Merry Christmas" in the margin for his entry on that day,
inured by his years at sea to lamenting the absence of a holiday dinner or
the plague of mosquitos. Instead he spent Christmas overhauling fluke
chains and added, "Bound to Okhotsk Sea I guess." It seemed too early to
head for still frozen bowhead whaling grounds. Two days later, however,
the ship's course was south by east. Then on January 3 he wrote, "Bound
for New Zealand I believe." A few days later Captain Davis's inept navigation resulted in a near disaster:

> January 9th: The watch were on deck. They thought they saw a
> light off the starboard bow. Shortly after they saw something in
> about the same direction they took to be an island. We found
> ourselves about 3 ship's lengths from the breakers. We imme-
> diately hauled slack in the wind and after a while under sail
> we managed to get past clear. The name of the island is Savage
> Island, inhabited by cannibals. They came very near having us
> for their breakfast.

Savage Island, now called Niue, lies about 1,600 miles northeast of New
Zealand. In 1774 Captain James Cook named it Savage Island because
the Polynesian natives who met him appeared to be stained with blood
around the mouth. In fact the so-called "cannibals" were not fearsome at
all; the red coloring of their teeth came from eating the native red banana
called hulahula. Moreover, several seamen listed in ships' crews in New

Bedford hailed from Savage Island, though such islanders were often simply listed as Kanaka.

After the near collision with land, the *Navy* continued toward New Zealand, and then near Sunday Island (now called Raoul Island), a strong east wind struck: "Blowing strong from the east. Laying still under close reefed topsails. Carried away the bow boat; she was left hanging by the after tackle. We managed to haul her alongside. After awhile hoisted her on deck after losing about all of the craft." As boatsteerer in charge of a whaleboat, Nathaniel Ransom took note of the significant loss of equipment: the oars, paddles, toggle irons, anchor, tubs of carefully coiled line, and a lantern keg filled with candles, ship's bread, and fresh water. In the fearful gale, Susan Davis could scarcely walk or stand still, and the seasickness that struck in its wake left her afraid she would not live until August when the *Navy* would return to New Bedford.

She marked her husband's fifty-eighth birthday as the ship crossed the International Dateline and approached the New Zealand whaling ground. "February 2: We have 7 months longer today; it seems as if I could not live so long and be as miserable as I am now. I do not know as it matters where one is when they die but I would rather be at home. One year ago today Caroline [her sister] died so we are passing away one after the other."

A cry from the lookout changed her tone: "They have just seen spouts for the first time since we have been here more than five weeks." Nathaniel Ransom too saw the spout and was astonished that Captain Davis did not shout an order to lower the boats: "Latter part raised a sperm whale. Old Jeff hadn't time to stop for him." The captain's passivity puzzled and infuriated him. His journal entries reveal an increasing scorn for Captain William Davis, whom he dubs "Jeff Davis," alluding to the president of the Confederacy during the recent Civil War. In fact Davis was no southerner—he hailed from Fairhaven. But later the epithet becomes "stingy Jeff Davis" or just "Old Jeff." Beyond uncertainties about the *Navy*'s course and the leaking hold, Nathaniel Ransom's dislike of the captain was rooted in Davis's poor management of the whale hunt and scanty rations for the crew. In his journal Ransom grumbled:

Old Jeff lost a barrel of molasses leaked out.

Sunday January 24th: Stingy Jeff skipper. Not much going on.

3rd Latter part wet hold. Saw two humpbacks. Hauled up mast and shortened sail. Old man had a row.

> February 9th: We've seen nothing as usual . . . Wet hole; making
> spun yarn, so much today . . . Humpbacks in sight.

Not far away sailed the *Henry Taber* from New Bedford, whose crew
caught, cleaned, and salted enough fish to fill an eight-barrel cask as the
ship cruised west of Australia. The fish enlivened the supper fare and
produced a more cheerful mood in the officers' quarters, where Captain
Timothy Packard relished a good dinner: "We live first rate having some
of the fish to eat that we caught at Amsterdam Island. They are splendid."[4]
A few weeks later he was smacking his lips over a dish of "good porpoise
balls for supper."

As both ships approached New Zealand the *Navy*'s crew saw a
school of blackfish, but again Captain Davis seemed no more interested
in them than in humpbacks. Instead he ordered the ship to anchor at the
port of Wanganui on the southwestern side of the northern island of New
Zealand, a port Nathaniel Ransom remembered from his visit eight years
earlier aboard the *Barnstable*. Susan Davis was anxious to spend a few
days on land, but at first the ship was forced to anchor ten miles from
shore in rugged seas. At last the crew was able to row her safely into the
harbor, where she was glad to walk on dry land once again. Among the
traders thronging the shore she sold her riding skirt and a thin dress she
had worn in Honolulu, for she would have little use for these clothes back
home. She was delighted to buy some peaches and grapes, a mouth-wa-
tering addition to the shipboard diet. Meanwhile the *Navy*'s crew got off
less appetizing rations, potatoes and onions and a raft of fresh water.
While Captain Davis and his wife spent the day ashore having tea with a
Captain Bartlett, the crewmen lowered their boats and went fishing.

At sea once more after leaving New Zealand Nathaniel Ransom
killed a sheep, and then smirked that "Old Jeff ate too much mutton
made him sick." As the ship sailed east southeast he continued pumping
the wet hold and working in the rigging. On Sunday February 28, 1869,
his journal ends abruptly as he ran out of paper, concluding in disgust,
"Course east by south. So much for this the Lord's Day. So winds up this
3 or 4 years lot of trash scribbled down by Nathaniel C. Ransom of Mattapoisett, Mass." Despite his disparaging his "lot of trash" he would resume
keeping a journal on each of his next voyages.

Susan Davis's tone brightened as she titled her early March journal
entry "Bound Home. Had chocolate for breakfast and Captain Davis
comes to eat with me. He seems to enjoy it." Her cheerfulness vanished in
the face of weather so stormy "one can scarcely creep about." It became
"so cloudy they have no observations, must calculate by dead reckoning,"

meaning that the dense overcast obscured the sun and planets so that the officers had no accurate means of measuring latitude and longitude. Another terrible gale struck on March 26 "but it is behind us and so we can run before it. Nearing Cape Horn and I shall be thankful when we are the other side of it for I have dreaded that place ever since we came from home." Days later a heavy sea stove in the bulwarks and she found three of her hens drowned. Usually chickens furnished eggs and an occasional Sunday dinner for the Captain and his wife, but only the smells of roast chicken reached the steerage or the forecastle hands as they settled around the kid of gravy, biscuits, and boiled beef or pork they called salt junk.

Susan Davis's thoughts lingered on human mortality as she marked the fifth anniversary of the death of baby Agnes. "She was taken away before she knew sin but her short life was full of suffering but there is a place where pain and sickness are not known and where friends part no more." Her daughter had never reached her first birthday; "had she lived she would have been quite a little miss."

Buffeted by a strong gale near Cape Horn she reported that first mate William Paige—a former neighbor from Hardwick, Vermont—was taken sick along with several in the forecastle. The weather remained calm, the water smooth as glass. She marked her thirty-first birthday in mid-April, recalling that two and three years ago she was ashore in Honolulu. Soon Captain Davis "was taken hard sick," but his wife was thankful to be able to wait on him, "for he does so much for me at all times." As the steward and cook were both abed with sickness she tried to prepare meals for the officers, making brown bread and white biscuit.

The unnamed illness abated after a few weeks, and in May Susan Davis's thoughts turned to homecoming. Progress was hampered by light winds and she complained that it took four weeks to travel forty degrees of latitude, an average speed of less than a hundred miles a day. Nearing Bermuda in early June she began to dread getting ashore as she feared trouble for Captain Davis over the poor catch of whale oil and bone. Indeed, during the months covered by Nathaniel Ransom's and Susan Davis's journals, the ship never lowered for a whale. While Captain Davis washed his wife's laundry and steered the ship on an aimless course, his crew found little to occupy their time. The captain's wife sensed their discontent as the *Navy* reached New Bedford on June 12: "Have taken but little oil and no great comfort in coming home I suppose the men think."

During its three-and-one-half year voyage, the *Navy* had taken 1,256 barrels of whale oil and 243 barrels of sperm oil and over ten tons of whalebone. Its yield for three Arctic seasons was about thirty percent

below average, reason enough to understand why William Davis never
served again as captain of a whaling voyage.

Perhaps Susan Davis's seasickness and dislike of life at sea also
contributed to her husband's decision to forsake the sea. On land once
more, she found her footing. Two weeks after reaching New Bedford
she went to a circus on Pope's Island with Captain Davis. Harvey Paige,
brother of the *Navy*'s first mate, paid a visit and brought news from Hardwick, Vermont. Susan Davis persuaded her husband to give up whaling,
and they returned to her family's roots, settling once again in Hardwick.
Two years later she gave birth to their son there. Unlike baby Agnes, he
grew to healthy adulthood and lived near his mother, who outlived her
older husband by many years.

"Darling Sarah"

On June 12, when the *Navy* reached New Bedford, Nathaniel Ransom
made his way to Mattapoisett and "spent part of the evening with my
Darling Sarah at home." The following day they visited James Ransom's
wife Almeida in nearby Wareham. On June 27, 1869, they married in a
simple ceremony witnessed by their parents, and Nathaniel's brother
Joseph, who was home from the sea. Reverend Leander Cobb, a Congre-
gational minister in Marion, signed their wedding certificate. It shows
Nathaniel wearing a stiff collar and bow tie, a horseshoe-shaped beard
framing his chin. Sarah wears her dark hair parted in the center, a lace
collar around the neckline of her dress. She was twenty-one, and her new
husband two years older. The day after celebrating July Fourth together,
they went to Fairhaven to visit Mr. Bourne, and that evening attended the
circus on nearby Pope's Island that the Davises had visited two weeks
before.[5]

Two days after arriving in New Bedford aboard the *Navy*,
Nathaniel Ransom returned to the city with his father. In the office
of Jonathan Bourne, owner of the *Sea Breeze*, father and son collected
Nathaniel's pay. The shipping agent's account book shows that he had
received a $100 cash advance, was charged $10 for fitting ship (bedding,
etc.) and had to pay $34 interest on these charges, a usurious rate of 31%.
He earned $1527.80, but charges from the slops chest for tobacco, a shirt
and the like were $156.09. His lay as boatsteerer was 1/100th share of the
whale oil taken, or $924.22. His 1/85 share of $51,304.49 for whalebone
amounted to $603.58. In total he earned $1227.71 net pay for his three
years and six weeks aboard the *Sea Breeze*. His father signed below him

Wedding Certificate Photographs, Sarah Dexter and Nathaniel Ransom, June 27, 1869.

to acknowledge payment. His seven months aboard the *Navy* probably brought him nothing at all.

The writings Nathaniel Ransom dismisses as his scribbled three or four years lot of trash reveal broad changes from the fourteen-year-old who first shipped aboard the *Barnstable*. He had acquired considerable skill as a boatsteerer or harpooner, learned to calculate latitude and longitude, and gained enough confidence in his seamanship to scorn Captain Davis's ineptitude. He had developed the boatsteerer's quintessential ability to work alongside officers, crewmen, Kanakas, and Eskimos. The coast of Siberia and exotic ports in the Falklands, the Sandwich Islands, and New Zealand had grown familiar and no longer thrilled him. He had learned the power of friendship, dependence on the love of family, compassion for the sick, and had conquered any squeamishness about laying out the bodies of the dead. Although one-fifth of the *Sea Breeze*'s original crew had perished of disease or by accident, Nathaniel Ransom considered his own survival scarcely worth mention. His daily record of life aboard ship reveals no repugnance at crowded conditions, or the squalor and vermin-infested food that plagued Susan Davis. Nor does he express any belief in divine justice punishing those who ignore the Sabbath or resort to strong liquor to alleviate their homesickness and misery. Nothing in his whaling experience affirmed any faith in divine rewards for the virtuous or punishment for evil-doers, sentiments expressed by Josiah Foster in the *Sea Breeze*'s logbook. Instead he saw that only the fortuitous combination of his own strength and skill and a sufficient portion of luck could bring a man safely home from the bowhead whale hunt.

Chapter IV: "May God Have Mercy on This Whaling Fleet and Deliver us from These Cold and Icy Shores."

Third Mate of the John Wells:
November 9, 1869–September 14, 1871

In November 1869, four months after their wedding, Nathaniel Ransom left Sarah Dexter at her parents' home in Mattapoisett and embarked on his third whaling voyage aboard the Arctic-bound *John Wells*. Marriage presented a painful dilemma: to support a family the young man needed earnings sufficient for a household of his own. Yet the surest vocation for a whaleman with two voyages behind him was to leave his bride and return to the sea. Necessity compelled him to continue the pattern of leave-taking and longing for home, treasuring a few mementos of his young wife, and awaiting letters from her in every port. The same dilemma confronted Nathaniel's brother Joseph Ransom, who also left his wife behind, with a baby daughter called Amelia. Two weeks behind the *John Wells*, Joseph sailed as third mate of the Atlantic sperm whaler *Marcella*.

The *John Wells*, an old spouter built in 1822, carried Nathaniel Ransom south and east from New Bedford, a now familiar route. His thirty-three shipmates averaged an age of twenty-five, three years older than the crews of the *Barnstable* and the *Sea Breeze*. Men from coastal Massachusetts filled the roster, their need for paying work crowding out the Azoreans and Kanakas. Nathaniel Ransom, just shy of his twenty-fourth birthday, advanced to the rank of third mate aboard the 357-ton bark, smaller than the *Sea Breeze*. Now he commanded the larboard (port) watch—about a dozen men—and the bow whaleboat.

Before Nathaniel Ransom departed, Sarah baked a cake for him to take along, and gave him some papers to read. Her homemade grape preserves and jars of dangle-berry juice would remind him of their few happy summer months together. Sarah remained always in his thoughts, tender sentiments that found their way into his private journal, for even after mocking descriptions of his first two voyages as three or four years of trash, he brought on board a third "Private Journal." He wrote the ship's name and "Aaron Dean, Master" at the top of every left page and the ship's location at the top of the right page. While he continued the logkeeper's habit of meticulously recording each day's weather, the setting of sails, and activities aboard ship, he confided to his third journal increasingly intimate glimpses of his sensations and emotions. Often he addressed Sarah directly, and perhaps he gave her the journal to read after he returned home. Monday after leaving port he mused, "Darling Sarah, I should have liked to help you wash today." Wringer washing machines had already made their appearance in the *Whalemen's Shipping List*, but the clothes had to be agitated and the wringers turned by hand crank. Any washerwoman welcomed a husband's help lifting wet bed sheets from the tub. "It is my birthday," he wrote on November 29. "I wish I were where my darling wife could pinch my ears." Two weeks later he shaved off the beard shown in his wedding photograph. "Sarah, I look like a boy now," he confided. He was twenty-four and had got his full growth, five feet seven and one-half inches tall. Sarah was taking music lessons in his absence and he played the accordion aboard ship, imagining harmonizing with her piano, but alone he heard only "dull music."

"Very Dry, Dry, Dry and Dull, Dull, Dull"

The *John Wells* toiled southward toward the equator for six weeks. Ransom made a mast for his whaleboat, painted the cutting falls, and found little else worthy of note, except that he and his shipmates "all partook of grape preserves for supper." The early stages of the Atlantic hunt for humpbacks and right whales brought little success. Although groups of finbacks swam near the ship, Captain Dean did not order boats to lower for them, for they swam swiftly and almost always escaped the harpoon gun. A few degrees north of the equator the crew chased a harem school of small sperm whales but gave them up as they escaped fast to windward. On December 18, working south along the eastern coast of Brazil the ship struck on a shoal with a bone-jarring jolt that shook every man aloft in the rigging. The crew was able to back ship and stood off shore immediately, relieved to find the vessel uninjured. A week later under a fine breeze from southward Nathaniel wished his dear Sarah a Merry Christmas without marking any celebration on the *John Wells*. He broke out fresh water and killed a pig; at least there would be fresh pork for supper. Next day he chased cowfish, small-beaked black dolphins, but took none. On New Year's Day a school of beak-nosed grampuses—ten or twelve-foot-long dolphins with a dorsal fin—swam nearby. They escaped the whalemen, who succeeded only in capturing seven porpoises.

Sailing about one hundred fifty miles a day, master Aaron Dean maneuvered his ship south of the Strait of Magellan through a winding passage between Tierra del Fuego and Hermite Island. Crewmen leaned over the railing trying to spear porpoises swimming close to the ship. The cook and steward caught some of the seabirds flying all over the deck but found them not worth the trouble to pluck and clean for dinner. For two weeks the *John Wells* struggled to make headway against the wind beating the ship to eastward. "Wind all around the compass heading likewise" reads the journal entry for January 26, 1870. After reaching the Pacific a few days later, the pre-dawn watch raised a school of large sperm whales. First mate Joseph Fisher, familiar from the voyage of the *Sea Breeze*, and second mate Frederick Prudent lowered their boats, but only succeeded in driving the whales off to windward. Next day, a Sunday, the *John Wells* gammed the *Thomas Dickason*, which had also left New Bedford in early November and already made a hundred barrels of precious sperm oil, real cause for envy.

Sailing north along the coast of Chile the crew caught eight porpoises and set about cutting off their blubber and trying it out, glad to feel useful at last. Oil from the jaw of the porpoise made a fine-grade lubricant for clocks and watches. South of the trading port of Talcahuano on the west coast of Chile, Captain Dean anchored at Mocha Island to buy twenty-five barrels of potatoes. Nathaniel Ransom went hunting on shore and shot a few wild pigeons at sundown. Ready to leave the harbor, the officers found five crewmen missing the "all aboard" call. Captain Dean decided to cruise for porpoise a few days and then go back after the runaways, reasoning that Mocha Island's uninviting landscape should move them to change their minds and return to the ship. The island covered less than twenty square miles, with a population of a few hundred native people, the Mapuche, who believed that it was visited by the souls of the dead. The runaways' decision to flee into such inhospitable surroundings says much about living conditions in the forecastle. Surrounded by sperm whaling grounds, Mocha Island lent its name to "Mocha Dick," famous as Herman Melville's white whale. Four of the *John Wells*'s original crew came from Brazil or Cuba; the nearness of Chile's coast made the island's location a logical place to run away from the ship. Nathaniel Ransom chafed at the necessity of trying to recapture the men: "Here we are hanging about here with a fair wind for the Sandwich

Islands waiting for the runaway scamps." Only the cook—who hailed from New Bedford—returned to ship. After dallying most of a week and returning twice to the island, Captain Dean gave up seeking the deserters.

En route to Hilo, the first and second mates caught two black-fish while Nathaniel Ransom struck others, "but the line drawed off from them." Missing chances to strike humpbacks, the crew found better success fishing for albacore and skipjacks. Otherwise they occupied their time making spun yarn and picking over potatoes. One idle Sunday in March Nathaniel Ransom groused, "Nothing doing, very dry, dry, dry and dull, dull, dull . . . I am getting about tired of *John Wells.*" The ship docked at Hilo on April second, and the week's layover gave him the opportunity to attend church and to send letters to Sarah and his parents, though he had to wait until docking in Honolulu, where the ship's office was, to receive any mail. Beneath Hilo's rainy skies the ship took on casks of fresh water, aromatic Hawaiian coffee, coal for the blacksmith's forge and the stoves that would be needed in the Arctic, bread, flour, and barrel shooks, heads, and hoops. The crew also brought aboard two new whale-boats made to order: shallow craft of thin cedar planking, seaworthy, lightweight, and pointed at both ends to reverse direction the instant a mate shouted "Stern all!"

Six passengers sailed aboard the *John Wells* between Hilo and Honolulu, where the ship docked for four days. There Nathaniel Ransom found letters from his family, and three from his Darling Wife. He wrote lovingly to her, to his parents and brother Sidney. He posted his letters at the shipping office when he went ashore to bring back newly hired crewmen and sixteen bales of tobacco, much of it intended for trade with Alaskan and Siberian natives.

In mid-April the crew of the *John Wells* squared away for the Arctic Ocean. By 1870, few whalers returned to the Okhotsk Sea where the *Sea Breeze* ranged a few years earlier. The lack of ice cover there in summer left whales vulnerable to attack, quickly depleting the stock of bowheads. Furthermore whalemen observed that bowheads appeared to learn from past experience, becoming very shy at the approach of ships or whale-boats. While their eyesight was poor, their hearing was acute enough to distinguish sounds of the natural environment, such as a chunk of ice slipping into the water, from the stroke of oars or the quieter lapping of paddles in the whaleboat. Upon hearing threatening sounds, even from fifteen or twenty miles away, they dove deep beneath the surface or swam rapidly away. This time Nathaniel Ransom's destination would be the Chukchi and Bering Seas, where he had first hunted aboard the *Barnstable.*

"I've Got the Blues As Usual."

During the month-long passage north to the Arctic, Nathaniel made a pen for potatoes between decks and aired his dusty straw mattress. He painted the new whaleboats green below the water line and black above, with a white rib running between; the use of color helped whalemen distinguish which ship boats belonged to as they peered through salt spray or ice fog. He found boredom harder to bear than heavy labor or danger, and idle Sundays while the ship carried him further into the hostile northern ocean were the worst of all. "Oh dear, it's rather dull music about this time with me," he confessed in late April. "I've got the blues as usual." On May 7, 1870, the ship passed through "72 passage," just west of 172 degrees west longitude, threading between the Fox Islands in the Aleutian chain. He marked six months out on May 9, wishing again that he could bother Darling Sarah about washing. The crew had set up a stove in the cabin in late April and two weeks later installed another in the forecastle as the ship raised ice in May, on Friday the thirteenth.

Approaching the bowheads' feeding grounds, the crew prepared for the whale hunt, slung the starboard whaleboat from its davits ready to lower, and rigged the Pierce guns. Because bowheads often fled beneath the ice when struck, Arctic whalers resorted to the most sophisticated weapons available in hopes of killing them immediately. The Pierce and Eggers bomb lance gun soon became the most widely used and effective weapon in the bowhead hunt. It measured one yard in length and weighed about twenty-four pounds. The shoulder-fired gun used a Winchester cartridge and a bomb lance that had to be loaded separately. Rigging the guns necessitated first loading the cartridge and a short harpoon staff that would be launched into the whale. A wire attached to the harpoon triggered the explosion of a sixteen-inch bomb lance—provided, or course, that the shooter succeeded in hitting his target. In May of 1870, those targets were nowhere to be seen from the masthead of the *John Wells*.

A half-dozen familiar whaleships from New Bedford or nearby ports, among them the *Champion*, the *Seneca*, and the *Henry Taber*, gammed one another south of the Bering Strait, waiting for ice to allow them to work northward. "Banging about just nowhere at all," Nathaniel Ransom amused himself by reading. North of the Pribilof Islands (St. George and St. Paul) the watch finally spotted whales, but the ice was too thick to lower the whaleboats, and the bowheads quickly disappeared beneath it. The lookout on the *Seneca* counted fifteen of them swimming northeast, and chafed at the lost chance to strike them.[1] Captain Timothy Packard tied his *Henry Taber* to the ice, although it continued to thump the ship, adding to the discomfort of the nineteen Hawaiian seamen he had taken aboard the previous December.[2] Captain Pease of the *Champion*, out of Edgartown, wrote of the 1870 season that his vessel entered the ice on May 17 about forty miles south of Cape Navarin in weather thick and snowing. Skies cleared three days later "showing about a dozen ships in the ice." By the time he worked the *Champion* out of the ice, "fifty ships were on a race to Cape Thaddeus; it was oak against ice . . . all came out more or less damaged in copper and sheathing." He reached Cape Thaddeus on the Siberian coast after four days, entering clear water, but saw no whales.[3]

Nathaniel Ransom passed the weeks of idleness in reading or mending clothes, and visited with Freeman Barrett, third mate aboard the *Benjamin Cummings*. Aboard the nearby *Seneca*, logkeeper George Duffy counted twenty-six idle whaling vessels with sails furled surrounded by impenetrable ice. A thick snowstorm in late May drove the *John Wells* into heavy ice, breaking off the martingale at the bow and tearing copper sheathing off the hull. Thick ice surrounding the ship would bear a man's weight, so that seamen could walk from one ship to another for a gam to alleviate their boredom. Homesickness plagued Ransom in early June as he waited for the ice to loosen its grip. "My Darling Wife, I'm lonely without you," he admitted. "I've got the blues of course." The *John Wells* was "Laying still for the very good reason that we can do nothing else." Fog "as wet as it is thick" obscured the view of nearby St. Lawrence Island, a treeless wasteland with a few thousand inhabitants. Under these conditions the only route northward lay along the Siberian coast, where the *John Wells* finally docked at Plover Bay on June 19. "Any quantity of Esquimeaux" from the tiny settlement came aboard to trade. The ship's cooper had made rum kegs to exchange with them, for wood was scarce in their barren homeland, and the Chukchi had already learned how to make rum from sugar or molasses bartered from the whaleships. Captain Dean offered tobacco, metal tools, and brightly colored calicos for the Chukchis' furs, walrus ivory, the lightweight boots whalemen called Masinkers, and fur-lined mittens. Meanwhile the *Champion* drifted northeastward toward Cape Agchen, moving about twelve miles a day in heavy ice.

At anchor near Plover Bay at the end of June 1870, the whalemen of the *John Wells* at last lowered their boats to cruise for bowheads. In contrast to this tardy beginning of the whaling season, Ransom's 1867 voyage into the sheltered Okhotsk Sea aboard the *Sea Breeze* had commenced whaling in early May. Now he remained aboard ship, feeling "quite unwell with a headache and cold chills running through my body. I quit using tobacco today." With too little wind for the vessel to maneuver, the crew had to tow the ship north of Indian Point using two whaleboats and lines, plodding, back-breaking labor. Near Indian Point (today Mys Chaplina, Siberia) Captain Barker from the English bark *Japan* came aboard and got a cask of bread and some slops. Later the same week, Captain Dean "let the *Daniel Webster* have eight barrels of beef" because, like the *John Wells* it was owned by William Brownell in New Bedford. Salt beef had grown tiresome after months at sea. Along the Siberian shore Nathaniel Ransom hunted ducks and shot eight, his mouth watering for the taste of roast fowl. He traded with the Chukchi and "got 3 pair of mittens and a pair of boots from them" on the last day of June. He bartered with real Yankee thrift, for clothing from the captain's slops chest cost dear money. Mariners on the *Thomas Dickason* who needed mittens paid $1.25 a pair, and rubber boots cost fifteen dollars.[4] As his ship passed through the Bering Strait, Ransom grumbled, "This is a high old 4th of July for me. I hope my darling wife is enjoying herself a little better than I am. I dare say she is and wonder if she is thinking of her husband at this time. I must play with the accordion a little," for Captain Dean granted the crew a holiday on Independence Day. Ransom's thoughts lingered on events of the previous year, when he and Sarah were newly married, visiting friends and relatives, and strolling through the circus on Pope's Island.

The Walrus Hunt

Memories of home and traces of depression were quickly driven aside in the pearly glow that passed for night: "At one o'clock this morning raised walruses. Mate got 5 second mate 5, third mate 7 and lost 2, fourth mate 8." Referring to himself obliquely as "third mate," Nathaniel Ransom tallied the walrus killed through the next month, as he and his shipmates shot 270, sometimes as many as thirty-nine in a single day. His skill can be measured against the record of the *Thomas Dickason*'s crew, who captured 187 walrus in the same season. Their daily catch peaked at twenty-one. Walrus were a novel quarry for Ransom, for their habitat lay north of the Okhotsk Sea where he had hunted bowheads on his last voyage. Captain Brownson of the *Barnstable* had taken a few walrus in July of 1862 and traded with the Chukchi for walrus ivory. Now improved methods of refining walrus oil enabled whalers to turn to profit the summer months before the bowheads appeared. In late May and early June, herds of walrus rode the ice as it broke up and drifted northward into the Arctic Ocean. Sometimes they slept in the water in a nearly upright pose, rising from

Etching on baleen, Oscar Sage, Kivalina, Alaska, 1992. Photo by Peter Randall.

time to time to breathe without waking. Their round heads, small black eyes, and drooping mustache-like tusks gave them an almost human face. Bull walrus basked on their backs in the sun like old codgers on a sandy beach, their flabby, shapeless bodies heaped together. Over nine feet long, they could twitch suddenly into motion, ready to plunge into the sea at the approach of a polar bear, their first enemy. Man was the second. Whalers began hunting walrus in great numbers in 1868, using the rifles developed in the Civil War to attack the stodgy, lethargic mammals. Weighing up to a ton, walrus yielded about three-fourths of a barrel of oil apiece from their three or four inches of blubber, far less than any whale, but their clear oil now cost less to refine than whale oil. Furthermore, the unsuspecting walrus were far easier prey than whales, for they usually fell on the ice where they were shot, with no need to make fast to them for a wild whaleboat ride.

Because the walrus reacted to scent rather than sound, hunters approached cautiously from leeward. They preferred a mild sunny day for the hunt, when walrus lolled about, dozy and listless. The gunman endeavored to row toward them from downwind, often dressed in white to blend into the brightness of surrounding ice. If he could land on the block of ice where the walrus lay, he fired his rifle as quickly as he could aim, targeting a spot between the eye and the ear, attempting to pierce the animal's brain. Sometimes he shot so rapidly that the rifle overheated and he had to reach for another, kept loaded and ready in his boat. Walrus seemed not to hear the crack of his rifle, but if a wounded animal caught the scent of man and tumbled bellowing and barking into the water, others became alarmed and shoved themselves into the sea to escape. Warm walrus blood sometimes melted rivulets into the old rotten ice where they bled to death, and the dead mammals and their hunters slid together into the sea. Whalers slaughtered nearly 4,000 in 1870, most of them females, who clung to their young. A. Howard Clark, writing for Goode's *Fisheries and Fishery Industries of the United States*, lamented that hunters could shoot entire herds of adult walrus, "and the little ones remain on the ice hovering around the carcasses of their mothers until death from starvation silences their moanings."[5]

Heedless of those cries, the whalemen took advantage of the Arctic sun that provided daylight around the clock. Working on the ice where the dead walrus lay, the crew cut off strips of blubber and hide. Some thought the walrus liver, heart, or tongue made good eating and took those organs back to the ship for supper. The walrus head was severed so that the tusks could be hacked out later aboard ship. Working efficiently on the ice, a good crew could butcher and load blubber from six or seven walrus into their boat to row their bleeding greasy cargo to the ship, making several forays a day. Captain Pease of the *Champion* lamented that his ship's company was inferior to many others in their ability to withstand exposure and cold. Nevertheless he succeeded in capturing about 400 walrus, making 230 barrels of oil. If natives approached the whaleboats, they salvaged the walrus hide for leather and took the meat for food, for the whalemen seldom bothered with either. Back aboard ship, the whalers skinned the strips of blubber and minced them before tossing them into the trypots. The entire walrus processing operation was far safer and easier than cutting in an enormous bowhead while clinging to the cutting stage slung from the side of the vessel as it pitched and rolled in the swells.

Further profit derived from walrus tusks. Those from an aged bull might measure a yard long and weigh as much as eighteen pounds apiece, but their core was often yellowish and pithy, making walrus ivory slightly less desirable than elephant ivory. Tusks from the female walrus were smaller, just a pound or two apiece, and finer grained. Whalemen looked forward to carving ivory (scrimshawing) during slack hours aboard ship. "Pleasant weather cutting out walrus tusks; I've picked out a pair that I caught for my darling Wife," Nathaniel Ransom wrote in early August. Carvers fashioned tusks into knife handles, dice, cane and parasol handles, crochet and button hooks, or small ornaments. Tusks were the walruses' chief weapon; they hooked both tusks over the gunwale to overturn a whaleboat, or drove them through its planking: "Got stove by a walrus, had to come aboard to repair damages; made out to get aboard, second mate holding my boat up with 4 walruses." Ransom's first concern was usually material losses rather than the danger of sinking into the frigid Bering Sea.

Not far from the *John Wells*, the *Seneca* too was hunting walrus. Her crew killed two hundred of them along the Siberian coast. There the ship struck the bottom so hard that pieces of the hull's copper sheathing (protection against teredo mollusks or ship worms) floated to the water's edge. Run aground in twelve feet of water, Captain Edmund Kelley lost some precious oil. He commanded his men to off-load casks of walrus oil and raft them together to lighten the ship, and then haul ground tier casks out of the hold. Two casks containing about 630 gallons of oil drifted away and were lost, together with four empty casks and twenty barrels before the crew could free the ship and resume walrusing.

"Somewhere in the Vicinity of the North Pole"

Nathaniel Ransom and his shipmates "got boats ready for whaling, gave up walrusing for this season," on August 5 as herds of walrus drifted south toward the Bering Strait. The *John Wells* plodded slowly north, still hugging the Siberian coast: "Quite a quantity of ice around. My Darling Sarah it is bitter cold, 16°. I should like to snuggle up to you about this time." While he imagined Sarah and her mother attending religious camp meetings on Martha's Vineyard, the ship sailed through the Bering Strait and continued north and east, reaching Icy Cape on the Alaskan shore on August 20. Arriving a full two months later than expected, he complained that they had missed the northward migration of bowheads toward the Beaufort Sea. "We saw quite a number of ships boiling ahead of us. We find ourselves with several other ships just about 2 days too late for good whaling." Captain Valentine Lewis on the *Thomas Dickason* counted twenty ships, four or five whaling, and four already boiling out oil.

Frustration plagued the third mate of the *John Wells* through the next week: "Lots of ships have taken whales today and we haven't even lowered for one." The more fortunate *Seneca* finally struck a bowhead on August 22, but competition was stiff: twenty-six ships hunted nearby. Envy gnawed at Nathaniel Ransom: "Chasing whales; did everything except strike one." And finally a quiet triumph: "Plenty of ice and snow.

Forenoon working to windward. Afternoon raised a bowhead lowered for him and struck. I got him at 10 PM finished cutting in," he reported with satisfaction.

Not all were so fortunate. Just after capturing that first bowhead of the season he "saw a ship in distress surrounded by lots of other ships but did not ascertain her name," for he was too busy cutting in. Foundering twelve miles northwest of Point Barrow, the *Almira* of Edgartown flew her flag upside down as a signal of distress. Captain Lewis on the *Thomas Dickason* saw the *Almira*'s signal, "steered aroun to her found her stove by the Ice." Captain Thomas Williams of the *Hibernia*, with his wife and children aboard, also hastened to aid the *Almira*. Others watched the *Hibernia* anxiously from a distance. "We think she got stove by ice. At 4 PM steering to southwestward cold enough to freeze a brass monkey," Nathaniel Ransom wrote. While trying to aid the *Almira*, the *Hibernia* had indeed struck ice, staving her hull, which immediately filled with water. Captain Williams managed to reach shallow water and anchored his ship two miles southwest of Point Barrow, while his crew frantically manned the pumps, and whaleboats from eight other ships hurried to aid both vessels. Their efforts failed as seawater filled the *Hibernia*'s hold and rose above the cabin floor, but everyone aboard reached safety. Next day the *John Wells* "got news of the ship *Hibernia* and bark *Almira* being lost." Captain Williams auctioned off the *Hibernia*'s cargo of five hundred barrels of oil and a ton and a half of whalebone. He took his family and crew aboard Captain Bernard Cogan's *Josephine* for the remainder of the season.

Loss of Thirty-three Vessels of the Arctic Whaling Fleet, Crushed or Hemmed in by the Ice. From a Sketch by Benjamin Russell. (Courtesy of the New Bedford Whaling Museum.)

At 550 tons the *Hibernia* had been one of the largest ships in the whaling business, and carried $32,000 insurance. The smaller bark *Almira*—built in Mattapoisett—carried no insurance and lost four hundred barrels of oil. Its captain, Charles Marchant, took refuge aboard the *Seneca* but later returned to Honolulu aboard the *Alaska* of New Bedford.

Captain Pease of the *Champion* at least kept his vessel and crew safe, although he had "not the right boys to whale in that ice," for his hands could not cut in one whale while their shipmates hunted another. They took only eight bowheads, four of them quite small. Meanwhile ships that had forty or fifty "men clad in skins and officers accustomed to that particular kind of whaling, did well." Indeed, for other ships the bowhead season proved to be a rich one despite its inauspiciously late beginning. The *Henry Taber* saw no whales until late August, and then captured seventeen near Point Barrow in just three weeks. The *Thomas Dickason* took no bowheads until August 31, then killed twelve more in the next month. Captain Valentine Lewis heard from Captain William Barnes that his *Aurora* was "full and in want of casks to put her oil in." Lewis sold him enough casks to hold fifty barrels of oil. The *John Wells* captured eleven bowheads after making its way fifteen miles north of Point Barrow and east toward Herschel Island, remaining in the Beaufort Sea throughout September. Nathaniel Ransom killed four of the bowheads, his matter-of-fact tone concealing the pride he took in his craft: "September 10th: Afternoon raised a large whale lowered for him I struck and got him at 4 PM got him alongside at 10 finished cutting got supper set the watch."

Intermingled with records of the catch come worrisome reports of threatening weather, for the ship lay further east and north than normal so late in the season. On September 18: "Plenty of hail and snow as usual." And the next day: "A thick snowstorm most of the time. Trying out oil. Afternoon lowered for whales fourth mate struck line got foul of an oar upset boat saved crew and boat lost whale evening laying aback." His cabin mate Benjamin Worth was flung out of the whaleboat together with its crew. Desperate seamen floundering in the hyperborean waters reminded him of the *Sea Breeze* boatsteerer's death two seasons past, drowned when he became entangled in the line made fast to a whale. Beyond the risk of drowning, being thrown into the freezing Beaufort Sea caused near fatal hypothermia. Everyone knew men could freeze instantly as they sank before they could move to keep themselves afloat, so that frozen corpses remained rigidly upright. Fifteen years earlier one whaler penned a gloomy rhyme:

In these dreary seas midst fog and frost
Poor whalemen oft in the boats are lost.
Unsheltered from the biting blast
With frozen limbs they breathe their last.[6]

September 24 found the *John Wells* "Cruising somewhere in vicinity of north pole . . . Afternoon working back to windward where we came from." Next day the crew finished boiling, "About time I think," Ransom muttered with relief as they were "bound for Herschel Island ground." On the 28th they experienced fine weather for the first time in a month, and took three more bowheads in the following four days. On October 3, the crew "saw several whales but did not lower for them," for the ship was blubber-logged by this time. They had run out of space to contain the enormous blanket pieces of blubber while they worked to cut them into horse pieces for mincing and trying out. The blanket pieces, weighing several tons, could de-stabilize the ship as they slithered around between decks. Meanwhile it was blowing a gale of wind from northeast, the seas so rough that the crew was forced to cool down the tryworks, for open flames could launch a spark into the rigging, and hot oil seething in the trypots could scald a seaman who stumbled too close to them.

Lumbering southward over the next two weeks in company with the *Champion*, *Seneca*, and *John Howland*, the crew of the *John Wells* restarted the tryworks several times, halting the boiling when there was a heavy swell on. A gale from northward drove the ship through Bering Strait on October 8, and carried away the fore topmast staysail near the prow of the vessel, still blowing the next morning. "About ten o'clock raised rock on St. Lawrence Island ahead hauled on wind barely went clear and that's all." It was a narrow escape from shipwreck, for flying spray and sea fog obscured any solid shape. The same gale struck the *Seneca* with a high sea that carried away its bow and waist boats with all their gear. The crew had no chance to finish boiling out the hundred barrels worth of blubber still on board until the winds abated enough to restart the tryworks. The *Thomas Dickason* too extinguished the fire in the tryworks as blubber shifted around heavily below decks. Seas sweeping over the decks carried away two of its whaleboats.

The *Champion*'s Captain Pease described with palpable terror the tempest raging near St. Lawrence Island and the damage it wrought:

On the evening of the 7th it blew almost a hurricane; hove the ship to south of Point Hope, with main-topsail furled; lost starboard bow boat, with davits—ship covered with ice and oil. On the 10th, entered the straits in a heavy gale; when about 8 miles south of the Diomedes, had to heave to under bare poles, blowing furiously, and the heaviest sea I ever saw; ship making bad weather of it; we had about 120 barrels of oil on deck, and all our fresh water; our blubber between decks in horse-pieces, and going from the forecastle to the mainmast every time she pitched, and impossible to stop it; ship covered with ice and oil; could only muster four men in a watch, decks flooded with water all the time; no fire to cook with or to warm by, made it the most anxious and miserable time I ever experienced in all my sea-service. [He had been whaling for twenty-five years.] During the night shipped a heavy sea, which took off bow and waist boats, davits, slide boards, and everything attached, staving about 20 barrels of oil. At daylight on the second day we found ourselves in 17 fathoms of water, and about 6 miles from the center cape of St. Lawrence Island. Fortunately the gale moderated a little, so that we got two close-reefed topsails and reefed courses on her, and by sundown were clear of the west end of the island. Had it not moderated as soon as it did, we should, by 10 a.m., have been shaking hands with our departed friends.

The *John Wells* dodged drifting ice in thick fog as the ship headed south, again combatting surging seas and fierce winds one week after the storm that nearly wrecked the *Champion:*

October 14th: Blowing a gale from northeast . . . Afternoon lost starboard boat at 7 PM hove to under main spencer fore topmast staysail. Carried away main topsail. Large cask of oil on deck fetched away; to prevent it going through bulwarks we cut a hole in the head let the oil run out; empty cask adrift cut one man's head open.

Oil poured overboard briefly calmed the seas closest to the ship. Ransom's inventory of damage to the vessel attests to the violence of the storm, weathered with his customary stoicism. Next day the gale blew "not quite so heavy as yesterday" and the ship reached the Fox Islands in the Aleutian chain. Under calmer winds next day the crew cleared up some between decks and "broke out a new main topsail . . . unrove cutting falls took in cutting stage got anchor on bow unbent cable run it below." They boiled out the remainder of the blubber—cold temperatures below decks had kept it from rotting—as they steered southeast, one sail in sight. The *Seneca* too lost another whaleboat, its fore topsail, and the gangway rail in the same gale near the Fox Islands. The *Thomas Dickason*'s Captain Lewis watched helplessly as his oil tank on deck near the tryworks broke adrift full of oil that spilled into the lower hold. Little wonder that he found "six men sick of duty." (Lewis was an erratic speller; he meant the men were sick and *off* duty.)

A far worse fate befell Captain Frederick Barker of the *Japan* who had gotten a cask of bread and some slops from the *John Wells* in June. The storm that carried away the main topsail and starboard boat of the *John Wells* in mid-October wrecked the *Japan* in heavy seas, roaring wind and dense fog near false East Cape (Mys Intsova) on the Siberian coast. No other whaling vessels were found nearby to take its crew aboard, and all men were feared lost.

Safely through the "seventy-two passage" among the Aleutian Islands, the crew of the *John Wells* set to work washing and scraping the long blades of baleen. Whalemen called scraping bone "slushing," for weeks in the hold softened the bowhead's malodorous gum tissue the way that thawing weather softened old snow. Men washed the whale-bone, blackish strips fourteen to sixteen feet long, and stood them upright in the rigging to dry on deck. Using lengths of spun yarn they bound the bone into hundred-pound bundles, ready to be shipped home from the Sandwich Islands.

As soon as the treacherous Arctic weather receded, Nathaniel Ransom found his journey to the south dull enough that boredom and depression returned. He knew that the voyage south did not mean a return home, for his ship would spend the next season whaling in the Arctic again. "Sunday October 23rd: I tried to amuse myself by reading my Darling Wife's letters and playing on the accordion but it was all rather dull music, only an aggravation." He passed the time washing and scraping bone, fixing up his boat, and washing his big coat. Aboard the *Thomas Dickason*, Captain Lewis likewise reported "wone watch employed in washing close."

"Any amount of rain as usual in Hilo," Nathaniel Ransom lamented in early November. "Darling Sarah I'm so lonely without you . . . This is a miserable place any time. Well we are now waiting for a breeze to go to Honolulu—perhaps we shall have to for a month to come." But four days later his ship reached Honolulu with its 1,208 barrels of whale oil aboard and spent the next month in port. There he was delighted to find eight letters, "5 of them from my darling Wife, one from my parents, one from Theo and one from Sid beside 2 papers from my darling and one from Theo. I had enough to keep me the rest of the day." While all hands went ashore, he remained aboard ship imagining himself in the company of his family. His brother Theodore with his Creole wife Josephine had settled nearer Boston, where he made a living as a traveling merchant. Nathaniel attempted to amuse himself by reading some of the letters sent by his darling wife and by playing the accordion, plagued by mosquitos that he pronounced "very troublesome." He wrote a few lines to Sarah each day, mailing his letters from the shipping office, though a real exchange of thoughts was impossible; news from home took weeks to cross the continent to California and then reach Honolulu by steamer from San Francisco. And by the time his letters reached Mattapoisett, months to a half-year had elapsed.

Together with fourth mate Benjamin Worth he attended meeting at Honolulu's Seamen's Bethel and services at the Fort Street church. The pair sampled other amusements ashore too, a "slight of hand performance" which he pronounced "rather dry" and a concert one Saturday night. "Evening I went to something accompanied with Mr. Worth which was called a theater but did not find it very interesting." Without Sarah's companionship, entertainment fell flat.

For some whalemen Honolulu meant the chance to sail for home, as did the first mate of the *John Wells*, Joseph Fisher of New Bedford. Nathaniel Ransom had known him for three years, as he had first come aboard as the *Sea Breeze*'s second mate in 1867. Laying aside any thoughts of returning home early himself, Ransom marked his twenty-fifth birthday on November 29, wishing in vain: "I would like to be with my Darling Wife today so I would every day but I cannot." Next day he watched a vessel depart that he had called home for three years: "The *Sea Breeze* with several other ships sailed for home."

Instead, he helped his shipmates bring aboard some small stores and wash the ship. They loosed sails to dry under the warm Honolulu sun. The crew counted and weighed their 171 bundles of baleen and loaded them aboard the bark *Polani*, a total of 17,228 pounds, over eight tons. But in Europe, the outbreak of the Franco-Prussian war reduced demand, and the price of bone fell to just sixty-five cents. At that price the summer's catch amounted to about $11,200. Walrus ivory was traded with the *William Rotch*. The whale oil was taken aboard the *Marengo* (another of William Brownell's whaling vessels) for shipment home. At 67¼ cents a gallon, it amounted to $25,590. A third mate's "lay" or share of the proceeds, perhaps one-fifty-fifth, might amount to six hundred dollars, once charges for his outfit and liberty money and tobacco were subtracted.

Nathaniel Ransom and his shipmates might have read a curious bit of whaling news in the *Honolulu Commercial Advertiser* that December. The crew of the *Cornelius Howland*, whaling near Point Barrow the previous summer not far from the *John Wells*, had captured a large bowhead. In the whale's head they discovered a harpoon head marked A.G.; the wound made by the weapon had healed over, leaving the iron embedded in the whale's blubber. Each whaling vessel marked its toggle irons to settle possible disputes about ownership of a captured whale. Initials proved this iron had belonged to the *Ansel Gibbs* out of New Bedford. That bark, however, pursued right whales in the North Atlantic regions of the Davis Strait and Cumberland Inlet during the 1860s. Somehow the injured whale must have traveled under or around the polar ice cap from east to west, a passage unknown to man at that time. Moreover, the discovery raised the question whether so-called polar right whales and bowheads were really two separate species. No one had a clear answer.

Among Tropic Isles

Aside from a few salmon and some turnips, the *John Wells* did not take on provisions before leaving Honolulu, for instead of heading for Baja California after gray whales as the *Sea Breeze* had done, Captain Dean sailed southwest by west among small Pacific islands where livestock, fruit, and vegetables sold cheap. His previous voyage—Dean had been master of the *John Wells* since 1865—brought home 639 barrels of sperm oil, and he hoped for another lucrative chase after sperm whales and humpbacks. Nathaniel Ransom remarked on December 25: "Pleasant weather. Got a porpoise . . . It is Christmas again and rather a dry one for me. I hope my Darling Wife will enjoy it a little better than I am doing. I quit smoking today but do not know how long it will last." Aboard the *Henry Taber* near Oahu, a boatsteerer named Abram Briggs wrote in his private journal that he marked Christmas with prayer and fasting and observed: "On this day our Redeemer of this wicked world was born."

Barely north of the equator the *John Wells* approached Baker's Island, claimed by the United States because of its guano deposits, bird droppings used as fertilizer. The crew repaired whaleboats and cleaned the mincing machine. The ship visited a number of tiny islets, most just a few square miles, now part of the Pacific island nation of Kiribati. Captain Dean seized any opportunity to hunt sperm whales, and lowered for them on December 30: "Fourth mate had one missed which started the whales off to wind'rd and we got no more chance at them." On New Year's Day the ship docked at Hopper's Island (today Abemama) where Dean bought two hundred pounds of bread and four barrels of beef from an English trading vessel. Nearby Ocean Island (Banaba) was nothing more than two or three square miles made of phosphate accumulated from centuries of bird droppings, rimmed by a coral reef, and a sandy beach. Its inhabitants offered little to sell except a few coconuts and chickens. Or perhaps Captain Dean offered too little in exchange. A few months later Captain George Bauldry shrewdly bartered tobacco for two thousand coconuts and 150 chickens. Three hundred miles to the west he anchored the *Navy* (Nathaniel Ransom's third ship) off Pleasant Island (Nauru) and traded flour and sugar for 150 hogs, eight thousand coconuts to feed them, and twelve boatloads of wood. The drab account of his voyage reveals nothing more about the purpose of his floating barnyard.[7]

On Pleasant Island, Nathaniel Ransom got a few small shells for Sarah and bought a parrot (which disappears from the journal without so much as a squawk.) Captain Dean traded for a lot of hogs and coconuts to feed them on, and several boatloads of wood. Between Ocean Island and Pleasant Island, the *John Wells* carried four passengers, one white man and three "squaws belonging to him."

In mid-January 1871, the ship landed two passengers from the Sandwich Islands on Strong's Island, where coral reefs edged a narrow passageway into the harbor. A mangrove jungle covered much of the volcanic island, where small bananas and coconuts grew abundantly. Ships took on fresh water here, and boats' crews hunted pigeons to enliven the shipboard diet of salt beef and pork. Narratives by other whalemen describe their encounters with scantily clad natives of these islands who offered strangers kava, an alcoholic drink concocted in a disgusting ceremony. Women wearing little more than a loincloth and a garland of flowers masticated the gnarly root of a certain plant, and then placed the pulpy mass in a vessel where it was mixed with water. They poured the liquid into coconut shells and handed them round. Kava's alcoholic content caused many a seaman to forget home and sweetheart, only to stumble back on board next morning lugging a head full of rocks and a sour belly. Such island welcomes sometimes resulted in epidemics of venereal disease in the forecastle a few weeks later.

Stopping to trade at MacAskill (now Pingelap) and Wellington Islands, Captain Dean picked up two beachcombers. Such men, sometimes fugitives from other whaling vessels or stranded misfits, could supply information about trading or serve as translators for captains dealing with the island natives. Herman Melville's *Omoo* describes captains' reluctance to hire on such men, often deserters from whaling ships or merchant vessels. On MacAskill Island, Dean traded for chickens, ducks, and some turtles. Nearby sailed the *William Rotch*, likewise on the lookout for sperm and humpback whales.

The *John Wells* spent ten days in late January and early February at Ponape, then called Ascension Island, at 340 square miles, the largest of the Caroline Islands. Surrounded by coral reefs, Ascension's distinctive basalt cliff at the north end of the island was visible from far out to sea. Captain Thomas Williams and his family (whose ship *Hibernia* had been wrecked in the Arctic) visited these islands several times, and both his wife and son depicted their lush verdant landscape. Some white inhabitants were British fugitives from Australian penal colonies or shipwrecked seamen and deserters who intermarried with the natives. The island's native people raised potatoes, corn, pumpkins, pineapples, and coconuts, and ate plantains, bananas, breadfruit, pigs, dogs, and fish. They built houses of vertical bamboo stalks, fastened with twine made from coconut husks, adequate protection from the weather in their warm, moist climate. The gourd-like fruit of the calabash tree served as their water dippers or containers, for they obtained metal goods only in trade with the whalers. Sometimes Captain Dean went "trading for himself" and at other times he bought stores for the ship, bartering tobacco, axes, small knives, pots, molasses, beads, and calico for firewood, coconuts, pigs, and chickens.

From the shipping office on Ascension Island, Nathaniel Ransom sent a few lines to Sarah, searching for words to express the unimaginable contrast between the familiar home he shared with her and the exotic landscapes where he found himself. On January 25, 1871, he and his boat and crew with Captain Dean aboard "started for one of the weather harbors for the purpose of the Captain's doing some trading. About 3 PM landed." The men spent the night on the island and next morning Nathaniel Ransom "went over to see Mr. Doane the missionary. Captain done a little trading." Missionary Doane tried to convert the natives to Christianity, hoping to gain their favor by persuading their chief or king, Nanigan, to worship with him. Doane had only indifferent success, as he focused on trying to cover the islanders' nakedness, while their own native garb was better suited to the tropics than the cumbersome western dress. Next afternoon Nathaniel Ransom with the captain and whaleboat crew "started for the ship; evening got aboard. Smoking ship—had to stay on deck all night." Whalemen smoked the ship by sealing up the area below decks and lighting smudge fires to drive out the rats that gnawed at their bundles of baleen and provisions. A plague of rats could imperil the seaworthiness of an old spouter or gnaw at the bungs of oil casks, causing them to leak and raising the danger of fire in the hold.

While some men from the *John Wells* went ashore, Ascension Island natives visited the ship. These Kanakas, of medium height with black straight hair and brown skin, went mostly unclothed, or men wore a loincloth of coconut bark, and women a yard of cloth pinned about the hips. Since women remained unclothed above the waist or below the knees, Nathaniel Ransom considered those who came aboard the ship "a lot of dirty squaws." No longer the naïve youth who first welcomed "ladies" aboard the *Barnstable*, he realized that these women and his shipmates were negotiating prostitution. Disgust and bitterness deepened his longing for home, and for Sarah: "I'm feeling somewhat homesick, tired of living such a life as this." Next day he was back to using tobacco. He went ashore with one of the other mates and shot forty pigeons, and got a pack of playing cards of the old man, as he called Captain Dean, all diversions from the melancholy yearning for home. He rowed casks of fresh water and boatloads of firewood back to the ship. Finally it was time to leave Ascension Island and put to sea once again. The day before weighing anchor, he went ashore for the last time and sold his accordion to King Nanigan. The chief of Ascension Island distinguished himself by dressing in one or more pieces of western clothing, acquired in barter from the whalers. Sometimes he sported a tall beaver hat, a tattered white shirt, and little else. Ransom's journal omits any price for the accordion, and says nothing of his reason for selling it. Perhaps his lack of skill discouraged him, for he called his attempts at making music with it just an aggravation. He leaves us to imagine how King Nanigan or his people learned to play the accordion. Maybe the pleated folds of its bellows and its pearly keys lay years later forgotten and half buried in sand at the base of some coral reef.

Six other ships from the Arctic whaling fleet also ranged among the South Pacific islands, hunting for sperm whales or anything else to refill their holds. Captain Valentine Lewis spent January and February trading for food supplies and looking for sperm whales, sailing the *Thomas Dickason* far south of Tahiti. While the nearby *Contest* killed two sperm whales, Lewis got only a few porpoise, as he watched blackfish, finbacks, and a sulphur-bottom swimming in the distance. The *Concordia* hunted in the Marquesas Islands. The *Seneca* took one sperm whale at the end of February southeast of Tahiti. Nearby, the *Champion* had made 180 barrels of sperm oil. The *Navy* could boast of taking five sperm whales, although three of them were small, and made 255 barrels of sperm oil.

The less fortunate *John Wells* sailed west from Ascension Island and anchored off Saipan "for the purpose of humpbacking. Seen several of the varmints, lowered 3 boats for them, got nothing," Ransom sighed. "Went ashore on a small island to get some eggs. Found plenty of them but they were about all live ones." His cabin-mate Benjamin Worth managed to get sweet potatoes and some lemons for the ship. In late February it lay near Palau, a group of small islets five hundred miles east of the Philippines, today part of Micronesia. "[February 22] Some of the natives of Pelew Island came aboard told us there never was seen a humpback anywhere about or around the Pelew islands so we find ourselves fooled by coming down here. Afternoon got anchors on the bows again put to sea with our foremast carried away." Ransom busied himself making spun yarn, sewing new canvas covers for the whaleboats' line tubs, repairing the cutting stage, cleaning the mincing machine, making a new cover for it, painting boats, and making a frame for the crow's nest.

Near Sulphur Island (today Iwo Jima), the crew chased humpbacks all day. "Got on to none of them. Sundown boats aboard." In late March they "saw a school of killer whales take a humpback; they took him down before we could get to him." All whalemen hated the pods of savage killer whales, whose six-foot-high dorsal fins sliced through the waves of every ocean. Charles Scammon in his 1874 description of marine mammals called them "wolves of the sea" for their sudden vicious attacks. Measuring about twenty feet, their combined strength enabled them to seize and destroy much larger whales, ripping their flesh with powerful conical teeth. They took only the humpback's fat oily tongue, leaving the corpse to sink before the whalers could salvage its baleen and blubber. The slaughter of the humpback galled the whalemen aboard the *John Wells*, for their between-seasons cruise among the Pacific islands captured only a few porpoises and one large turtle, which Ransom caught somewhere between Palau and Iwo Jima. As April began, Captain Dean abandoned his fruitless hunt for sperm whales and humpbacks and turned the ship, now "bound to northern regions," hoping this time to reach the Arctic before the bowheads swam through the Bering Strait on their summer migration toward the Beaufort Sea.

"The Trials and Troubles of the Arctic Ocean"

Amidst "pleasant weather and plenty of ice" the crew set up a stove in the cabin. Near the ship floated a bowhead stinker but the captain passed him by. "Not much doing of note" summed up the passage north: "My Darling Sarah this is tedious indeed," Ransom confessed on April 8. Hogs bought in the tropical Pacific had to be slaughtered before they died of cold: "Killed a few hogs to save their lives." With a heavy swell on and a thick snowstorm all day the butchering continued for a week, for it was cold enough to keep fresh pork. Killer whales and finbacks swam after the hog entrails thrown from the ship and the crew made a few attempts to capture them, without success.

Nathaniel Ransom put a bomb lance in a finback on April 12. Although they measured as much as eighty feet in length, and produced high quality oil, finbacks were seldom hunted, as they sank when killed, and sharks robbed most of the blubber before the dead whale could be raised. The introduction of Pierce's bomb lance gun first made it possible to attack finbacks, for they swam so swiftly that a whaleboat could rarely approach within range of a harpoon gun. Given their low value—finbacks' short baleen was of poor quality—he probably shot the finback because there was no other prey in sight.

Through late April and into May, the *John Wells* plowed north-ward, struggling to keep free of ice, which appeared April 20 near Cape Navarin on the Siberian coast. Other whalers nearby; the *Concordia*, *Reindeer*, and *Elizabeth Swift*; also worked slowly to the north. Nathaniel Ransom took out some ivory to carve a picture frame for Sarah, dispar-aging his artistic efforts: "I spoiled a little ivory . . . I damaged a little more ivory." On May 17 he accompanied Captain Dean aboard the ship *Contest*, for fourth mate Prince Nye of Mattapoisett had brought him letters from his parents, from his brother Theodore, and most importantly, one from Sarah. Because whaling voyages often lasted several years, ships that left New Bedford often carried letters for those that had left for the Arctic the previous year. The *Contest*, built in Mattapoisett, departed in July 1870, and the letters it carried were eight months old by the time they reached Nathaniel Ransom. But there was no possibility of sending home a reply until he reached port in Honolulu once again, and the letter from Sarah only intensified his longing for her: "Oh how I should admire being with my darling wife today and always." Not far from the *Contest* ranged other familiar whaleships, the *Thomas Dickason*, *Lagoda*, *Massachu-setts*, *Midas*, and *Progress*. Immobilized by ice surrounding the *John Wells*, the crew shot a few seals, minced their blubber and put it into the ship's cooler, for it was not worth starting the tryworks until they had taken several walrus or a whale. They found some satisfaction in being "head of navigation," meaning furthest north of the half-dozen whalers in sight as they engaged in a friendly competition to be first to reach the bowheads' feeding grounds.

Near Plover Bay on June 5 a canoe appeared paddling toward the

John Wells, carrying bearded, shabbily dressed men hardly recognizable as fellow New England whalers. "Captain Barker, late Master of wrecked ship *Japan* reported 9 men lost of ship's company: 7 of them drowned and 2 died ashore." Ransom's brief journal entry summarizes a tale of horror and frozen death. The previous year in late June, Captain Barker had gotten a cask of bread and some slops from the *John Wells*, whose crew now felt astonished to see him emaciated, filthy, and clothed in ragged fur and skins. His account of the loss of his ship struck terror into the hearts of every listener. The October gale of the previous fall that tore away the *John Wells*'s topsail near St. Lawrence Island had driven the *Japan* ashore near false East Cape on the Siberian coast. As his vessel filled with icy seawater Captain Barker hurried below to salvage what he could of its provisions, for it was too late in the season to expect rescue by another whaling ship. His men swam or scrambled to shore as best they could. Two of those who managed to swim in the bone-chilling sea and reached shore, collapsed in their wet clothing and died of hypothermia as soon as they staggered onto the land. Barker himself reached shore half frozen. There Chukchi natives laid him on a sled and hauled him into their hut as he drifted into unconsciousness. He told the crew of the *John Wells* that his life was saved by the chief's wife, who opened her fur-lined clothing to warm his frozen feet at her breast. It was three days before he could bring himself to taste the only food his rescuers had to share, raw walrus blubber, some of it putrid, some still attached to the skin, bristling with hairs. Worse than the revolting food, the cold, and the threat of starvation was the isolation Barker suffered during that interminable winter. "Oh horrible! Horrible! The contemplation rendered me nearly desperate enough to take my own life," he confessed to his journal.[8] Now in the summer of 1871, he rejoiced to return to men of his own kind. The *John Wells* also took the *Japan*'s second mate aboard, and Nathaniel Ransom "broke out slops for the wrecked men." Captain Barker accompanied Captain Dean aboard the *Henry Taber* to tell his story, for the whalers from Massachusetts ports had been charged to find out what had happened to the *Japan* and her master, who hailed from New Bedford.

Aboard the *Henry Taber* near Plover Bay boatsteerer Abram Briggs wrote that "Captain Barker of the bark *Japan* and 1st officer Mr. Irving came on board with his boat's crew to whale it for us." A week later, his ship gammed the *John Wells* near the Diomedes Islands, where both the American and the Asian continents could be seen on a clear day. There Abram Briggs confided in his journal, "In the ARCTIC once more, I hope for the last time," as he reflected on the plight of the *Japan*'s crew:

> Now I am glad to state here that all the survivors of the ill-fated
> ship *Japan* are kindly cared for as circumstances will admit
> and distributed among several of the fleet. From the time of
> her stranding up to the present day they lost nine of the ship's
> company and let us all trust they are better off than in this world
> of trouble. And let us hope the all wise Being will permit the
> rescued ones to return to their friends no more to pertake of the
> trials and troubles of the Arctic Ocean.

On June 17, the *John Wells* "anchored close to where ship *Japan* went
ashore. Took last shipwrecked man aboard. We've now 15 of the *Japan*'s
men aboard including Captain and 2nd mate." Chukchi from the small
whaling settlement at East Cape came aboard the whaleships to trade
and Nathaniel Ransom "purchased a few pairs of boots and mittens for
tobacco."

Visiting among the whaling fleet Captain Barker continued to
relate his tale of rescue by Chukchi natives, who had kept his crewmen
alive through the bleak isolation of the dark Arctic winter. In his months
with the Chukchi, Barker had shared the winter hunger they suffered
from the scarcity of walrus. Now he pleaded with the whalers to cease
slaughtering them. The fifty-five vessels in the 1870 Arctic whaling fleet
had butchered nearly four thousand walrus. At least Captain Timothy
Packard or Abram Briggs on the *Henry Taber* could truthfully say that they
had refrained from hunting walrus during the 1869 Arctic season. Packard's motive then was simply to save precious cargo space in his small
ship for bowhead oil. The *Henry Taber*'s hold could contain only about a
thousand barrels, and the huge whales yielded valuable baleen in addition to their blubber. However, in the 1871 Arctic season, the crew butchered about 175 walrus; a month after welcoming Captain Barker aboard,
the *Henry Taber* measured 104 barrels of walrus oil.

Nevertheless Barker persisted in pleading for the Chukchi. After
returning home he wrote to mariners' newspapers in Honolulu and New
Bedford urging an end to the slaughter threatening the very survival of
the natives who had rescued him. Neither his letters nor his impassioned
pleas to his hosts among the Arctic fleet aroused much sympathy for the
natives. A week after collecting the last of the *Japan*'s men, the crew of the
John Wells commenced walrusing about five in the morning and continued
"walrusing all day and night got about 75 in number."

Laying aside Captain Barker's gloomy tale, Nathaniel Ransom had
other troubles on his mind. The letter from his parents informed him that
the youngest of the seven Ransom brothers, twenty-year-old Andrew, had

followed him to the Arctic. Andrew had signed on as boatsteerer aboard the *Progress,* now hunting walrus not far from the *John Wells.* Going to sea at fifteen, Andrew had made two voyages chasing sperm whales and right whales in the Atlantic. Home from an unsuccessful hunt in September, 1870, he had waited in Mattapoisett less than a month before embarking on the *Progress* after a more lucrative catch of baleen and bowhead oil. On a Sunday in mid-June 1871, Nathaniel Ransom "got news that [Captain] Dowden put Brother Andrew into the forecastle because he was sick." When the blacksmith of the *Progress* came aboard the *John Wells* a few days later, he "sent a few lines by him to give Andrew when he went on board his own ship again." Three weeks later—Sunday was his only day of freedom—Nathaniel was at last able to go aboard the *Progress* to see Andrew himself: "Poor fellow—he has had rather hard usage aboard of her." Andrew gave him some things Sarah had sent him and a letter from her written nine months earlier. While the *Contest, Progress,* and *John Wells* hunted walrus near one another, crewmen visited among the three ships. Nathaniel sent Prince Nye from the *Contest* aboard the *Progress* with some of the skin mittens and boots he had bought from the Chukchi to take to Andrew. For the time being he could do nothing more. He found himself "about sick with headache, cold, chills, and sore throat" and thought of "taking a rum sweat." His chills and sore throat lasted for ten miserable days, and he finally "took an alcohol sweat." It was "a rather rough 4th of July aboard" as the crew slaughtered forty more walrus. "I wonder what my darling is doing about this time. I hope she is enjoying herself and taking comfort," he mused.

He was soon back at the brutal hunt after walrus: "got several and got my boat stove all to pieces by one of them." Both male and female walruses used their pointed tusks for defense, and easily broke through the whaleboat's thin planking. In mid-July he got his boat stove again, "came very near to losing her." The walrus hunt appeared worth the risk, at least for the moment: the *Seneca's* logkeeper reported the *John Wells* in sight on July 13, having taken four hundred walrus and one bowhead. Captain Thomas Williams of the *Monticello* could boast of three hundred barrels of walrus oil; in less than a month, his four boats' crews killed over five hundred. But later in July, Ransom again "started on the ice in search for walruses. Saw none of any account. I got catched in a gale of wind 20 miles from the ship. At 12 o'clock at night I managed to get aboard of bark *Paiea* of Honolulu Captain Newbery. I came very near getting swamped several times. In hoisting my boat on deck they stove her all to pieces." Next morning he found "Captain Newbery's mechanics to work" on his boat and in the evening, as the weather moderated, he "managed to get on board of old *John Wells*." It was a relief to find a change of clothes and a hot supper and to sleep in his own bunk again. The following Sunday he shot about thirty walruses. "I got my boat stove by one of them as I usually do."

Interspersed with remarks on damages to the whaleboat come observations that the walrus were becoming very shy. "[July 10] Evening after walrus. Got one whole one." In fact, as Captain Barker had warned, the walrus were growing scarce after years of the whalemen's plunder. Two weeks later the boats were again "off cruising for walruses got nothing." And by August first, Captain Dean gave up walrusing for good. The *Henry Taber* killed 240 walrus, making nearly 104 barrels of oil by July 8, and then turned instead to chasing bowheads. The *Thomas Dickason* managed to capture ten gray whales—Captain Lewis called them ripsacks—and made almost three hundred barrels of whale oil before turning to walrus. The ship took 184 walrus before leaving their habitat on August 6. While there were a dozen fewer whaling vessels in range than the previous season, they took altogether fewer than half as many walrus.[9]

Not only were walrus growing scarce. Nathaniel Ransom observed ominous signs too that provisions were dwindling aboard the *John Wells*, for Captain Dean had not restocked in the Sandwich Islands as whaling captains commonly did. In mid-July he got casks of bread from the *Progress*, and a chance for a brief visit with Andrew. Days later he "got what potatoes the *William Rotch* had for us which is very few, the greater part of them having rotted." At the end of the month the *John Wells* "let the *William Rotch* have 8 barrels of beef." Weather and navigation commanded his attention as a strong wind from the northeast drove ice away from the Alaskan shore, allowing ships to progress north of Cape Lisburne, the last high point of land along the coast. Further north the land became monotonously featureless, marshy and treeless. Captains who had navigated this route before watched warily for the sand bars running parallel to the shore, as they feared that drifting pack ice or wind from the west would drive their ships aground.

Grim news came from the *Henry Taber* on August 10, for Lewis Kennedy, a twenty-four-year-old Englishman from the *Japan*'s crew, died "of the scurvy on the lungs," according to Abram Briggs: "From leaving this World of Troubles and Woe he has entered into a Heavenly mansion where love's peace forever reigns . . . Oh death where is thy sting? Oh grave where is thy victory?" Two months after taking Kennedy aboard, men buried him halfway between Wainwright Inlet and Point Belcher, a world away from his native London.

The *John Wells* passed Icy Cape on the Alaskan coast on August 9, threading through "a very narrow passage between the land and ice. Afternoon a little more room to work ship." It was a harbinger of the next month's struggles to keep ships from running aground between the land and ice closing around them or coming down suddenly on the fleet, crowding vessels toward shore. A pair of bowhead carcasses, stripped of their blubber, drifted past the *John Wells* from the "fleet of 16 ships ahead of us 4 of them boiling." Among them, Nathaniel Ransom recognized the *Arctic*, built in Mattapoisett; his older brother Charles had signed on as cabin boy for its maiden voyage in 1850. In those early days of bowhead whaling, the *Arctic* returned after three summers with 2,549 barrels of oil and over twenty-two tons of baleen. Now after taking only one bowhead Captain Dean of the *John Wells* managed to sail north of all sixteen rival vessels and "came to an anchor at the head of navigation. 2 ships got whales; about 80 boats cruising in ice for the sarpents."

The Arctic pack ice hemming in the fleet was later pictured by William Fish Williams, then a twelve-year-old aboard his father's *Monticello.* Young as he was, Willie had already seen plenty of ice, for he was aboard the *Hibernia* the previous season when it grounded and wrecked off Point Barrow. He described:

> [A]n enormous accumulation of cakes or floes of snow-covered sea frozen ice, of all sizes and shapes, but containing very few whose highest points are more than ten feet above the sea level, and those have been formed by the crowding of one floe on top of another. There are very few level spots of any extent, the general effect being very rough. There are no icebergs, as there are no glaciers in these northernmost parts of either America or Asia. The pack is not, therefore, in its individual parts imposing, grand, or beautiful, but as a whole, under all the varying conditions of an Arctic sky, from brilliant sunshine to a leaden gloom, it is a magnificent spectacle; and when you stop to consider that it represents ages of accumulation, and that there is beneath the surface nearly ten times more bulk than what you can see, you realize that there is something to be considered beside beautiful effects, that there is within it a power which cannot be expressed and can only be partially comprehended.[10]

To the whalemen, ice presented a formidable obstacle, little admired for its beauty. Soon the wind turned against the fleet and began to blow from the west, forcing ships eastward closer to the Alaskan shore and into shoal water. George Duffy counted thirty ships anchored nearby in mid-August, as his *Seneca* lay in six fathoms (thirty-six feet) of water. Valentine Lewis fretted that his *Thomas Dickason* lay anchored to ground ice in just nineteen feet of water. Captains had no choice but to send their men out after bowheads by hauling whaleboats over the uneven plates of ice and into more open water. Captain Lewis saw four bowheads in the ice, and nearby ships took five whales, evidence that persuaded him to persist in the hunt. But ice solidified whenever the temperature dropped, trapping whaleboats and their crews far from the mother ship. Abram Briggs of the *Henry Taber* described a sharp northwest wind that blew in on August 12 shifting the ocean current "packing in where the ships lay. Several ships came up making twenty-one in all . . . Ice coming down foul of us. Fourteen boats belonging to other ships got blocked up in the ice. The crews all left the boats and walk[ed] over the ice to where the boats were in clear water and they took them on board of their ships." Ransom "went ashore with several other boats after men that while in scattering ice chasing whales had to haul their boats on ice and leave them there on account of ice closing up and go on shore. There were fourteen boats crews been away from their ships for twenty-four hours." Away from their ships meant away from cooked food, fresh water, dry clothing, and the stove in the forecastle. A week and a half later the *Seneca*'s crew mated with the San Francisco bark *Carlotta* to capture a bowhead; men cut off the blubber and bone and camped on shore for a brief, shivering sleep before hauling their catch twenty-five miles to the *Seneca* over the ice.

"It Commences to Look Very Gloomy About Here."

As ice impeded the cruising for whales, bowheads grew more elusive. "Saw nothing and lost boat trying to catch it," Ransom snorted. "Got nothing" and "saw nothing" he groused, as ice or wind hindered the hunt: "Blowing a gale from northeastward. All 5 boats pulling along shore to windward. Stopped on beach all night." Camping ashore with no shelter beyond a whaleboat turned on its side as a windbreak, his boat's crew huddled together sleepless and shuddering with cold. The following day: "Lots of whales close to the ship several of them taken by other ships' boats while ours were all 40 miles away. Evening got aboard." No better luck favored the *Henry Taber*, jammed in the ice nearby. Its crew and that of the bark *George* each struck bowheads and lost them under the ice. When the crew finally succeeded in hauling the *Henry Taber* out of the ice and into clear water, Briggs rejoiced: "God be praised for his good and glorious works."

"Laying to an anchor off Point Belcher" on August 27, the *John Wells*'s men cruised for whales but "found no chance to strike." Men could hear bowheads moving and spouting as they swam beneath ice thick enough to protect them from attack. Gloomily the men comprehended that the adult whales had grown shy, evading capture as soon as they heard the ships or their whaleboats approach. In the previous season they had rounded Point Barrow and sailed east beyond Herschel Island. Now weather and wind held them nearly a hundred miles southeast of Point Barrow. They mated with one of the *Henry Taber*'s boats helping to tow a dead bowhead, each whaleboat claiming half the stinker. They took some satisfaction in finding that it was a large one; half of it made forty-five barrels of oil. A thick snowstorm swirled around the ship all day on August 30. On board "minsing and boiling" decks became slippery and treacherous. Shivering crewmen elbowed one another out of the way for a chance to work at the seething trypots, breathing their greasy smoke. A "fresh breeze from southward" would have driven the *John Wells* further north, except that the ship lay "hard and fast in ice."

As they gammed among the fleet whalemen discussed the worsening ice trap, weighing that danger against the temptation to continue hunting bowheads. After days of dismal remarks that the *Navy* lay at anchor in the ice, thick fog and nothing doing, Captain George Bauldry at last reached for his whale stamp as the mate struck a whale. The kill lay thirty-five miles from the ship. Two of the *Navy*'s boats' crews mated with two from the brig *Comet*. The two dozen men spent most of two days cutting up the whale on the ice, and three more days dragging their boatloads of blubber and baleen over the slick, uneven ice pack back to their ships. At anchor in nine fathoms of water, Captain Bauldry counted thirty ships in sight, two cutting in whales and six trying out blubber. As August neared its end, the *Navy* captured two more whales, and stowed down eighty-five barrels of oil, reason enough to stay put, it seemed.

Or perhaps not. On September 1, Nathaniel Ransom entered in his journal a laconic account of the first event in an impending disaster: "The bark *Roman* got stove by ice and went down all crew saved." Obscured by a thick snowstorm, ice moved slowly toward the land. As the *Roman*'s crew worked cutting in a whale, the ice to which they had anchored the ship drifted southward toward the Sea Horse Islands (between Point Franklin and Point Belcher) where it grounded. Men stood helpless as pack ice several miles in width approached, first lifting the *Roman* and then driving her swiftly astern, breaking the rudder and pintails. Ice stove in the stern of the ship and threw her over on her starboard side, masts crashing onto the ice. Quickly the crew lowered whaleboats from the larboard side as the pack ice shoved the *Roman* bow first beneath the sea. In forty-eight minutes only the shattered stern and the mizzen mast stood above water. Those close enough to watch stared in disbelief as its crew, including Captain Jared Jernegan's wife and two children, scurried into the whaleboats and were taken aboard other ships. Several ships clustered just north of the *Roman*, anchored in three to five fathoms of water as a southwest wind drove them closer to land, so densely packed together that they could scarcely swing freely without ramming one another.

Next day the brig *Comet*, tied up to the same piece of ice as the *Henry Taber*, "got stove" by the ice coming together. She was "sold by auction to Capt. Knowles of the Bark *George Howland* for thirteen dollars," Abram Briggs wrote. That paltry price reflected how little use anyone expected to make of more equipment, given the worsening predicament of the ships nearby. "Our Captain got a cask of bread and nine bags of flour and a boat with all her gear," Briggs added. Men towed the *Henry Taber* three miles from the wreck and into clear water, tore up one of the older boats for firewood, and opened the cask of bread from the *Comet*, for they too were short of provisions. "It commences to look very gloomy about here," Briggs reflected. Captain Packard took Captain Sylvia of the wrecked *Comet* aboard his *Henry Taber*, and also found room for ten mariners from the *Roman*.

Whalemen were not the only eyes watching the *Roman* and the *Comet* sink. Along the Alaskan shore stood Inupiaq Eskimo huts, some crude structures of whalebone covered with animal skins, others dug partly into the earth. The inhabitants of the small settlement often paddled out to the whalers to trade furs or deer for rum, rum kegs, tobacco, and metal tools. Now the Eskimos warned of ice moving toward shore, where winds would drive it into the vessels and crush them. The ships' masters gave their words little credence and continued hunting whales, for they regarded native people as primitive and superstitious. Many shared the opinion of young Willie Williams, aboard his father's *Monticello*. He commented sardonically that the natives had already taken "the first two degrees in civilization by learning to use tobacco and drink rum," commodities they obtained from the whalemen.[11] Willie found the Inupiaq particularly revolting for their habit of making a hole near the corner of the mouth to insert an ornament of ivory, polished stone, or even an empty brass cartridge shell. Sometimes the hole stretched to the point of tearing toward the lip, leaving a gap that moved eerily as they chewed tobacco. He considered the natives shiftless to the point of starving in the winter because they failed to store up adequate food—ignoring the fact that the five hundred walrus killed by the *Monticello*'s crew would have fed several Inupiaq families for an entire winter.

Now instead of heeding the Inupiaq, the whaling captains judged their predicament by the experience of past seasons. They expected northeast winds would soon drive the ice off the Alaskan shore, widening the narrow channel where the remaining ships lay at anchor. Besides, some whalers succeeded in capturing whales, despite their increasingly worrisome imprisonment in the ice. The *Thomas Dickason*'s men found a dead whale in the ice and cut him in on September 2. The same day that they heard of the loss of the *Roman* and *Comet*, they killed two more whales. First mate John Stivers on the *Henry Taber* continued to send boats off cruising for whales, even on September 4 and 5 as a thick snowstorm raged about the ship, now anchored a mile from land and a scant quarter mile from the ice. "One of our boats would probably have struck a whale had not the chief mate of the *Florida* drove him down with his steering oar," he wrote angrily. Stivers' frustration accompanied deepening fears about the position of the fleet. He knew that the forty-five miles south of his *Henry Taber* offered no open water, and the narrow channel between pack ice and the Alaskan shore was only about nine feet deep, too shallow to float his bark. "Nearly everyone in the fleet despairs of getting their ships south this fall which is a cause of much uneasiness with everyone," he admitted in his logbook entry for September 7.

Nathaniel Ransom on the *John Wells* felt keenly the fleet's precarious situation, and fear manifested itself in illness: "Surrounded by ice as usual and no prospect or chance for lowering a boat or getting anywhere with the ship being any better as I see. I am not feeling very well." Next day he broke out provisions, the shrinking stores another cause for alarm: "our ship hard and fast in ice of course. I'm feeling quite unwell." Fields of jagged ice sheets amassed by pounding waves stretched further than the eye could see. "The ice remaining about the same," wind-driven spray froze instantly on the rigging of the *John Wells*, immobilizing the furled sails. Whenever a gleam of sun broke through the leaden sky, the forest of half-empty masts lit up with a sudden icy sparkle. Ransom busied himself carving walrus ivory and tried to think of something other than his worsening prospects for survival: "I made a frame this afternoon for my Darling Wife." It was a way of conjuring Sarah's image, envisioning the moment when he would hand her his gift, a moment when he would be safely at home once more.

Next day he and his shipmates worked "all day freeing around trying to do something with the ship, I don't know what. Forenoon hauled her out of ice after using up about all of the rope in the ship." Men chopped a hole into a block of ice closer to open water and set their single-flued ice anchor into it, running the line back to the windlass at the bow of the ship. Pumping the windlass steadily, they tightened the line as the ship inched further from the looming pack ice. Their backbreaking labor accomplished nothing in the end. "Afternoon got her ashore where she now lays it is about 11 o'clock at night." Next morning "got ship afloat let go anchor old man aboard *J. D. Thompson*; she lies hard and fast on bottom." Attempting to re-float ships that the wind had driven ashore was made more difficult in the Arctic because tides close to the north pole rise only about six inches, offering only the slightest advantage. To stabilize the *John Wells*, which had failed to produce any amount of bowhead oil, the crew stowed down about 150 barrels of salt water.

As whalemen battled the encroaching ice, they exchanged the grim news that flew thick and fast among their thirty ships. Nathaniel Ransom reported, "*Emily Morgan* got a whale. The second mate of her going to bomb the whale the gun went off the bomb passing through his neck killing him instantly." Abram Briggs on the *Henry Taber* heard "that the *Awashonks* is a wreck, the *Julian* is ashore by or close to her; the *Eugenia* has lost her rudder." Ice crushed the *Awashonks* on September 8 about six miles south of the *Henry Taber*, but the ship did not sink, since it already lay on the bottom, dismasted and ruined in plain sight. George Duffy on the *Seneca* judged that the eight ships near the wrecked *Awashonks* were also "in a perilous condition." Captain Packard went to the aid of the *Elizabeth Swift*, which had run aground near his *Henry Taber*. Little wonder that her captain, George Bliven, was very sick. The *John Wells*, caught in the narrow channel between the shore and drifting pack ice the other side of a shoal, could move in no other direction than further north. "The way things look now the ship will have to winter up here this coming Winter season." Nathaniel Ransom knew what the ship held by way of provisions; it was nowhere near enough. Captain Barker's tale of gnawing at putrid walrus blubber haunted his mind. And as the *Thomas Dickason* lay "Ice boun on wone side and Land on the Other," Valentine Lewis, who was not a religious man, confessed his fears to his journal: "God have Mercy on this Whaling Fleet and deliver us from these cold and Icy Shores."

"We Have Left Our Home for Parts Unknown"

On September 9, Captains Leander Owen of the *Contest* and James Fisher of the *Oliver Crocker* came aboard to consult Lewis. Other meetings followed as captains of the twenty-eight remaining whaling vessels contemplated the unthinkable necessity of abandoning their ships. The fleet now crowded so closely between the land and the shoal separating it from shifting pack ice that it became difficult to prevent neighboring vessels from colliding. Wind blew from the southwest, driving the ships further inland and northward. And the water between the land to the east and the shoal to the west varied unpredictably in depth, as captains saw each time they dropped the lead line to the ocean bottom. The only variation in their uneasy predicament came as fog and snow obscured their surroundings or sun illuminated what they began to call their "dreadful situation." Under these circumstances the whaling masters decided upon two courses of action. First, they concluded to send Captain David R. Fraser of the *Florida* and three whaleboats south from Point Belcher toward Icy Cape to explore the possibility of escape, searching for any whaleships remaining south of the trapped fleet. Second, men from several ships' crews went aboard the brig *Victoria*, at 149 tons, the smallest and lightest of the trapped vessels. They attempted to lighten it enough to float the brig over the shoal and into clear water, but the *Victoria* sailed only three miles south before running onto ground ice on September 11. That same day Nathaniel Ransom watched warily as "the second mate of the *John Wells* with lots of others from our different ships" off-loaded casks of oil and provisions from the *Kohola* "breaking her out to try to get her outside of the ice to let the ships' conference know what kind of a fix we are in so they will not clear out and leave us here to winter in case we have to abandon our ships which is quite likely the way things look now." Imprisoned in the ice, old *John Wells* creaked and groaned, as if dreading the ice-crush that had wrecked the *Roman* and the *Comet*. In daytime the crew busied themselves with the common tasks, cleaning equipment, running the last of their oil below decks, wondering whether any purpose would be served in standing mastheads to sight bowheads, wondering, indeed, whether there was any purpose to anything anymore. During the night, the cruelly luminous Arctic half-dusk, worry solidified in them like the young ice that hardened further each day around the fleet, an insidious, scarcely visible submarine growth. The effort to lighten the *Kohola* failed, as the ship grounded off Wainwright Inlet. Now crews anxiously awaited news of the ships to the southward that appeared to be their only chance for rescue.

Those seven whaling ships—among them the familiar *Lagoda*, *Europa*, *Daniel Webster*, *Arctic*, *Midas*, and *Progress*—lay seventy or eighty miles to the south, but they were far from safe. Their captains too would have left the whaling grounds, except that they also were caught in the ice, which gripped them hard for ten days. The British vessel *Chance*, damaged by striking ice, had sprung a leak, but all seven ships were eventually able to free themselves. Ironically, it was this thinner, weaker southern ice that kept the rescue ships within range of the desperate mariners to the north, whom they were now preparing to rescue. Captain Fraser brought them a petition from the captains of the trapped fleet, acknowledging that their plea for help meant that the ships to the south would have to abandon whaling for the season. And in the previous year, about half of the catch had been captured in late September, a chance at gain they would have to forfeit.

Nathaniel Ransom heard the news of these negotiations, for the northern ships lay so close together that it was no trouble at all for men to commiserate on their dire prospects as they hauled their whaleboats over the ice. He watched as some crews from other ships began to freight provisions south to land them on shore, even before word reached them that the whalers to the south would wait for them. Captain Fraser's party returned with a reassuring message from Captain Dowden of the *Progress* to the whalers trapped seventy miles north: "I will wait for them all as long as I have an anchor left or a spar to carry a sail." Ransom's diary gives little sense of the depth of his relief when the news came that rescue was at hand. "Making preparations for leaving the ship and taking to our boats. Got news from ships to southward. They seem to think they are safe enough as yet." His brother Andrew, aboard the *Progress*, would be safe as well.

The captains of the trapped vessels now united in writing a declaration to justify their abandonment of the fleet. They described their dilemma, having provisions for no more than three months, yet anticipating a wait of eleven months before they could look for help from the next season's whale fleet. They found themselves in a barren country where neither food nor fuel could be obtained. Already they counted three ships crushed, two others lying hove out, stove by the ice and leaking badly. The remainder of the fleet lay in just three fathoms of water, with crews of five wrecked ships distributed among them. The grim tone of their declaration—no complete copy has been preserved—appeals to ship owners and investors for their reason and understanding. Of course several of the captains themselves owned shares in their vessels, and all would forfeit the stores of whale oil, walrus tusks, and baleen already stowed below decks. They headed their agreement "Point Belcher, Arctic Ocean, and signed it September 12th, 1871." Nothing else could be done.

First mate Stivers mourned: "Our beautiful *Henry Taber* lying at anchor close to the beach and close to the ice." Abram Briggs and his shipmates "[t]ook the starboard bow boat in on decks and commenced to put on a false keel and rising boards." Over the next few days they also reinforced the four other whaleboats—now lifeboats—with copper sheathing to protect their hulls from ice. They raised the gunwales against the heavy seas that might swamp the over-laden boats, for they were only a few feet deep and would have to carry extra men, clothing, provisions, and gear. Packard got some corn, pork, and codfish from the *Navy* and set his men to work sewing sailcloth bags to carry food and boiling beef and pork in the trypots, work Stivers called "making preparations to flee for our lives." "Four boats of one ship have left for good," Briggs noted anxiously, as he continued "cooking meat making bags for grub." As the current set to the north he heard whales, and it commenced to snow. Captain Valentine Lewis sent two of the *Thomas Dickason*'s boats loaded with provisions southward to the rescue ships. He penned one final, desperate entry in his journal: "May God pleas [sic] send us a N. E. wind or all is lost."

On the *John Wells*, Captain Aaron Dean commanded Nathaniel Ransom to take charge of a whaleboat heavily laden with provisions, rowing and sailing seventy miles south to transport supplies to the *Progress* and six other ships that agreed to rescue the whalemen now trapped between Wainwright Inlet and Point Belcher. "This morning I started south with a load of provision; evening, tied up ashore for the night." It seemed a relief to prepare an escape, despite the prospect of camping ashore while his whaleboat crew dozed fitfully on the frozen coast. He led them further the second day battling scattering ice and an unpredictable sea. "Morning started to southw'rd in search of ships. Found the *Lagoda*, put our traps [gear] aboard of her with lots of other boats. Afternoon started back to ship, got news all hands packing up getting ready to leave."

Thursday September 14, 1871, was a day Nathaniel Ransom and his shipmates would never forget:

> I got aboard *John Wells* found all hands with their dunage [belongings] packed up ready for a start for ships in clear water. I packed up some of my traps and started strait off again. There were 28 ships' company abandoned their vessels today. I left quite a number of my things aboard on account of having to take so much grub with me.

GENERAL VIEW OF THE ARCTIC WHALING FLEET IN THE ICE

Native huts. Native summer tents. Winter huts.
Roman. Point Belcher. Barks Concordia,
Gay Head, and George

Massachusetts. Henry Taber. Florida. Navy. George Howland. Carlotta
John Wells. Contest. E. Swift. O. Crocker. Fancy. Monticello. Paiea.
J.D. Thompson. E. Morgan. Champion. Seneca. Reindeer

Kohola. Julian. Minerva. William Rotch. Victoria. Mary.
Eugenia. Awashonks. T. Dickason.

Destruction of the Arctic Whaling Fleet, sketch 1 of 4. Sketched by Captain William H. Kelley of the *Gay Head,* ca. 1872. (Courtesy of the New Bedford Whaling Museum.)

Abandoning the Barks "George," "Gay Head," *and* "Concordia" *in the ice off Point Belcher, September 14, 1871. Destruction of the Arctic Whaling Fleet,* sketch 2 of 4. Sketched by Captain William H. Kelley of the *Gay Head*, ca. 1872. (Courtesy of the New Bedford Whaling Museum.)

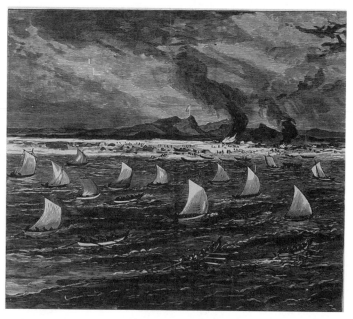

The Rendezvous at Icy Cape—The Boats Effecting a Landing. Destruction of the Arctic Whaling Fleet, sketch 3 of 4. Sketched by Captain William H. Kelley of the *Gay Head*, ca. 1872. (Courtesy of the New Bedford Whaling Museum.)

Without a pause to sleep he set out for Icy Cape with the remainder of the crew of the *John Wells*, leaving the deserted ship, in company with twenty-seven others, their flags flying upside down as a signal of distress. He knew he would never see the possessions he left behind again. Discarding their whaling gear, abandoning bundles of baleen and barrels of oil in the ship's hold and taking leave of the vessel that had been their home for the past two years violated every whaleman's instincts. Every mariner's heart sank at the last sight of the deserted vessels. Among the abandoned ships was the 385-ton bark *Navy* that had carried Ransom home from Honolulu in 1869. "We have left our home for parts unknown," wrote Abram Briggs grimly.

The logkeepers of the abandoned ships *Navy*, *Thomas Dickason*, and *Seneca* closed their books for good, as did first mate Stivers of the *Henry Taber*. Despite the confusion and disarray of leaving ship, Nathaniel Ransom salvaged his journal, witnessing each day's harrowing events in pencil now, more lasting than ink in the fog and salt spray. Abram Briggs of the *Henry Taber* also continued writing in his journal:

> At 12 noon all the ships boats left the ships with our provisions and clothes and started down the lead of clear water between the land and ice to the ships down to Icy Cape that are in clear water . . . At 12 midnight halted on the land until 5 AM then started [off again]. At 9 AM got through the ice into clear water started for the ships. The ships that are out into clear water are *Europa*, *Daniel Webster*, *Midas*, *Arctic*, *Progress*, *Lagoda*, *Chance*; the rest, 31 in all are in the ice. At 10 AM we came on board the *Europa* of Edgartown as shipwreck mariners. So ends the log journal voyage & also the end of the bark *Henry Taber*.

Nathaniel Ransom too found refuge aboard the same rescue vessel:

> I've just come aboard of ship *Europa* Captain Mellen after being out in a hale and rainstorm pulling and sailing for last 24 hours. I had to throw my bomb gun a box of bomb lances with a musket and lots of ammunition with several other things overboard, my boat and all, lots of Esquimeaux garments with some others.

Sacrificing the warm clothing and weapons that might be needed to save his life, he clung to his journal. Gale-force winds and heavy seas rocked the rescue vessels. The *Arctic*, the *Midas*, and the *Progress* each lost an anchor while they struggled to hold their positions as the deeply laden whaleboats approached. Ocean swells tossed the boats like corks, as whalemen clambered aboard the rescue ships. No system functioned to keep crews together; Captain Aaron Dean boarded the *Lagoda*, while several of his men went on board the *Europa*, along with some 270 other shipwrecked mariners. Ransom would have preferred taking refuge on the less crowded *Progress*, where he could at least look after his brother Andrew. As soon as the crews of the abandoned ships were safely aboard, their whaleboats were cast adrift, an aching loss for Ransom, who took unbounded pride in "his" boat. Physically and emotionally, he was all spent. All told about twelve hundred souls were distributed among the seven rescue ships that set out next day for Plover Bay in search of fresh water. These whaling vessels normally carried thirty or forty men. Now with two or three hundred aboard they were seriously overloaded as they began their five-week journey south toward safety.

Aboard the unfamiliar *Europa*, Ransom persisted in his methodical record-keeping, noting that the ship "got under weigh headed for Behring Strait with about 300 people aboard," ten times the usual number. Among them were Captain John Heppingstone and his wife from the *Julian*, Captain Benjamin Dexter and his wife from the *Emily Morgan*, and four other captains of the abandoned ships, who later expressed their "heartfelt thanks" to the *Europa*'s Captain Mellen:

Barks "Arctic" and "Progress" Receiving the Crews of the Wrecked and Abandoned Ships South of Icy Cape. Destruction of the Arctic Whaling Fleet, sketch 4 of 4. Sketched by Captain William H. Kelley of the *Gay Head*, ca. 1872. (Courtesy of the New Bedford Whaling Museum.)

We would also tender our sympathy for the loss of his season's catch, and return extra thanks for the generous manner in which he invited us on board by setting his colors fore and aft when he saw us coursing in our boats. And the welcome on board in the Arctic Ocean in our destitute condition will long be remembered by all, and may his future prosperity in life be measured out to him after his own bounteous manner of ministering to ourselves while on board.[12]

Now the most pressing need was to reach "Plover Bay as fast as possible for the purpose of getting water." Despite "not feeling very well" Nathaniel Ransom "got off a large raft of water" when the *Europa* reached port. He and his shipmates also salvaged "a lot of provisions and other stuff from the wrecked ship *Oriole*." Stove by ice at the beginning of the bowhead season in mid-June, the *Oriole* had put into Plover Bay, where the damage was found too serious to repair. Its cargo and equipment were auctioned off, and its crew distributed among other vessels. Now the rescue ships took any remaining gear and much needed provisions.

At Plover Bay it was a relief to find the "*Arctic, Progress, Midas* in sight" for Nathaniel Ransom was at last able to go "aboard of bark *Progress* to see Andrew; found him sick and looking quite bad," for he had lain in his bunk below decks for three months, too ill to work. His vessel harbored 221 rescued whalemen, and the crowded conditions likely worsened living conditions for everyone. Nathaniel continued to track his brother's ship, unable to do anything else as the *Europa* "passed through 72 passage of Fox Isles all sail set." He himself was "not feeling well; quit smoking tobacco altogether . . . smoked only 3 times a day for some time past which was immediately after eating." Nevertheless, he made himself useful to the *Europa*, helping to scrape, wash, and stack the 5,000 pounds of whalebone aboard. The chance to do something to earn his keep lessened a bit his feeling of being beholden to Captain Mellen and his crew.

All seven rescue ships and the twelve hundred-odd whalemen and four families reached Honolulu safely; the last, the leaking British vessel *Chance* traveling over two months. On October 23, five weeks after leaving the Arctic, the *Europa*, with Ransom aboard,

> Came to an anchor in Honolulu. I went ashore in search of Captain Dean who arrived here today in bark *Lagoda*. I received 8 letters: one from my parents, 1 from Theo, and 1 from James and 5 from my darling Wife. I was happy to learn they are all quite well. Evening went aboard of bark *Progress* awhile to see Andrew. After I went aboard of *Europa* I read as many of my letters as I could. I had to quit reading before I finished them

on account of not feeling able to proceed any further. I have felt
very bad all day.

The letters from his loved ones at home reminded him painfully of his
own wreckage, of which they knew nothing. Immediately the *Honolulu
Gazette* printed news of the destruction of the Arctic fleet, and the story
spread rapidly through the offices of shipping agents and seamen's board-
inghouses. In fact, the entire Arctic season amounted to a loss; when abandoned the *John Wells* had only 330 barrels of whale oil in its hold, and the
rescue ships fared little better. The *Europa* brought just 230 barrels back
to Honolulu and Andrew's ship *Progress* just 340. Bowhead whaling had
become less profitable even as it became more life-threatening. Twenty
years earlier whalemen had taken bowheads at sixty degrees north latitude. Now all of the abandoned vessels lay trapped more than ten degrees
further north.

Next day Nathaniel Ransom prepared to leave Honolulu aboard
the steamer *Moses Taylor*:

> Got $150 from Captain Dean to pay my passage home. I was
> ashore with brother Andrew a good part of the day. Forenoon I
> purchased a ticket to go to San Francisco as first cabin passenger.
> I got some medicine of the Doctor, packed my clothes with
> Andrew's help. Afternoon I had letters from my own precious
> darling Wife. 9 o'clock in the evening we started for Frisco. The
> brass band company favored us with music before starting. I feel
> a little better today.

Left behind in Honolulu, Abram Briggs yearned in vain to go home
aboard the "Rolling Moses." With a full passenger list of 170, among them
Nathaniel Ransom, the steamer left for San Francisco, and Briggs turned
to the American consul, who gave him fifteen dollars, a suit of clothes,
and sent him to the Sailors' Home to board. Time crept slowly onward,
as he visited the cemetery and attended a minstrel show in the hot, sultry
weather that left the town almost dead. Glumly Abram Briggs watched
the *Europa,* the *Arctic,* and the *Progress* depart for the between seasons
cruise in southern waters.

Aboard the steamer *Moses Taylor* bound safely homeward,
Nathaniel Ransom's spirits recovered: "I have felt quite like myself again
today—that is quite smart." He busied himself by reading some of Sarah's
letters, and passed the time with other men from the abandoned whaling
fleet. He bought a watch and chain for thirteen dollars before arriving
at San Francisco on November 5. In company with James Carter, second

mate of the abandoned *Gay Head*, he took a room at the St. Nicholas Hotel:

> I went from there to see Dr. Dupuy but did not find him at home.
> Afternoon went again found him at home, got some medicine of
> him. I feel a little better this afternoon and evening we spent at
> our boarding place . . .

> Mon. 6: Pleasant weather; this afternoon I drew $30 of Captain
> Dean bought my ticket for Boston. I traded a watch chain with
> Colson afternoon bought a lot of food to carry with me. Evening
> I went to a kind of Theatre. I have felt some better today.

He had the company of Herbert Colson, second mate of the bark *Massachusetts* and a fellow refugee from the abandoned ships. Next day he departed from San Francisco at 7 o'clock in the morning and took a "steamboat to take the cars. At 11 o'clock started from the station. I feel a little better again."

The railroad, completed only two years earlier, carried Nathaniel Ransom homeward through Omaha, Union Junction, and Chicago. There he "had a good view while riding from one depot to another of the ruins caused by the great fire" that had burned much of the city one month before. Here at least were grounds for comparative consolation, for the Chicago fire had taken three hundred lives and left a hundred thousand residents homeless. In contrast, all of the whalemen in the Arctic fleet survived, and their homes on land had been spared, though their shipboard homes were a complete loss. As he journeyed eastward, Ransom's sardonic humor recovered: "My pains and aches it seems have about left me and a bad cold has taken their place, but I prefer having the cold, bothersome as it is, if one of the other troublesome comrades will stay away." On November 13, he "arrived at Pittsburgh, PA from where we started for New York via Philadelphia. I've got the toothache for a change."

"Tuesday [November] 14: We arrived at New York this evening at 7 AM in time to get to Mattapoisett tonight but on account of our baggage not being here at the depot had to wait till midday trains. I expect we shall have to weather it out one more night. I've got the toothache of course." That same day the American public learned of the loss of the Arctic whaling fleet in a *New York Times* article. The New Bedford *Whalemen's Shipping List and Merchants' Transcript* tallied the loss of 13,605 barrels of whale oil, 965 barrels of sperm oil, and 50 tons of whalebone, though all lives were saved. The *John Wells* lay amid the other ships, trapped between Point Belcher and Wainwright Inlet among ice floes that the newspaper reported as thirty-five to fifty feet high.

Nathaniel Ransom's journal ends abruptly, without recording his arrival in Mattapoisett or Sarah's joy and relief at finding him safe once more. New Bedford's *Republican Standard* reported however that his group of whalemen did in fact arrive at dawn the next morning, just a week after leaving San Francisco. Back at home in mid-November, he would weather out the entire winter there. Since he had left home at fourteen, he had spent eight whaling seasons in the Arctic, and only once remained at home for an entire year. He longed to see a Mattapoisett spring again, and summer with his darling Sarah.

Baleen, photo by Peter Randall.

There is an odd postscript to the famous whaling disaster of 1871 and New Bedford's loss of the Arctic fleet. As the whaleboats pulled away from the abandoned ships, the whalemen took one last look at the vessels that had been their home for the last several months. They watched as one boat-steerer jumped free and soon disappeared among the immense ice floes surrounding the trapped ships. He knew there were ample provisions for a single man stored on board, because only the bare minimum could be loaded onto the whaleboats, already heavily laden with people. And there were rifles on board, firewood, drinking water, and the clothing and belongings his shipmates had left behind. If he could survive winter alone in the Arctic, the valuable cargo of whalebone and oil stored in the twenty-eight ships that were still intact would be his according to the laws of salvage.

It was a sudden gamble, the decision made abruptly as the whale-boat carried him away from the abandoned fleet. This boatsteerer was a young man, likely in his early twenties, promoted out of the forecastle after one previous voyage as seaman, and now facing the end of the Arctic whaling season for the third or fourth time. But he had no experience of the Arctic winter beyond what he had heard from Captain Barker.

Three days after the whaleboats departed, the young boatsteerer watched numbers of Inupiaq men gathering near the fleet, which they could now reach by walking cross the new ice. They began to plunder the ships, salvaging firewood, axes, pots, rope, sails, knives, harpoons, lances, and other valuable metal goods. The captains, knowing the effects of alcohol on the natives, had agreed to pour all of it into the sea before leaving their ships. The only bottles the Inupiaq found were medicine stored in the captains' chests: chloroform, tincture of opium, iodine, calomel (mercurous chloride used to treat syphilis), bismuth subnitrate (an astringent antiseptic powder), collodion (a viscous liquid used to dress wounds), and emetics such as ipecac. As they guzzled the unknown substances, some became violently ill. Others died. Believing that evil spirits inhabited the ships where they found the poisonous liquids, they set fire to the *Florida*, the *Gay Head*, and the *Concordia*.

Two weeks after their crews abandoned the fleet, a favorable northeast gale freed the remaining ships from the ice that trapped them, later giving rise to accusations that the ships' masters should have remained a few weeks longer until they could escape under sail, their vessels and cargo intact.

The boatsteerer who stayed behind took shelter in the *Massachusetts*, driven by the Arctic winds further north than any of the fleet had reached under sail. He defended his booty as best he could, fatally outnumbered by the natives, who began rolling out the heavy casks of whale oil and carrying away bundles of dried baleen. A second heavy gale in early October sent the abandoned ships crashing into one another. "Of all the butting and smashing I ever saw, the worst was among those ships, driving into each other. Some were ground to pieces, and what the ice spared, the natives soon destroyed."[13] Alone, he faced the cruelest Arctic months: October, November, December, January, February, and March. Until the fleet returned in late April or May, the Inupiaq, whose language he did not understand, would be the only other human presence in the vast wasteland of ice and sea.

Against those odds, the lone white man did survive, and ships from New Bedford found him the following spring, "pretty well used up." In the end, the Inupiaq saved his life, as the Chukchi had saved Captain Barker and his crew from the *Japan* the winter before. "They set out to kill me," he said, "but the women saved me and afterward, the old chief took care of me. A hundred and fifty thousand dollars would not tempt me to try another winter in the Arctic."

This lone gambler remains an enigma. Several sources tell his story, even quoting his words, but none gives his name. The returning sailors who found him in the spring of 1872 and listened to his story certainly knew who he was. He was one of them. He had succumbed to that kernel of greed that slept in all of them. He had stepped outside their midst, rejected their common resolve to abandon their valuable cargo and head for safer waters. He had almost paid with his life, but not quite. They took him back, erased his name, and the brotherhood closed around him.

In contrast to the grim version of his story recounted in Alexander Starbuck's *History of the American Whale Fishery*, a brief, less ominous account appears in the *Whalemen's Shipping List* for October 1, 1872. That issue prints a letter from the Arctic, where two New Bedford ships were salvaging what remained from the ships abandoned the previous September. This source writes simply:

> The boatsteerer that stopped here is alive and says that 14 days after the ships were abandoned a heavy north gale set in and all the ice went off, and most of the ships dragged off [the bottom where they had run aground.] This winter to all appearances has been a very mild one, and we have encountered nothing but small ice.

This article and the *Whalemen's Shipping List* itself, written for New Bedford's merchants and whaling industry, depict the early ice threat of 1871 as an anomaly, detailing salvage efforts and emphasizing the continuing profitability of Arctic whaling.

But five years later, a second whaling disaster dealt another heavy blow to New Bedford's Arctic fleet. This time twelve vessels were abandoned in the ice near Point Barrow. Three hundred men saved themselves by dragging whaleboats over the ice, finally reaching the *Florence* about eight miles to the south. Trapped in a quarter-mile of ice, the *Florence* had to be cut free with spades before it and the *Rainbow* and the *Three Brothers* could make their way southward through the Bering Strait. Of the fifty-odd men who chose to stay behind with the abandoned vessels near Point Barrow, only three were found alive the following year.

The magnanimous response of Captain Dowden, Captain Mellen, and other rescuers of the 1,219 whalemen and the few families who abandoned their vessels in 1871 earned only a meager reward. In 1891—twenty years after the disastrous loss—Congress awarded the owners of each of the five rescue vessels registered in the United States $25,000. Owners of the *Arctic*, registered in Honolulu, and the *Chance*, registered in Australia, received nothing. The money amounted to just over a hundred dollars for each person carried to Honolulu on the five American rescue ships, an odd recompense for saving human lives.

Chapter V: "Among the Wrecks"

Third Mate of the Illinois,
March 18–November 13, 1875

After reaching Mattapoisett in November of 1871, Nathaniel Ransom settled on land for the next three years. He kept no journal, and nothing tells us whether he suffered nightmares of the crushing Arctic icepack, or felt his arms ache with rowing a frail whaleboat against the thickening wavelets of young ice. He bought a small house at the northeast corner of Foster Street and Beacon Street, just a few strides from the waterfront. Jonathan Hiller, who sold him the house, worked installing a new line for the water pump and putting up gutters, while a mason plastered and laid brick. Ransom shaped new doors, laid flooring, and painted the woodwork, for years of carpentry and boat-building aboard ship had honed his woodworking skills. From his front door he could walk down Beacon Street to the lighthouse at Ned's Point. He needed to breathe salt air, to live close to the town's docks, although the shipbuilders' wharves had gone quiet. The pounding of caulkers' hammers and the roll of heavy casks of shooks no longer rang in the air. In his second summer at home, Sarah gave birth to a daughter on August 16, 1873. They named her Laura Elma Ransom, for Sarah's mother's name was Laura Snow Dexter. When a second daughter was born in February 1875, they named her Eunice, for Nathaniel's mother. Eunice Cushing Ransom had died the previous November at the age of sixty-five. She had given birth to eight children; three lived.

The economic crisis called the Panic of 1873 drove many Massachusetts men back to the hazardous back-breaking labor of whaling. Completion of the transcontinental railroad in 1869 had been followed by rapid expansion and financial speculation. When some railroad companies failed to meet their credit obligations in September 1873, they ignited a wave of bank collapse and financial uncertainty. Anxiety was fueled by political disagreement over the use of silver and gold to back the paper currency issued to fund the Civil War. Business failures idled scores of workers, and the over-supply of labor further depressed wages.

To support his wife and daughters, Nathaniel Ransom signed

on as second mate aboard the *Rainbow* as 1875 began, eager to work under Captain Bernard Cogan, one of the best-liked and most successful whaling captains in New Bedford. All of the ship's officers and skilled tradesmen were Yankees, and many of the twenty-five seamen aboard were either New Englanders or European immigrants from Germany and Ireland. The availability of Anglo-European laborers pushed out the Kanakas, Azoreans, and Cape Verdeans who had comprised much of the crew during whaling's heyday twenty years before. On January 19, 1875, the *Rainbow* sailed out of New Bedford, crossing the Atlantic to dock at Brava in the Cape Verde Islands in February. Perhaps it was there that Nathaniel Ransom left the ship. It is unclear why he changed his plans or whether he returned home before Sarah gave birth to Eunice in February. However, he embarked again less than a month later, this time shipping out on the bark *Illinois* under Captain David Fraser. The transcontinental railroad that had brought him home after the abandonment of the *John Wells* carried him westward to Oakland, California to meet his ship.

Much of the North Pacific bowhead whaling fleet had moved to the West Coast, saving New Bedford's thrifty ship owners the considerable expense of sending vessels around Cape Horn. These businessmen disliked investing new capital in an aging industry, and the North Pacific fleet decreased from forty ships in 1871 to just sixteen in 1875. Because larger, older bowheads had been killed in the earlier years of the hunt, the average catch now yielded a hundred barrels of oil and about 1,500 pounds of baleen. As petroleum reduced the demand for whale oil, the value of a single whale—once as high as seven thousand dollars—now fell to half that amount. Yet with fewer prospects for good earnings on land, whalemen like Nathaniel Ransom returned to the Arctic, where the scarcity of bowheads forced them to push further north and hunt later into the darkening autumn.

The disaster of 1871 was not the final voyage for these mariners, nor for the whaling captains who had been forced to abandon their ships between Alaska's Wainwright Inlet and Point Belcher. Already in 1872, Captain Thomas Williams of the wrecked *Monticello* returned to salvage what could be found in the wrecks. The *Champion* had been burned, and the *Thomas Dickason* lay grounded on shore. From the old *Reindeer*, stove and driven up into shoal water, he off-loaded casks of oil and took them aboard the *Minerva*. He managed to get the *Minerva* afloat and attempted to salvage the *Seneca* as well. The *Seneca* sank in a heavy gale as it was being towed to Honolulu, but the *Minerva* and its cargo of oil and bone arrived, earning a profit of about $10,000. The ship itself continued in service for another decade.

Like Williams, Captain Charles Allen, whose *J. D. Thompson* had run aground in the early stages of the disaster, also returned to the Arctic in 1872, as did Captain William Kelley of the lost *Gay Head*. Kelley's eyewitness drawings of the abandoned fleet were published in the *Atlantic Monthly*. Captain Benjamin Whitney of the *William Rotch* returned as captain now of the *Arctic*, which had rescued crews of the abandoned ships in 1871. Whitney no longer returned to New Bedford, for the *Arctic* now used Honolulu as its hailing port. Of those thirty-two captains who lost their ships in September 1871, more than half resumed Arctic whaling within the next five years, as Nathaniel Ransom did. Numerous officers likewise returned undaunted. For instance, Herbert Colson (who had been second mate of the abandoned *Massachusetts* and had traveled homeward from Honolulu with Ransom) returned the following year as captain of the *Java*. These fearless men, returning to the site that nearly became their frozen grave, strike later generations as heroic. Their courage accounts for the trust that ship owners continued to place in them, despite their aban-donment of the fleet. In fact Leander Owen, master of the wrecked *Contest*, and West Mitchell, captain of the *Massachusetts*, assumed command of other whaling vessels after only a month or two in port. Furthermore, four of the captains who returned after the 1871 disaster persisted in the whaling industry long enough to weather the transition to steam power, which eventually allowed ships to winter over near Point Barrow or at Herschel Island in the Beaufort Sea. Bernard Cogan, for instance, master of the abandoned *Josephine*, returned as captain of the *Rainbow*, and perse-vered in the Arctic whaling business, later as master of steam whaleships based in San Francisco. Even Captain Frederick Barker, who had survived a winter of near starvation among the Siberian Chukchi, returned to Arctic whaling and continued into the steam age.

Returning to the Arctic as these men did, Nathaniel Ransom left his darling little family in Mattapoisett on March 8, 1875. Sarah waved from the doorway of the little house on Foster Street, holding tiny Eunice in her arms, with Laura wobbling unsteadily and clutching her skirt. He traveled by train from Mattapoisett depot to Taunton, Massachusetts, where he "took a lunch" at the home of his father's younger half-brother, Nathaniel Morton Ransom, a physician. Dr. Ransom then brought him to the railroad station where he met John H. Rogers, who also signed on aboard the *Illinois*. John Rogers, a short black man, had been first mate of the abandoned *Reindeer* in 1871. He and Nathaniel Ransom probably met as shipwreck mariners aboard the *Europa*, for Rogers became its second mate on a return voyage to the Arctic only three months after abandoning the *Reindeer*.

Even in familiar company the usual misery befell Nathaniel Ransom as soon as he left home: sore throat, a terrible cold, and feeling rather lonesome, his little family always in his thoughts. He stopped in Chicago, and passed through Council Bluffs and Omaha, re-tracing the same route that had brought him home three years before. While transcontinental railroad travel was faster and safer than the long voyage around Cape Horn, it was by no means free of difficulty. The train spent five hours stuck in a snow drift on the western side of the Rockies before reaching Ogden, Utah, and the journey to Oakland lasted eight days.

In Oakland, he met his brother Andrew and shared a hotel room with him before Andrew left for Panama. Given the slow pace of travel and of transcontinental mail service, the brothers had to plan their meeting months in advance as a rare opportunity to come together. Nathaniel Ransom notes only the briefest facts, and that he "went back a short distance with Andrew to see his girl. Gave my carpet bag to a rascal with the instructions of Andrew and when I got to the hotel could not find it. Andrew stays with me tonight at the Brooklen Hotel. A mean place I guess."

After Andrew left for Panama, Nathaniel Ransom got his bed tick filled with straw and took his things aboard the *Illinois*, which had sailed from New Bedford three years earlier. With San Francisco now its hailing port, the bark returned from its Arctic seasons to California rather than shipping its cargo home from the Sandwich Islands or journeying around Cape Horn home to Massachusetts. He signed on as third mate under Captain David R. Fraser, whom he had encountered in 1871 when Fraser, captain of the *Florida*, led the expedition of whaleboats seeking rescue south of their icy entrapment near Point Belcher. Before the *Illinois* sailed from San Francisco, he found Captain Aaron Dean, and their conversation turned inevitably to their ill-fated voyage on the *John Wells*. Aaron Dean would sail as master of the *John Carver* in a few months, whaling in the warmer waters of the Pacific. Nathaniel Ransom recorded: "cruised around a while. Wrote a few lines to my wife. Evening went up to Platts hall awhile with Rogers and Capt. Fraser." On March 18 the *Illinois* pulled away from the dock:

> This morning I wrote a few lines to my darling wife. Mailed the letter about 7 o'clock. Went on board the ship. Changed some of my clothes. About 11 o'clock the Capt. came off on a tug boat

which took us in tow. Afternoon stowed away chains, washed
off deck. I am feeling rather lonesome with a bad cold on me.
Hope my darling little ones at home are well. We have started
for Arctic I suppose.

The routine of departure, hauling up the anchor and chains, did nothing
to lighten his heavy heart.

"A Regular Dog's Life"

By now life aboard a whaling bark was familiar, and the dreary passage
to the Arctic hunting grounds was filled with mundane tasks. As third
mate, Nathaniel Ransom had charge of the larboard watch and of his own
whaleboat, as he had on the *John Wells*. It took the *Illinois* five weeks to
reach whaling grounds from San Francisco, longer than the voyage from
Honolulu, which lay further to the west. In his journal, he confided the
effect of this solitary part of the voyage on his spirits. At twenty-nine,
he composed entries far longer and more revealing than those of the
immature adolescent who left home aboard the *Barnstable* fifteen years
earlier. After leaving port he felt "awful lonesome laying here rolling
and tumbling about in a dead calm not two weeks from home. I miss my
darling little family." Next day: "I look at my wife and little girls' pictures
every day. Come as near seeing them as I can."

One week later he reminisced tenderly on his last day at home: "On
wind heading to North. Heavy squalls . . . Three weeks ago today I was
with my darling little family. Took little Elma [daughter Laura] to brother
James in forenoon." James, his wife Almeida, and fourteen-year-old Etta
lived in New Bedford. "Afternoon stayed with my wife and little ones
at home. Today I have got a wet jacket. Several times water flying over
the rail. Our latitude today is about 44-30 [still well south of the Aleutian Islands]. Crawling to North'rd slowly. I have not changed my under
clothes since I left home."

The slow pace of travel lowered his spirits even further:

Not much wind today. What little we've had has been dead
ahead. Repairing larboard boat today. Painted my boat & 4th
mates. No sleep for me today. I washed out my white shirt some
of the dirt. Broke out small stores, got a set of oars put in my boat.
Working in rigging. I am not feeling very well today. Homesick,
etc. Have some cold on me yet. 3 weeks today I left my darling
little family. Hope they are all well tonight . . .

[March 30:] Wind westward on wind heading to North and working in rigging. Getting ready to put in cutting gear. I drank the last of the dangle berry juice my darling wife put up for me. Have felt quite well for me today only lonesome as ever.

To occupy his melancholy evenings, Ransom mended and altered his winter clothing. "This evening I turned up the bottom of my old black coat about one foot, basted and commenced sewing it as it was much too long for sea wear." A man who could mend sail knew how to patch his own gear. "Discovered this afternoon my old Arctic gear about worn out. The bottoms are about gone. I want to try and patch my old salt and pepper pants." Most of his Arctic gear and Eskimo garments had been thrown overboard in September 1871 as he struggled to sail his over-burdened whaleboat south from Point Belcher toward the rescue ships. Now he heard an unwelcome voice interrupting his sewing: "The old man is calling me to work up the ship's line."

Although the captain was able to figure the ship's latitude himself, he called upon Nathaniel Ransom to calculate the longitude: "Capt. Fraser wants I should help navigate. Doesn't like it because I did not bring an epitome with me." In 1837 Nathaniel Bowditch published *The New Practical Navigator, Being a Complete Epitome of Navigation*. Ransom's scorn for the captain began with recognizing the old man's ineptitude as a navigator, his failure to provide the proper equipment on board, and the demands he made at inopportune times for working up the ship's line, which he noted on April 8 as latitude 51°30′ N and longitude 160° W. The ship, "spray flying and decks covered with ice," sought the seventy-two passage, threading among the Fox Islands in the Aleutian chain to enter the Bering Sea.

Unlike the *Barnstable* or the *Sea Breeze*, the *Illinois* carried no livestock aboard, and therefore had no source of fresh meat. Nor did the ship dock at the Sandwich Islands for fresh water and vegetables or fruit. The diet remained unappetizingly uniform until men went in shore near the Aleutians' Fox Islands "in pursuit of codfish. Got about 30 in our boat and about 50 more on board the ship . . . We had fried codfish for supper." The months spent cod-fishing on the Grand Banks after returning from his first voyage had taught him the craft, now supplying a tasty addition to the *Illinois*'s monotonous diet of salt beef and pork.

Hampered by a "dirty wet fog" and lack of wind, the ship idled for several days before passing through the Aleutian archipelago to reach the islands of St. Paul and St. George. Ransom sheathed his old red mittens and broke out the Pierce's bomb lance guns. He worked at carpentry, making new steps for the steerage and bulk heads for the blubber-room cooler. As the cold sharpened he complained, "I have not experienced any warm weather since last summer . . . It seems to me a regular dog's life here same as ever. The weather continues quite cold yet thermometer down to 20 above a good part of the time." The stove below decks drew poorly, filling his cabin with smoke. Within sight of Cape Navarin on the Siberian Coast "officers commenced standing mastheads" to watch for drifting ice, which was "getting quite thick and heavy. We have been butting it some all day. No whales been seen by us yet."

He felt unwell and dreaded worse suffering as the cold and labor of whaling loomed ahead:

> My nervous trouble has been on me quite bad today. Could not sleep this forenoon but very little. Opened the second & last box of ointment. I wish I had a dozen more boxes of it. I think it does more good than anything else I can apply on the outside. I am feeling better now than I did this forenoon. It has been 14 degrees above zero today. My face shows and feels the effects of cold winds. Chilblains.

His frostbitten face grew splotchy and red, itching whenever he got into the warmth below decks. His fingers and toes smarted and burned in the cold, and everywhere the coarse woolen clothing chafed against his skin. He slept fitfully or not at all, "too much dreaming to attend to . . . [April 25]: Butting ice some. I saw quite a number of walruses . . . I have felt very bad all day. Palpitation, faintness etc. Can not sleep any of any account. On the whole it seems to me I am having rather of a rough time of it. I dreamt James had gone whaling in the old bark *Willis*." That dream of James evoked happier times, although it was his brother Sidney who sailed on the *Willis*. The old Mattapoisett bark had plied the Atlantic hunting sperm and right whales without ever venturing into the hostile Arctic waters; it was condemned in the Azores in 1866. Bound northward now into bowhead grounds as the *Illinois* butted ice, Nathaniel fretted, "My old nervous trouble has been on me quite bad today."

Everything changed at once on April 26:

> Morning raised bowhead. Lowered for him about ½ past 5 o'clock. Saw the second one after we got down but no chance to strike on account of so much young ice being in the way. Chased until about noon. Came aboard. Lost my forenoon watch below but that did not amount to anything. Afternoon sent up cutting blocks falls, etc. Broke out fresh water. Ship laying in ice.

Hoisting Aboard the Head of a Bowhead Whale, Showing the Whale Bone; Albert Cook Church. (Courtesy of the New Bedford Whaling Museum.)

As the bowheads migrated north the chase began early with the predictable frustrations and failures:

> At 5 o'clock this morning lowered for whales all going fast to wind'rd showed no chance for a striking. After breakfast tried them again. Chased all the forenoon without success. It is now 4 o'clock in afternoon. Several whales in sight to wind'rd. It is now ½ past 8 o'clock in the evening. We have just got on board ship from another wild goose chase.

On May 1, the second mate struck a whale, and the first mate killed one two days later. On May 4 it was Ransom's turn: "Fine weather. Got two hours sleep this morning after finishing cutting. Afternoon went in shore after whales. I struck a large one close to the heavy ice. Saved him. Commenced cutting about ½ past 3 o'clock, finished about ½ past 7. It is now about 9 o'clock. I have just come below to try for a little sleep." Next day he killed another bowhead: "Morning my watch on deck. Raised whales. Old man sent the mate down alone. Kept the others all aboard. After a while struck a whale. I went down. Killed the whale for him. His boatsteerer got knocked overboard by the whale. I picked him up all right." Rescuing the boatsteerer evoked the loss of the man thrown overboard from the *Sea Breeze* years before; this time every man in the whaleboat sighed with relief as they hauled the boatsteerer aboard.

Striking bowheads in early May was exceptional luck, for the hunt usually began much later. Only in the sheltered Okhotsk Sea in 1867 had Nathaniel Ransom's ship captured bowheads in early May. The *John Wells* failed entirely at profiting from the northward migration of the whales and instead its crew shot walrus to fill their trypots with blubber.

As third mate of the *Illinois*, Nathaniel Ransom usually took charge of cutting in blubber, mincing and boiling down, and cutting out baleen from the whale's head.

Near the Siberian coast, the crew tried out blubber, watching warily for ice near the ship:

> Morning raised two whales. Mate, 2nd & 4th mates lowered for them. Did not strike. I stayed aboard and boiled oil. All hands on deck all day and biggest part of the night. Lately looking [at] one another the great part of the time. Evening a canoe of Esquimeaux came aboard. Had nothing of any account to trade. Ship close in to land. Becalmed & still going in shore. Ice coming down on us, etc.

> May 7th: Wind from N. East'rd. Boiling all day. Mate, 2nd & 4th mate as usual lowered for whales. Chased all the afternoon. Got nothing. I stayed on board and boiled. All hands on deck all day and good part of the night wending along the ice part of the time. I had about 1 hour & ½ to myself, just time enough to have a warm dinner which I did & changed my clothing. Washed the dirty ones.

The four bowheads that the *Illinois* captured in early May were following their food source, krill or plankton, toward the Beaufort Sea. For the next three months the whalemen had no further chance to strike whales as the ship idled near Cape Thaddeus and Plover Bay on the Siberian coast. For most of the month the *Illinois* was "laying in the ice same as ever."

Captain Fraser prepared for walrusing, building himself a small dinghy (the journal spelled it "dinky") and practicing shooting his rifle with John Rogers. Ransom helped the blacksmith get out his forge to make walrus irons and lances. The second mate "went to shoot a seal on the ice. Fell overboard in the operation. Got on board all right only with wet clothes." When he saw a bowhead that same evening, Ransom went for him but saw no more of him and had to leave his boat on the ice to return to the ship, waiting for the ice to open. Wondering what his little family was doing, he felt very lonesome, and dosed himself with "nervous root tea."

Familiar New Bedford whaling vessels approached—the *Onward*, *Triton*, and *St. George*—bringing news from home and welcome sociability. Captain Fraser bought a hog from the *Triton* and treated the officers to the novel taste of fresh pork. Andrew Robinson from the *Onward* came aboard to visit Nathaniel Ransom in mid-May. The two men had become acquainted on the *Sea Breeze*, and Robinson was another shipwreck mariner from the 1871 disaster, when he had been aboard the abandoned *Eugenia*. By June of 1875, several other familiar vessels were hunting near the Siberian coast: the *Florence*, the *Helen Snow*, the *Acors Barnes*, and the *Arctic*. The *Acors Barnes* brought letters for the *Illinois*, though none for Nathaniel, keenly disappointed at receiving nothing from Sarah. He went on board the *Arctic* to visit Captain Benjamin Whitney, "an old shipmate . . . from the bark *Sea Breeze*," now based in Honolulu. He knew the shape and smell of the familiar old Mattapoisett *Arctic* where his older brother Charles, now long dead, had begun as cabin boy so long ago. Whitney too reminisced with him about the 1871 disaster, when he had been captain of the abandoned *William Rotch*.

Close to Plover Bay, the *Illinois* rammed ice hard enough to stave a hole in the bow, further evidence of Captain Fraser's inept handling of the vessel: "The ship has sprung a leak caused by butting ice foolishly." The usual procedure when a leak was discovered in the bow was to shift cargo in the hold to lower the stern of the ship and raise the bow above the water line to repair the leak. Therefore the crew "broke out a lot of casks forward, tried to find the leak," and discovered it eighteen inches under water. "Think of getting water to roll aft to get the ship's head above water to try & stop it." Repairs did not succeed in plugging the leak: "The old ship leaks about 2000 strokes [of the pumps] every 24 hours laying to an anchor." The collision and resulting damage caused Ransom to think Fraser was no more competent than Captain Davis of the leaking *Navy*.

Between Plover Bay and St. Lawrence Bay Captain Fraser hired four Chukchi natives for the duration of the season, eager to gain more hands for walrusing. Captains had learned that Pacific Islanders accustomed to tropical weather were ill suited to the walrus hunt on the ice, which began June 8 and lasted for the next five weeks. In the Arctic summer light, the crew toiled shooting and skinning walrus and boiling their blubber around the clock:

> [June 8:] . . . [A]ll hands after walruses. Shot and got 3. I have had all night job of it skinning them. Nice medicine for my cold which is bad enough today.

> [June 9:] All hands up all day and night. Shot & got 33 more walruses. Done enough work on them to take care of 200 in most ships. The old man goes to work the hardest possible way to do anything.

Nathaniel Ransom was not the only man aboard the *Illinois* who disliked Captain Fraser. "Old man yelling most of the time, as usual about nothing," he groused in early April. The crew showed no respect for a master unable to lead them. Fraser put a man in irons for twenty-four hours, though Ransom does not mention his offense. Isolated aboard ship, men who felt they had been wronged had no recourse to justice. It was a situation well adapted to unscrupulous exploitation of the unwary or unlettered.

> [June 10:] . . . [O]ld man put carpenter in the rigging. Bashed him with a rope for a while then put him in double irons and down in the hold. He claims the carpenter drew a knife on him when he went to haul him out of his berth. He has ordered his clothes packed and says he is going to put him ashore up North here.

Putting a seaman in the rigging was a form of torture, as his hands were tied, sometimes so high that his feet scarcely reached the deck. As the ship rolled beneath him swinging his feet above the deck, his entire weight hung suspended from his bound wrists. While the cat o' nine tails whip had been outlawed at midcentury, the captain easily found a rope to lash the carpenter. Captain Fraser's cruelty, imprisoning the carpenter in the dark hold with hands and feet shackled, and his threat to abandon the man in the Arctic intimidated and embittered the entire crew. Fraser occupied the seamen in pointless labor, depriving them of the energy to mutiny: "Men employed in filling casks with salt water etc. for sake of having it to pump out again to make work. My cold hangs on about the same."

Furthermore, provisions grew scarce aboard the *Illinois*: "Forenoon broke out bread & flour. All there is on the ship." It reminded him ominously of the shortage of provisions on the old *John Wells*. And venturing down into the hold, he saw each time that the ship continued to leak.

Nevertheless, the walrus hunt went on throughout the endless hours of daylight near the summer solstice. Captain Fraser could take two or three men to row his dingy close to the ice where the walrus lumbered about, the dingy often followed by a whaleboat whose crew took charge of butchering the dead walrus and hauling their blubber and tusks back to the ship. Approaching walrus to leeward to avoid alerting them by his scent, the captain or another gunner—often Nathaniel Ransom himself—could creep onto the ice and begin to shoot. "All hands of us all day walrusing. Shot and got about 25. I got my boat stove by a walrus. Patched it up with canvas. I had a very poor day. Severe pains in breast, etc. Everything must have gone wrong with me." A crack shot himself, Ransom scorned poor marksmanship in others: "[June 15:] Morning saw quite a number of walruses. The mate started off shooting at them on the ice. Shot away about 200 cartridges. Got seven walruses which made 10 with 3 the other boats picked up." Captain Fraser "got the end of one of his little fingers blown off by cartridge accidentally going off" in late June. A week later only six of Fraser's twenty-eight shots at walrus hit their mark.

Nathaniel Ransom's own slaughter of walrus continued unabated as summer daylight dimmed into the brief Arctic night:

> [June 16:] About 12 o'clock AM the old man went off shooting walruses. Got a few. After breakfast started off again. Kept to work 'till about 6 o'clock in the evening. It is now about 7. We have made over 59 walruses. About 68 hours to work at it . . . I am wet through with sweat. It is a thick fog.

> [June 19:] Saw a few walruses. All hands went for them. Got none. Old man went on board the Bark *Florence*, Capt. Williams; got several letters. None for me, same as before . . . We commenced boiling walrus.

> [June 24:] All hands on deck as usual walrusing. We have been at it all day & I expect will keep it up all night. It is now after 9 o'clock & we are in the midst of walrus. My boat is alongside with 16 in waiting for another boat to unload. I have felt bad all day, the worst I ever felt in my life. Severe pain in my breast, etc . . . It has been 24 hours now since I had my 77 walruses.

Even the chest pain that grew more alarming meant no respite from work.

[June 25:] All hands again today walrusing. Got about 60. We are at it now. Hardly below enough to get our meals. It has been quite good weather today. I have felt a great deal better than I did yesterday.

[June 26:] All hands again all day walrusing. It is now 7 o'clock in the evening and the chance is good for all hands all night. We have got 50 walruses so far. Could have twice that amount if [we] had worked it right.

[June 27:] It is now about 7 o'clock. I have just got my dinner. One boat's crew at a time. We have shot & got something in the neighborhood of 100 walruses today. The chance is good of all of us being at it all night.

Nearby a dozen other ships were also fully engaged in walrusing. Weather "too rugged to walrus it" provided the only pause in the shooting, skinning, mincing, and boiling as day turned into night and night turned to dawn once more. "[June 29:] Commenced mincing walrus. Getting ready for boiling again. No chasing walrus today." By July 1, the labor and lack of rest had destroyed any sense of well-being: "I am feeling very bad. Am not sleeping when I get a watch below. Severe pains, palpitations. Sometimes I get discouraged almost to death & others I feel a little better. I commenced using my last bottle of Gold Seal." Worry over his health brought on insomnia, and the constant Arctic daylight and ongoing toil on board made sleep difficult at any time.

[July 2:] Finished boiling. All hands on deck stowing down. Shot some walruses & a bear. It is now six o'clock. Boat off shooting. The prospect bids fair for all hands being up all night. I have felt better today than I did yesterday. All hands up all night for 15 walruses & be all hands again today.

[July 3:] All hands as usual walrusing. Got 19. I have been 40 hours without any sleep. Hard to work all the time. Ship in the ice. Walruses very shy. I'm in hopes I shall be able to sleep a little tonight. Run down balance of oil.

After running walrus oil from the cooling tank on deck into barrels in the hold below, Captain Fraser gave his crew a holiday as Independence Day fell on a Sunday. "A hard old fourth of July. For one hope my darling ones at home are well & happy." Next day the hunt resumed at daybreak:

Commenced walrusing about 4 o'clock this morning. It is now 4 o'clock in the afternoon. We have got 57 walruses on board. A lot more on the ice to get. Probably an all night job of it at least.

Later it is now 11 o'clock at night. I have just got on board with a load of walruses. Found a letter from my darling wife. I was pleased to hear that she and all were well. I am going right off again after more walrus.

The good news from Sarah chased away his weariness and worry, although the letter had been written months before.

[July 6:] All hands day and night for walrusing. Got about 60 today I believe & 185 yesterday. While I was unloading my boat alongside the old man ran into a large cake of ice with the ship. Stove my boat quite badly. It is now 12 o'clock at night. One watch just went below for a little while.

[July 7:] Morning strong breeze from South'rd. All hands on deck skinning walrus. At night old man shot 6 out of 28 shots or cartridges & skinned them. I have just got aboard ship. It is now 2 o'clock Thursday morning.

[July 8:] It is now about 5 o'clock. We have got about 60 [walrus] today on board & are after more. At 12 o'clock at night about 100 walruses. After more. I am feeling rather sleepy.

[July 9:] Walrusing as usual. All hands of course. All the time day and night. It is now 5 o'clock in the morning. I have just got my last night's supper. Later it is now 10 o'clock PM. We have just got through skinning walrus & I have been 40 hours without sleep. Got about 160 walruses in the time.

On July 10, Nathaniel Ransom tallied his record: he had killed 123 walrus over five days. In addition, he shared the labor of rowing to and from the walrus grounds, butchering the animals, cutting out tusks, hauling the blubber on board, mincing it, and boiling out the oil. Beneath the Arctic skies, darkness amounted to little more than dusk, and work continued around the clock:

[July 11:] A rain storm and thick fog at 12 o'clock a.m. Got all walruses on board. I got my boat stove all to pieces between ship & a cake of ice. We tied the ship up to a cake of ice. Afternoon got 20 walruses.

The next day, the crew shot forty-eight more walrus, and thirty-one more on July 15:

All hands on deck boiling. Breaking out shooks, etc. Stowed the last walrus blubber in the lower hold. Have been bothering at something all day same as we always do.

[July 17:] I have been on my feet nearly 24 hours on a stretch with the rest of my watch. Run down over 100 barrels oil [3,150 gallons] this afternoon. It is now a thick wet fog. We are still boiling.

[July 18:]: Boiling walrus oil. All hands on deck as usual just for the sake of being on deck to suit the old man. Afternoon run down about 30 barrels of oil. A thick fog about all day. At noon cleared up a little while. Saw ice and several ships. No walrus in sight.

"I am not particular about seeing any more for the present," he added drily.

The *Illinois's* crew killed between eight hundred and a thousand walrus in June and July of 1875, three times as many as Ransom's 1870 season aboard the *John Wells*. The years between 1874 and 1878 marked the high point of the walrus kill, when close to 70,000 were captured.[1] In addition, untold numbers were lost as they fell from the ice, or escaped capture, wounded, only to die later. Captain Frederick Barker's pleas in 1871 to stop the walrus slaughter after he had suffered the Chukchis' winter hunger obviously had little effect. By the end of the 1870s, whalemen discovered that whole villages of Eskimos, as many as fifteen hundred, had starved to death because of the shortage of walrus meat. Some became seriously ill after resorting to gnawing the sealskin used to cover their lightweight boats. Some ate their dogs. Chukchi mothers stripped their babies naked and left them on the icy shore to hasten their frozen death rather than watch them perish slowly from hunger. Among the settlements decimated by winter hunger was Plover Bay, a village the whalemen depended upon to obtain fresh water and trade goods. Starvation reduced its inhabitants to a few skeletal wraiths. Like Nathaniel Ransom, Captain Fraser had listened to Frederick Barker during the summer of 1871, yet he and his crew remained unaffected by the human deprivation they caused, or simply felt greed stronger than remorse.

In the midst of boiling and stowing down oil, the crew struggled to keep the *Illinois* from further ice damage: "July 13. Strong breeze. Afternoon trying to get out of the ice. Carried away one of the bobstays & some of the back rope. Butting ice pretty hard. Shall be lucky if [we] do not tear the ship all to pieces. Evening got jammed in the ice while two other ships almost along side of us got clear." The next day the crew "got the ship out of ice" and steered eastward toward the Alaskan coast "in company with several other ships. All hands on deck of course. Boiling and stowing down oil. Afternoon shortened sail. Evening made all sail again. We've had quite a rain storm today. I changed my clothes tonight, the first time since the first of June I think." The whalemen finished boiling walrus oil and stowed it down as the ship neared Cape Lisburne on the Alaskan shore and anchored there to take on fresh water. Nearby lay the bark *Europa* that had carried Nathaniel Ransom to safety in 1871. Captain Fraser boarded the ship for a visit with the *Europa's* Captain James McKenzie.

"Close to the Wrecks"

On July 25, the *Illinois* "came to an anchor close to the wrecks" of vessels abandoned in 1871. At the sight of them Nathaniel Ransom felt "very bad today severe pains, etc." No longer stranded between Wainwright Inlet and Point Belcher, the hulks of the two-dozen-odd ships not sunk or burned by the Eskimos had drifted northward near Point Barrow, further than ice had allowed them to range in 1871. Next day he "went ashore and got a boat load of wood and some shifting boards. Afternoon got underweigh. Steering to North'rd. I am feeling better today than I did yesterday. I got the wood among some of the wrecks." After four winters wracked by drifting ice and howling gales, the remains of hull and stern could scarcely be identified. Eskimos had already taken everything usable that could be wrested from the ships, including rope, sails, and iron tools. Salvagers who arrived in spring 1872 carried away as much of the whale-bone and oil as they could extirpate. Nevertheless, anyone who knew these ships as well as Ransom did would again see in his mind's eye their proud shape under full sail, or imagine the home-like cabins that once housed the ships' officers.

But the safety of this year's vessels presented a more acute cause for concern: "Found the bark *Arctic* aground Capt. Whitney is in hopes to get her off all right the *Triton* & *James Allen* are also laying on anchor here." Whitney, his old shipmate, did succeed in getting the *Arctic* afloat once more, but the grounding reminded whalemen of the perils of sailing east of Point Barrow, where they saw "plenty of ice around us, a small strip of clear water for the ships to go along." As the *Illinois* edged cautiously northeast the crew scraped and washed walrus ivory. Nathaniel Ransom suffered another bout of his heart ailment: "[I] could not sleep a wink. Lay'd in my bunk in misery all the time, my heart beating so hard I could scarcely get my breath." His journal does not acknowledge any connection between the heart irregularities that struck him and the consciousness of his precarious situation, so much like the ice trap four years earlier.

The end of July found the *Illinois* anchored east of Point Barrow waiting for bowheads, which would not begin their migration south until mid-August. With neither walrus nor bowheads in sight, frustration and idleness plagued the crew once again:

> Old man on board Bark *Triton*. Left word to smoke ship. Purpose to keep all hands on deck no doubt as there was nothing else to do. For there was no need of our smoking the ship as there is only a few mice on board. We did not raise smoke enough to harm a mosquito. Afternoon fog lifted. Washed off decks. Washed two dirty garments. We are still laying to an anchor close to low land at about 72 degrees North Lat[itude] . . .

> [July 31:] Morning 3 boats off in the ice cruising for whales. One ashore wooding. Smoked ship again just to keep things moving. About 7 o'clock in the evening boats got on board. We saw one whale or rather the mate says he saw one but I have my doubts . . . as none of the rest saw him. It is now quite a big rain storm.

Rain was a rarity, since the frigid Arctic air held little moisture, and what precipitation fell was more often snow. August second brought a welcome sight:

> The *Rainbow* in all of her glory appeared to us. Went on board for letters & papers but found none for me. Had to stay all night on account of its blowing so hard. Slept in the berth where I had my things before. Everybody likes Capt. Cogan.

> [August 3:] Strong breeze from S.W. again today. All hands on board the *Rainbow* for late news. I might have had late news from home just as well as not if I had only thought to tell my folks to write. Well it cannot be helped now. It is now a rainstorm. Broke out fresh water. Filled the casks with salt water. Got back from the *Rainbow* 6 o'clock this morning.

Clearly Nathaniel Ransom wished he had remained as the *Rainbow*'s second mate, serving under a captain who—unlike David Fraser—was competent and well respected.

Waiting for bowheads to begin their southward migration, boredom settled over the fleet.

> [August 4:] Morning got the Carpenter of the *Onward* to come on board to work on my boat repairing her where the old man got her stove when we were walrusing. Afternoon Capt. Hayes was on board a while . . . Evening got underweigh in company with several other ships steering to the West'rd. Plenty of rain . . .

[August 5:] This morning let go anchor. Lots of rain again. Wind
S.W. Carpenter of the *Onward* still on board to work on the boat.
Afternoon old man went on board the *Onward*. Took the cat with
him. Evening sun shining. Fog banks around.

The *Onward* hailed from New Bedford, and its crew passed along old
newspapers, among them a *New Bedford Standard* of May 20. Ransom
groused that there "doesn't seem to be much news in it. No Mattapoisett
news. Only Silas Snow has changed his programme a little."

Nonetheless, change was afoot. The New Bedford *Whalemen's
Shipping List and Merchant's Transcript* from the same week listed the usual
prices for sperm oil and whale oil and the whereabouts of the fleet. In
addition readers were informed that Britain had organized an Arctic
Exploring Expedition ready to sail for the Davis Strait. Captain Nares
would be deceived, however, in the hope of finding an ice-free polar sea
as he navigated between Greenland and Ellesmere Island. And despite
the assertion that his "hardy mariners" were supplied with the stoutest
clothing and healthiest food, the men became ill with scurvy and Nares
was forced to return home in 1876. Perhaps, the reporter implied, the
British explorers should have consulted Yankee whalemen about how to
survive the Arctic. Another Englishman, Mr. Axon, estimated that by 2000
the population of the United States would reach 546 million. He opined
that our civilization would not "be eclipsed as that of Rome was, by the
triumph of the barbarians, the danger of the future being from interior
demoralization and vice."

As the *Illinois* lay anchored near Point Barrow, Nathaniel Ransom
busied himself with more mundane problems, repairing the port pump,
picking over potatoes, and patching an old pair of pants. "About all the
fleet" lingered nearby, shifting position to avoid drifting ice, "as close into
land as we can float. A lot of natives on board . . . Quite a number of ships
close by. I've scratched the gratings on the skylight ready for varnishing
as there is nothing else to do." Northeast of Point Barrow the crew "got
in 4 small boat loads of wood. Second & 4th mates went after a second
load. Found none. One man ran away from the 4th mate's boat. We saw
him from the ship going back in the country." The deserter, a man named
Brady, was later picked up by the *Europa* and returned to the *Illinois* on
August 19. Life ashore on the barrens of Alaska's north coast could be
harsher than life aboard a whaleship under Captain Fraser's command.

[August 12:] Forenoon broke out potatoes. Picked them over.
Afternoon stowed them away. Broke out small stores. Put my

boat on the cranes. All the ships to South'rd of Point Barrow. I
changed and washed my clothes.

[August 13:] . . . Men picking oakum . . . Evening old man dealt
out tobacco to those that wanted it. I've got a severe headache. I
put on my muskrat skin coat to wear for the first time.

In late June, he had traded a spare cap with the blacksmith for the muskrat
coat that the blacksmith had gotten from the Chukchi. Whalemen might
scorn natives' beliefs about weather or the spirit world, but they recognized from experience their skill at clothing themselves to meet the
elements. Animal skin clothing worn fur side inside helped insulate and
wick moisture from the body, keeping them dry and windproof.

Bored by inactivity and surrounded by "Plenty of ice, heavy cakes,"
in mid-August, his thoughts turned to the last Mattapoisett summer.
"Two years ago tonight I went for the Doctor. Bought some peaches." On
that evening, he had fetched a doctor for Sarah, who gave birth to Laura
Elma Ransom on August 16. "Monday . . . This is little Elma's birthday,
two years old. As I trust the Lord has spared her life & will all of my little
family for me to meet with them again soon. I hope to find them all well."
The cry of "There blows" interrupted his daydreams, as the starboard
watch raised whales. The second mate got a small one, and Nathaniel
Ransom was called from his watch below decks to help with the cutting
in. The late season bowhead chase now began now in earnest.

The *Illinois*'s first efforts led nowhere, while other nearby ships
easily took several whales:

Somebody is catching whales not a great way off while we are
doing nothing.

[August 25:] Capt. Hickmott of the *Acors Barnes* came on board
begging. Got some blacksmith coal, a lead line & some iron . . .
Afternoon one ship chasing a whale. Evening came up with a
lot of ships all boiling I think & some whaling. Spoke *Cornelius
Howland*. Reports *Rainbow* with 5 whales, others in proportion.
We saw a few spouts going fast to windward. Lowered. No
chance. One ship to leeward got a whale.

[August 26:] Old man went on board the *Helen Snow*. Found her
with 3 whales.

Finally on August 27 the crew took another bowhead and by eight o'clock
in the evening got him alongside. The work of cutting in commenced at
10 o'clock in the evening. Boiling began next day, interrupted by a heavy

rainstorm that forced the crew to cool down the tryworks, only to fire them up again toward evening. Meanwhile nearby, the *Cornelius Howland* ran aground in the mud, an unwelcome reminder of perils to be avoided through vigilance and skillful navigation.

"We Seem to Have Very Hard Luck Just Now."

As September began the weather turned cold: "Freezing quite hard . . . About noon raised a spout. Lowered for it. Saw no more of it. Afternoon saw the *James Allen* take a whale. I've got an awful headache. Evening let go anchor in 10 fathoms water," a reassurance that the *Illinois* was in no danger of running aground. Battling a "severe headache & cold" Nathaniel Ransom "raised a whale. Chased him 3 or 4 hours. Lost run of him. Went on board the ship after working ship to windward." Next day he fared no better: "Chased a few whales in the morning. Did not get any. I got within 6 fathoms of two different ones. Several ships got whales. Afternoon & evening chasing whales. Got nothing." And the following day: "Quite a number of ships got whales in sight of us. We lowered several times. Got nothing. We seem to have very hard luck just now."

At last on September 5, a Sunday, he "got a whale and got through in the operation about 10 o'clock. Commenced cutting. Blowing almost a gale wind." The wind blew from the northeast, the direction that could have saved the icebound fleet in 1871. Now it blasted the *Illinois* with such force that the crew had to let go part of the whale, and the ship dragged on the bottom so that the captain gave orders to slip the anchor to avoid colliding with the nearby *Europa*. Nevertheless the *Illinois* struck the *Europa*, which carried away all of the *Illinois*'s headgear, jib boom, sprit-sail, and bobstays and sprung the bowsprit. Officers went on board the *Europa* to assess the damage; it had lost one of its whaleboats and broken the windlass gear in the accident. From the *Europa*'s deck they saw the *Illinois*'s anchor and chain were gone; a cake of ice parted the buoy rope. The ship lost forty-five fathoms (nine thousand pounds) of chain and a three thousand pound anchor.[2] Although the crew saw a bowhead, they could not lower the whaleboats for him, for all hands were employed in clearing away the wreckage, setting storm sails, and close-reefed topsails. Once the *Illinois*'s damaged gear was patched together, the men resumed mincing and boiling blubber from the whale caught before the storm.

On September 9, the *Illinois* took a small bowhead toward evening and finished cutting him in about 10 o'clock at night. Without a respite, the second mate and Nathaniel Ransom each killed a bowhead the following day. Once again the wind blew so heavily that it seemed necessary to cut away part of the bowhead. "Tried to cut the whale the second mate got but could not without losing the head. Old man made a mess of it—& the chances are we shall lose the head now. We are now waiting for better weather to make another attempt. Latter part started the tryworks." The weight of a whale's carcass, as much as seventy tons, could capsize a vessel. Shifting the carcass to windward could counterbalance the wind's force pushing the ship to leeward, but once the whale had been brought alongside and made fast to the ship, shifting its immense bulk was nearly impossible.

On September 10, he wrote: "All hands on deck fooling about at 10 o'clock. Moderating. Commenced cutting. Saved all of the second mate's whale. Afternoon boiling. Wind S.E. Mate & second mate off chasing whales. 4th mate and I on board as common. Evening fine weather. Second mate fell in with a lot of scooping whales. Got one. Took him along side." These were the smaller California gray whales, also called mussel diggers for their habit of feeding near the ocean bottom, described here as scooping. They migrated north in summer, following plankton near the coast, and traveled south toward California or Mexico in the winter. The next day brought fine weather:

> Old man sent the mate and second mate in shore for whales. Any amount of them in there. The 4th mate and myself on board cutting and doing the work as usual. Got two ripsacks, one of them alongside. The other cut in.

> [September 14:] Saw lots of whales scooping as usual. Got two little ones. Cut in two. Got ship under weigh. Took them on alongside in evening . . . Here's hoping the old man doesn't send none but mate & second mate for whales. He says that is his style . . .

> [September 15:] Fine weather. Got two whales. Could have taken a dozen if we could take care of them. We have now got about 700 barrels on board and a whale along side. No trick at all to catch whales now here. Ship laying to an anchor.

> [September 16:] Pleasant weather. Boiling and stowing down oil. Any quantity of whales in sight but did not lower for any of them as we have not been able to cut in yet. We are still laying to an anchor.

> [September 17:] Light air from the land. Caught one whale. Cut him in. Boiling oil. Whales are not quite so plenty today

as they have been. The mate & second mate are the only ones
has lowered for whales. I have felt quite bad today. Pains in my
heart, etc. Evening we boiled a little oil.

Amidst the profitable hub-bub of killing whales, cutting them in, and
boiling blubber mid-September had passed. Now, a few days later than
the fateful September 14 when the 1871 whaling fleet was given up for
lost, the Arctic winter sent an icy blast down upon the *Illinois*:

[September 19:] Evening wind from north and blowing a gale.
Lots of heavy cakes of ice in sight. Cooled down the works about
½ past 12 o'clock. Struck a large cake of ice. Stove the port bow.
Caused her to leak badly. Have to keep pump going about all the
time to keep the ship free.

The risk of sinking now added to the difficulties of maneuvering out of
the growing fields of ice, the ship powered only by the fickle northern
winds:

[September 20, Monday:] At daybreak steering to Westward.
Blowing a strong gale of wind from N.E. Heavy snow squalls.
Had lots of ice to combat with. We began to think one while we
should not get along with the ship between ice & land but we
did after carrying away the head gear on the ship. Evening no
ice in sight. Laying still under short sail. Blowing fresh yet.

The ice butting the ship at daybreak skinned a hole in the forward hold.
All hands were called shortly before a second collision with a cake of ice
that carried away the headgear, damaging the rigging in the same area as
the earlier accident with the *Europa*. The crew manned two pumps, the
ship rolling and pitching badly and the water coming in streams forward
in the lower hold. The ship continued to leak two hundred strokes every
twenty-four hours until it reached port in San Francisco.[3] Ransom remembered the *Navy's* leak on his homeward voyage in 1869, and concluded
that Captain Fraser was as inept as Captain William Davis.

Regardless of the perils of sailing a leaking ship north of Point
Barrow, he continued calmly entering weather and work details in his
journal:

[September 21:] Blowing a gale from N.E. Morning started the
works. All hands breaking out and stowing down oil. Ship under
a close-reefed main topsail. Saw several whales. Evening moderating a little.

[September 22:] Strong wind from N.E. Boiling oil. Forenoon

made a little sail. Snow squalls in plenty. Afternoon saw two whales & boats went for them. I stayed on board ship, kept the works going. Boats returned without success. Point Barrow in sight.

The ship struggled to make headway out of the Beaufort Sea while all hands labored "on deck as usual, all day & a good portion of the night. Boiling & stowed down a little oil in the hold. I am feeling rather bad. A bitter cold day this."

Overall, the 1875 season proved milder than the short 1871 summer, allowing several of the sixteen ships in the Arctic fleet to sail over 260 miles east of Point Barrow, and within fifty miles of the mouth of the Yukon's MacKenzie River. But by late September, the fleet moved cautiously westward along the northern Alaskan coast. On September 25, the *Illinois* struggled to approach Point Barrow:

> On the wind trying to work up a little toward Point Barrow. All hands on deck as common boiling and setting up shooks. The steerage boy & my boatsteerer are off duty on account of illness. Boy quite bad.
>
> [September 26:] Wind from Westward. Steering N.E. Boiling and stowing oil. All hands as usual. Setting up shooks, etc. Afternoon saw quite a body of ice. Quite good weather but very cold. Saw a whale, one rising only.
>
> [September 27:] Monday. Light baffling winds. All hands working, about as common. In each other's way. The tryworks are still in operation. I cut one of my fingers with a minsing knife. Some ice in sight. Trying to work ship to S.E.
>
> [September 28:] Strong wind from Eastward. All hands as common on deck looking at one another a good part of time. Stowed down a few barrels of oil & boiled out a few more. At noon started to Westward in company with *Helen Snow*. Saw one or two whales going fast. Old man got a cask of bread from her.

"In an Awful Pickle"

As September ended the crew finished boiling blubber and stowed casks of oil below decks. Nathaniel Ransom, marking the change by bathing (presumably in sea water), worsened his skin irritation: "I had a wash all over & changed my clothes. I have lots of scratching to attend to." Chasing whales without success on October first, he complained that his itching skin gave him no peace: "I am almost wild with the itch. I have to scratch about all of my watch below instead of sleeping." After a few days the itching subsided as he and the second mate were called out to lower for whales: "Afternoon second mate struck a whale. Got capsized. I took his line. Saved the whale for him. I have no boatsteerer yet as mine has not been able to do anything. I have a green hand to steer me or had today." As boatheader, he shot the whale himself, handicapped by the lack of an experienced hand to manage the boat after he struck. Other ships took whales as well, a sign that the bowheads were migrating south for the winter. "Saw the ships *Java & St. George*. Capt. Knowles had 8 whales. *St. George* 6, *Java* 6. Reports *Rainbow* with 12." For the next three days, the *Illinois* boiled blubber, cooling down the tryworks in heavy wind. "[October 10:] Blowing strong gale from N.E . . . Tried to stow down oil. Got one or two casks below. Gave it up for a bad job. Made sail again on the port tack. Evening took in some sail. Blowing a gale. Heavy sea on, etc." The gale continued next day as the crew dropped the lead line every two hours to measure the depth of water. Ransom reported, "I am about crazy with the itch and chilblains."

Plagued by a relentless skin irritation, he scorned Captain Fraser's uncertainty about navigating the ship through the Bering Strait, which was only sixty miles wide. "Old man would like to leave out of this but afraid he can't find the Strait." Wind drove the *Illinois* perilously close to East Cape on the Siberian shore where Captain Frederick Barker's ship *Japan* was wrecked in 1870:

> [October 13:] Blowing fresh from N.E. Forenoon got into the [spot] where the *Japan* went ashore & if it had not been very clear should have gone ashore the same way on account of the old man not knowing anything. At noon stowed down [some] casks of oil. Afternoon went ashore. Got a few casks of water. In St. Lawrence Bay the *Rainbow* came to an anchor close to us about midnight. We got our water on board. Got ship under weigh.

Given Captain Fraser's incompetence, Ransom took comfort from the reassuring presence of Captain Bernard Cogan.

On October 14, the *Illinois* docked at Plover Bay on the Siberian coast to return the four natives who had labored aboard since early June. Ransom tried to row them ashore in his whaleboat but failed:

> Afternoon let go anchor. Carried [off] all the windlass gear. Set to work repairing it. Blowing hard all the while. At midnight I tried to set the Natives ashore but could not on account of it blowing so hard. I had to fight [to get] back to the ship.

[October 15:] At 4 o'clock this morning drifting off fast. Hove up anchor. Found it completely stove. Stock gone and flues spoilt. Made sail trying to hold on 'till it moderates so as to land the natives who are very anxious to get on shore.

[October 16:] Morning managed to land the natives with a part of their provisions but not to their own settlement, but we were lucky to get them on shore at all.

The Chukchi had nowhere to turn in their anger against Captain Fraser and his officers who had shortchanged them. Ransom too turned his back and forgot them, for he was eager to head south. "About 3 o'clock this afternoon made sail & squared away for San Francisco I suppose. Steering S.S.E. I think it about time to go Southward as the decks are all iced up. Evening carried away 3 top gallant sheets and one topsail." Next day, it was still blowing strong from the northeast, and the ship continued to leak very badly. "It takes about one half of time to keep the ship free from water with one pump going in rugged weather like this. Broke out beef & pork today. Repaired damages on sheets, etc. Very cold. Everything aloft one glair [sic] of ice." The rigging remained rigid in the coating of ice, compounding the hazards of climbing aloft and the difficulty of shifting sails.

As the crew took in the cutting stage and stowed away blocks and tackles Nathaniel Ransom was still "in an awful pickle itching & scratching about all the time." Mixing ashes from the tryworks with sea water, the crew stirred up a caustic lye solution and washed off decks. The lye and its caustic vapors exacerbated his condition. The mariners sent down the crow's nest and stowed away all of their iron whale gear except the boat craft. Finally, on October 20, the crew celebrated the end of another season of Arctic whaling: "Hove try works overboard. Evening passed through one of Fox Island passages." He still suffered from his skin malady: "The itch still hangs on me. I have to tare lots of skin off myself every watch below." As the weather continued to moderate the crew hauled baleen up from below decks. "All hands on deck from daylight to dark splitting and scraping bone. My head has ached about all day. Feels some better tonight, but I am half wild with the itch." To his annoyance, Captain Fraser slowed the ship's travel so that the crew could clean and bundle the thirteen tons of bone on board. "Not carrying much sail. Letting the ship go easy to have plenty of time to do the work in. All hands splitting and scraping bone." On Sunday he washed and changed clothes, still itching and scratching. With more time on his hands he felt the return of "Some of old pains on again" and fretted that the "ship leaks very badly."

Approaching California, he fidgeted as the ship lay nearly still and Captain Fraser kept the crew "bothering around from one thing to another. Anything to make work." November 4 favored the ship with "fine weather. Finished drying & bunching bone, 260 bundles of it which will probably average 100 pounds each." The next day they "Overhauled & weighed the walrus ivory. Doing a little of all sorts. Evening I shifted clothes. Set to work. Washed dirty ones."

On November 7, the ship "raised land. Afternoon hauled up chain. Bent on the anchor. Stowed away boat gear, etc. About 4 o'clock p.m. took a pilot on board ship. About 10 miles from 'Frisco with a fair wind. Old man went on shore on the pilot boat. Left the ship to lay off and on to avoid getting hauled up by the crew." Next day the ship was "laying off & on to accommodate old Fraser, give him a chance to skedaddle. The evening came to an anchor on the bar with a fair wind to go in the harbor while all the other ships that were in sight went in. But this kind of work will not be allowed to last much longer." When the *Illinois* docked the next day, Nathaniel Ransom quickly forgot his rancor against the captain: "I got four letters from my darling wife and was made glad to learn that she with my little ones were well as common. Thank the Lord for such good news." As soon as possible, he went ashore to the offices of ship owners Ivory Bartlett and Son: "Sent a letter to my Sarah. Saw Mr. Bartlett. Got $20.00 from him. Afternoon I came on board. Got a gang of men from on shore to carry on the work. I heard that Andrew was in the steamer *Salvadore*."

Once Captain Fraser left the ship, Nathaniel Ransom and the cooper acted as shipkeepers and took charge of the vessel. "Afternoon I went on shore. Got a chain & anchor on board. Came off in a tugboat. The ship *St. George* came in. I am still staying on board the ship with the cooper. It is now evening. Very pleasant. I have been reading my letters again." He went aboard the *Rainbow* to visit Captain Cogan, still regretful not to have remained as part of that crew. At the shipping agent's office on November 13 he "Heard they had got old Fraser in jail."

The charges against Captain Fraser remain unclear. His misman-agement of the *Illinois*'s crew, the damage to the leaking ship, and his lack of navigation skill may have been reported to the owners, but did not end his career, for Fraser was still master of the *Illinois* in the spring of 1876. Under his command, it was struck by the *Marengo* south of Bering Strait and sank at once. That year's summer season saw a second disastrous blow to New Bedford's Arctic whaling industry as twelve ships had to be abandoned in the ice. The *Marengo* was among those lost off Point Barrow.

Ironically, Captain Fraser continued as a whaling captain into the steam age, sailing out of San Francisco into the Arctic for another eighteen years.

For his part, Nathaniel Ransom had finished with whaling for good. He "settled with Wright & Brown for my work in the *Illinois* which did not amount to but little considering what oil I helped take. Evening I put up to the Galt House" in San Francisco. The *Illinois*'s catch of bowhead and walrus oil, baleen and walrus ivory should have earned its third mate a handsome payment for the season's work. The account book of Ivory Bartlett's firm credited the *Illinois* with 2,200 barrels of oil and 26,000 pounds of bone.

The *Whalemen's Shipping List and Merchants' Transcript* for January 11, 1876, estimates the average catch of Arctic vessels in the 1875 season as 1,384 barrels of whale and walrus oil and 14,091 pounds of whalebone. In comparison, the *Illinois* did very well indeed. Despite Captain Fraser's inept navigation and poor management of the work and his crew, he brought home a greater catch than the *Acors Barnes, Java, Onward, Triton, Rainbow,* or *St. George.* The *Whalemen's Shipping List* counted eighteen "fairly profitable" whaling voyages of the past season, and sixteen that resulted in "quite a large average loss."

The newspaper priced oil at 65½ cents per gallon and bone at $1.12½ per pound. Using these figures and a price of forty-five cents per pound for 5,000 pounds of walrus ivory, the season's catch amounted to a value of $75,390. With a third mate's lay averaging one-fiftieth to one-sixtieth, Nathaniel Ransom should have earned perhaps $1,400 for his season's work, as much as his three seasons' voyage on the *Sea Breeze.*

The account book of ship owner Ivory Bartlett's firm calculates the *Illinois*'s cargo value twice; oil at thirty-five cents gold, or at seventy cents; bone ninety cents a pound or $1.25; ivory at forty-five cents gold. In one set of figures the crew receives thirty per cent of the cargo's value; in a second version the crew earns one third.[4] The owners' intent was to recoup the costs of repairs to the vessel after its collision with the *Europa* and the later ice damage, but the account book reveals a system that rewarded labor arbitrarily and incommensurate with the effort of individual crew members.

Ashore in San Francisco, Nathaniel Ransom went to his hotel, where he met his friend Herbert Colson, just arrived in port as master of the bark *Java,* returning like the *Illinois* from the Arctic bowhead season. While Colson had risen from second mate to captain, Nathaniel Ransom—although he signed on under Bernard Cogan as second mate of the *Rainbow*—never served at a rank above third mate.

The next day, Ransom went aboard the *Illinois* with a boatsteerer to whom he sold some of his gear. Then he returned to the mail dock to see if Andrew had arrived, but he had not. "To see him is all that keeps me in 'Frisco. Now I have been writing a few lines to my Darling Wife." Next morning he "carried two shirts to a Chinaman to do up." He found his brother, spent a part of the afternoon with Andrew, and finished a letter to Sarah. That evening he "put it in a letter box & went down town awhile waiting for Andrew to get through courting." Nathaniel and Andrew shared a hotel room and next day went "cruising about from one place to another. We called on Maggie, Bridget's sister in the forenoon."

Together in November of 1875, Nathaniel and Andrew "went to Oakland to see Jim Cushing and his folks." Aboard the *Sea Breeze*, he tended Joshua Cushing, who sailed in company with his older brother Edward. Several men named James Cushing lived in the environs of Mattapoisett, and one or two of them later settled in California. Now Andrew and Jim Cushing accompanied Nathaniel to the Oakland ferry to begin his homeward journey. While Andrew continued longer in his seafaring career, he had now settled permanently in California. He and Nathaniel, separated by the entire North American continent, would never see one another again.

Nathaniel Ransom's third transcontinental railroad journey again brought interruptions caused by weather and accident:

> [November 18:] A heavy rainstorm all day. We were detained 18 hours on account of the freight train off the track. Evening we found ourselves in Truckee [Nevada] 24 hours behind hand in a thick snow storm & on account of a sandslide on the track ahead of us. Have got to stay here all night & another 24 hours longer. The slide struck a train of cars and held them fast, smashing the engine all to pieces.

> [November 19:] About 8 o'clock got started on our journey East. About 38 hours behind hand. We are now [in] Reno & we hear of 2 miles of the track to Virginia being washed away.

The distance from San Francisco that the train should have covered in twenty-four hours had instead taken sixty-six. Impatience and frustration manifested themselves in illness:

> I have got a frightful cold or at least a very uncomfortable one. Could not sleep any last night.

> [November 23:] Near St. Louis. I feel about as sick as they make

them tremendous headache typhoid fever I was 8 hours about
dead.

[November 24:] I didn't succeed in getting asleep in car last
night. But perhaps just as well as I was vomiting all night . . . I
haven't eaten anything. Have got a terrible sore throat.

He arrived in Philadelphia the following day, continued by train to
New York, and shipped home on board the *Propeller City of New Bedford.*
"November 25: This morning I arrived home to Mattapoisett. Was happy
to find my little family all well. As usual I am not feeling very well today."

In his fourth and last whaling journal Ransom complains often of
heart palpitations, chest pains, cold, sore throat, chilblains, "flees" that had
gotten into the straw bed ticking he had filled in Oakland, "sever headache" and sore muscles, feeling "stiff as a board." Aside from arduous
toil without sleep, long spells of boredom and friction with the captain,
several other causes account for his complaints. First, the diet aboard the
Illinois included almost no fresh fruit or vegetables. By April in Mattapoisett, he would have eaten parsnips wintered over in the vegetable garden,
soon followed by dandelion greens and rhubarb. But Nathaniel Ransom
and his shipmates left Massachusetts in March, "spring poor" after a
winter diet with little if any fresh produce. Under these conditions, men
were likely to develop scurvy, the disease that killed one of the survi-
vors of the *Japan* shipwreck who had survived the Arctic winter on the
Eskimo diet of walrus blubber and little else. Not until 1932 was scurvy
clearly traced to a deficiency of vitamin C. It could be prevented with
an adequate supply of fresh produce, or fresh meat, particularly organ
meats, but the whalemen often lacked both. Food poisoning from spoiled
meat or bacteria in contaminated water also caused the vomiting or diarrhea that Ransom and fellow crew members suffered from time to time.

Unsanitary conditions likely caused or at least exacerbated skin
conditions. Constantly wet by salt water and chilled through, Ransom
lacked every comfort. Skinning walrus on deck or working at the trypots
caused a sweat that clung to him beneath his heavy fur clothing. As the
weather grew colder and days abruptly shorter, Ransom changed his
clothes only every four to six weeks, and likely slept in them regularly.
Fresh water was rationed aboard ship, so that washing clothing or himself
in anything fresher than seawater became a rare luxury. While the crew
was actively chasing whales and boiling down their blubber, men worked
ceaselessly beneath the midnight sun. On June 19 he wrote, "I've felt
stiffer than a board all day long. Back ache, etc. Have had 3 hours sleep

out of 24." The most frightening ailment was the rapid heartbeat that robbed him of breath and strength. Even for a young man—Ransom was not yet thirty—whaling labor was killing. He would never return to it.

Nathaniel Ransom at home with wife Sarah.

Epilogue: Home from the Sea

At home in Mattapoisett after he returned from his fourth and final voyage aboard the *Illinois*, Nathaniel Ransom considered how best to support his precious little family. In addition to Laura (little Elma) and baby Eunice, Sarah gave birth to sons Clarence, in 1878, and Everett, the following year. Nathaniel and Sarah Ransom's little Cape Cod house stood close to the Mattapoisett shipyards that had built so many whaling vessels—the *Clara Bell*, *Elisha Dunbar*, *Europa*, *Reindeer*, *Onward*, *Plover*, *Contest*, and *Almira*. One after another the shipyards closed. Caulkers laid down their mallets, riggers put away their tools, sailmakers rolled up huge sheets of canvas and laid their needles in a nest of oily wool inside a wooden case. As whaling declined, what trade there was drew toward New Bedford. Nathaniel Ransom hung his muskrat coat in the woodshed, for Sarah objected to the smell of blubbery smoke and whale oil that clung to it.

Her father Ephraim Dexter was grateful for his son-in-law's work alongside him in the fields and the barn. After years of repairing whaleboats and cobbling together pens for potatoes or a platform in front of the tryworks, Nathaniel Ransom loved carpentry, the feel of the wood smoothed by his plane, or the scent of fresh sawdust under his saw. He and the old ship's caulker agreed on making every seam and joint tight against the wind and weather. He earned a little cash working on Mattapoisett's roads for his own father and for Father Dexter and others, for each household was charged a highway tax, or required to supply labor in payment. He carried schoolgirls to Tabor Academy in Marion in his horse and buggy, and he cut ice from fresh water ponds in the wintertime.

In 1880, Nathaniel Ransom sold his little house at the corner of Foster Street and Shipyard Lane. In the promising month of April 1881, he bought a farm in Dextertown on the Marion Road running toward New Bedford. The land had belonged to Joseph Dexter, one of Sarah's uncles, and bordered her father's farm. The large barn could shelter the horse and buggy, with a spacious hayloft above. The house, gable end toward the road, was painted mustard yellow, with cranberry trim for the window frames and doors. A broad stone slab served as doorstep, with tall white and purple lilac bushes either side of the doorway. Behind the main room stood a summer kitchen with a hand pump to draw water from the large cistern into the soapstone sink. Upstairs were bedrooms enough for the children and a front parlor with shelves for the shells he had brought back to Sarah, the walrus ivory picture frame, and a few other oddments from his travels.

Here Nathaniel Ransom earned a living from farming and gardening on his own land and tilling Ephraim Dexter's farm and part of the old Gideon Dexter land on Pine Island Road. In four whaling voyages he had missed nine growing seasons at home, the gentle lift of air that signals spring, the fattening lilac buds, the spurt of yellow forsythia, and then the cycle of garden plants. He sowed peas and cabbages as soon as a sharp spade could open the earth. Sarah dug dandelions, washed the bitterness out of them, and boiled them with a bit of salt pork. Nathaniel cut spears of asparagus, shaded from green to mauve, to ivory, and then the red stalks of rhubarb, his mouth watering for a tart rhubarb pie. After years of subsisting on hardened sea bread and salt junk, his taste buds ached for whatever grew from the earth.

Summer visitors who frequented Marion and Mattapoisett to escape the heat of throbbing cities like Boston and Providence appreciated fresh milk, fresh eggs, and garden vegetables. Where Prospect Street met the County Road that ran over Hammond Hill on its way from Marion toward New Bedford, William Dexter opened a store handy to the carriages and travelers passing by. He was some relation to Sarah, and his small general store readily took Nathaniel Ransom's vegetables in trade for household supplies.

Pondering how the Dexter family absorbed Nathaniel Ransom, I came at last to solve the riddle of my grandmother's story of the frozen seamen who had lost their lives going to the aid of others. As the trajectory of my study looped back to its beginning, I visited a Hiller cousin, like me a great-granddaughter of Captain Matthew Hiller. She immersed herself in the history of Marion and Mattapoisett, attracted to genealogies of their families, few more numerous in their branches and descendants than the Dexters. In the genealogy she lent me, I read the story of Ephraim Dexter's father, Gideon, born in 1781, a caulker by trade. A clipping from an unidentified New Bedford newspaper reported his tragic death on the last day of January in 1827.

On that day the sloop *Betsey* of Wareham took shelter in Mattapoisett harbor, hauling in as far as possible due to ice. Soon the sloop could be seen drifting out toward Buzzards Bay and away to sea. Several people went to her assistance. About 7 p.m., the sloop's crew lost a small skiff overboard, and Gideon Dexter, age forty-six, and Caleb Dexter, thirty-four, apparently cousins, took a boat and went to recover the skiff. Battling a strong north wind and extreme cold, they failed to return to the ship, which was run ashore, and the persons aboard were landed with much difficulty wet and much exhausted. The next morning a search was mounted for the two Dexter men, one in the lost skiff and one in his own boat. The skiff was found on Goat Island a half-mile away, and the body of Caleb Dexter found lying on the marsh frozen. The other boat drifted across Buzzards Bay and was picked up near East Chop off Holmes Hole (today Woods Hole on Cape Cod) with the body of Gideon Dexter, also frozen. "His hands were much lacerated and the oar battered to pieces from which it appears that he exerted himself to return until exhausted." Gideon left a wife and nine children; Caleb had a wife and aged parents to mourn their loss.[1]

Not every feature of my grandmother's story squared with this event, for the dead men had not perished on a North Atlantic whaling voyage. Nevertheless, the substance of the story—men frozen to death in attempting to rescue others—proved true. As for Gideon Dexter's wife, Mary, even without the second sight she knew that her husband had not returned by morning, and must have assumed he was dead or drowned. Their fourth child, Ephraim, Sarah Dexter's father, was one of the nine whom she would have to rear alone. And before he settled down to the trade of ship's caulker, Ephraim himself made two whaling voyages and was once shipwrecked. My grandmother's story, the death of her great-grandfather, the persistence of men in the seafaring that took their lives, lent a tinge of fatalism to the craft of whaling. At the same time, once I realized that Gideon Dexter's death had nothing to do with Nathaniel Ransom, I was left to wonder why my grandmother had in fact never shared any memories of her father with her grandchildren.

Whaling changed Nathaniel Ransom's family forever, scattering the seven brothers from New York to California. Over a quarter century, the Ransom men embarked on twenty-two whaling voyages. None rose to the rank of captain; none grew rich from oil and bone. Charles died of spinal injuries after two journeys in pursuit of sperm whales. James, Sidney, and Theodore left whaling after the Civil War. James and his wife Almeida had two daughters, Frances and Etta, and the family moved into New Bedford, where James worked as a carpenter. After the death of his wife, James put in to the Sailors' Snug Harbor in New York City, and when he died at the age of seventy-three, he was laid to rest in Mattapoisett's Pine Island cemetery. Nearby, Charles, dead at twenty-one, already lay beside their parents. After Sidney's wife Lucy died on Martha's Vineyard, he moved to California, where he married a woman who had immigrated from Norway with her parents. The couple lived first in San Francisco, whose seaport grew and prospered as New Bedford's whaling fleet declined. Sidney turned to farming in Hayward, California, and like James, he stayed for a time in a home for disabled Union volunteers, naming his illnesses as asthma and heart disease. He outlived his brothers, dying at the age of eighty-nine, and lies buried in the Lone Tree cemetery in Hayward, a continent away from his family's Mattapoisett resting place in the Pine Island burial ground.

Theodore's travels as a merchant trader retraced some of the whalemen's routes. His old canvas trunk bears labels from London, Paris, and more distant ports. When he died in Brooklyn of pneumonia at the age of fifty-three, Aunt Josie brought him home to the cemetery in Mattapoisett, where she lived alone for the next seventeen years.

Sidney Ransom.

Theodore Ransom.

Joseph Henry Ransom, the brother closest in age to Nathaniel, remains something of an enigma, for the two men never exchanged letters, and Nathaniel's journals do not mention him. Home from the 35th US Colored Infantry in March of 1865, he married Mary Sampson Faunce, daughter of an eminent family of Baptist pastors that included the ninth president of Brown University. They lived with their four children in Mattapoisett, and then in Pembroke, Massachusetts. At thirty-two Joseph decided to return to whaling, departing in December 1876 aboard the *Pacific* for the Arctic bowhead hunt. Apparently he never returned to his wife. Perhaps Mary's religiosity alienated Joseph, for she became a preacher like her father, William Faunce. By 1900 Joseph lived in a Sacramento boardinghouse among Irish and Canadian immigrant day laborers, listing his occupation as carpenter. Before dying at the age of eighty-three, Joseph too took refuge in a newly established California veterans' home, in Yountville in Napa County.

Andrew, the youngest of Nathaniel's brothers, did not marry his sweetheart Bridget, whom he had introduced to Nathaniel in San Francisco. He did wed a woman named Marcella, who was born in Ireland,

Joseph Ransom.   Andrew Ransom.

and they named their son Joseph. Andrew never returned to Mattapoisett after sailing as boatsteerer on the *Progress* in October of 1870. He left the sea, earning his living as a journalist and editor in Santa Clara. Later he published a "Pacific Calendar" in San Jose.

For a time the brothers apparently kept in touch, with their parents at least. All three sent home to Mattapoisett studio photographs of themselves, in identical cardboard frames. One of Nathaniel's children, perhaps Eunice, labeled each one in the family album: Uncle Sidney, Uncle Joseph, Uncle Andrew, and noted beside the two last, "Cal." She had never seen them. Andrew's letters reveal that although he was only about thirty miles from Sidney—a distance either could have rowed in a whaleboat—they lost touch with one another.

In May of 1876, sixty-five-year-old father James Ransom married for the third time, a woman named Desire Adams. When he found himself in financial need a few months before his death, it was Andrew who provided assistance, turning over to his father the small balance in his New Bedford bank account. "Dear Father, I received a letter from you a few days ago" Andrew wrote in 1897. "[I] was glad to know that you still live but am sorry to hear that in these your last days you are in want financially . . . Since we have met dear Father more than a quarter of a century has elapsed, and the chances are we shall never meet again in this World." Six months later Andrew wrote to his father again and wanted to know if:

> Sidney & Joseph [are] still in Cal[ifornia]. I have not heard from them in years. The Boasted McKinley Boom has not struck us yet. But in 1900 we hope to have a Bryan Boom that will sweep the trust and Monopolies from this Country. I am on the reception Committee to receive him in San Jose July 8th. I don't like to mix in Politics. But it is a case of Root Hog or Die.

Versions of that old folk song circulated throughout the nineteenth century. The Ransom brothers heard it often during the Civil War years. One variant typified their hardscrabble lives in whaling, farming, carpentry, and other trades:

> Sometimes it's dreadful stormy and sometimes it's pretty clear
> You may work a month and you might work a year.
> But you can make a living if you'll come alive and try
> For the whole world over, boys, it's root hog or die.

Although my knowledge of Nathaniel Ransom's daily existence dims with the end of his whaling journals, I imagine him trudging down to

Mattapoisett's Pico Beach, where he ties his boat safely above the high-water mark. He has built himself a trim little sailboat, two-thirds the scale of a whaleboat, and turned hull upwards, or he would say, hove down. This morning sun sparkles on the wavelets curling in from Ned's Point, and he sniffs at the wind as he fills his pipe, for he has never been able to really quit using tobacco. Coming across the wet sand he recognizes a familiar shape, his childhood schoolmate Lilburne Hiller. Lilburne wears a full beard now and an old slouch hat. A clamming fork, tines upward, rests on his left shoulder, and in his right hand he swings a clamming basket of quahogs, just half full, because he lives alone. No one pesters Lilburne over his housekeeping; he just opens the front door and the back door of his old farmhouse and lets the wind sweep the floors. He plants a big garden, three rows of sweet corn for himself and three for the crows. Now he nods to Nathaniel Ransom, his eyes crinkling at the brilliant sun. Together the two old friends turn the sailboat over and carry it down to the water. Nathaniel Ransom nods his thanks and swings his dinner pail into his boat. Sarah has packed him a little bread slathered with grape preserves, and an apple or two. He arranges his fishing pole and bait and coils his line and locates the bucket used for bailing. He still thinks of these things as his boat craft. He pulls up the sail and settles himself at the stern, one hand on the tiller. Sometimes those old aches plague him still: the left side strained hoisting oil casks aboard the *Polani*, or the scar where he cut his hand with the mincing knife. But mostly these former comrades leave him in peace once he is a cod-fishing. His boys are old enough to pull an oar now, but Clarence and Everett are at school, so he has the day to himself. Steering out toward Strawberry Point he muses that there is no finer prospect than an outgoing tide and a fair breeze on a day of pleasant weather.

The whaleman—who had watched other shipmates slide down to a watery grave—died at home on land. Nathaniel Cushing Ransom lay abed in February of 1907, wracked by kidney disease and weakened by heart failure. At least he waited to meet death in his own warm bed, with Sarah's aging face above him, and Eunice, Clarence, and Everett nearby. Laura lived a hundred miles to the north, with her spindly-legged husband and her five-year-old son. He was a handful, that boy. The old man's thoughts turned to companions from the *Sea Breeze* who never reached home again: the two mates felled by typhoid and buried at Port Stanley in the Falkland Islands, boatsteerer Jack Mather left in a makeshift hospital in the Sandwich Islands, another hapless boatsteerer who became entangled in the line and vanished in the Bering Sea, and Charles Cornell, who died days after falling from the rigging. He himself would have a grave near his own home in the little Pine Island cemetery, where Sarah's parents and Philander and Phebe already lay, and his own brothers Charles and Theodore with their parents not far away.

In the year of Nathaniel Ransom's death, 1907, Susan Davis also died, long resettled in Vermont after the unproductive voyage of the *Navy*. In New Bedford, the *Whalemen's Shipping List and Merchants' Transcript* had shrunk to just two pages; the list of whaling vessels at sea and in port, prices of oil and bone, and advertisements for clothing, whale oil, spermaceti, and whalebone take up all of page one, with page two devoted to human interest stories and fiction. In the February issue the editor complains of international "tramps" who immigrate to America in search

Nathaniel Ransom, Christmas 1897.

of higher wages, then return to their native lands to live in idleness. In New York, a new forty-two story Singer building causes the newspaper's editors to question whether it is really safe from fire, for stories of the 1906 San Francisco earthquake and ensuing inferno are fresh in readers' memories. The writer fears that in the event of fire people in the Singer building's upper stories will have to wait "with as much calmness as they can muster" for the fire to be put out—or the alternative. The 1871 whaleship crews confronting the prospect of winter in the Arctic mustered such calm in the face of impending starvation.

The March 12, 1907, *Whalemen's Shipping List* reviews the whale fishery for 1906: only twenty bowheads and one right whale were captured in the northern Pacific the past season. The vessels imprisoned in the ice in 1905 were all released without loss of life. One San Francisco steam-powered whaleship was lost in fog, together with two bowheads just taken. The northern Pacific whaling fleet for 1907 consists of nine steam-powered vessels, two barks, and two schooners. The Atlantic whaling fleet numbers nineteen ships. Their success for 1906 showed a preponderance of sperm whaling, though prices for sperm oil averaged just fifty cents a gallon, and no price was quoted for whale oil. Surprisingly, Arctic whalebone sold for five dollars a pound, a rate that made bowhead whaling pay, despite the diminished catch. Fifteen steamers and sailing barks continued to name New Bedford as their hailing port, with eight hailing from San Francisco and a very few from Norwich, Connecticut, and Provincetown at the tip of Cape Cod. Smaller Buzzards Bay ports and Nantucket had disappeared from the list altogether.

A century has passed since the whaleman's death. Everyone who ever knew him has now followed him into that last unknown place. Perhaps there is a non-human witness. Today marine zoologists have evidence that some Arctic whales may live as long as two hundred years. Bowheads have been found in recent times with old Inupiaq and Chukchi spear points made of bone or stone embedded in their flesh, overgrown by protective layers of blubber. These weapons were last used in the 1870s, before the Eskimos obtained iron weapons from the whalemen, before they salvaged the toggle irons, guns, and lances from the 1871 wrecks. More recently marine scientists have dated bomb lances from the old Pierce's whaling guns used in the 1880s and found in bowheads taken in 2007. And so perhaps somewhere a bowhead calf who escaped death from Nathaniel Ransom's bomb lance gun still exists, an ancient spirit now, still swimming the frigid waters of the Okhotsk Sea, the Bering, the Beaufort, or the Chukchi.

End Notes

Notes to Chapter I: A Man at Fourteen

1. Edward F. R. Wood with Judith Navas Lund, *The Ports of Old Rochester; Shipbuilding at Mattapoisett and Marion* (New Bedford: Quadequina Publishers, 2004), p. 83–84.

2. The price of sperm oil and estimate of Sidney Ransom's earnings are derived from the account of the voyage given by his shipmate, Matthew Hiller. See Grace Crombie Woods, "Captain Hiller Tells Capture by *Alabama*," *New Bedford Sunday Standard*, January 5, 1930.

3. For the names, sizes, ranges, and habits of various whales and dolphins I rely upon Charles M. Scammon's *The Marine Mammals of the North-western Coast of North America together with an Account of the American Whale Fishery*. (San Francisco: John Carmany, 1874). Modern descriptions of marine mammals often give smaller sizes for the various species, and the names of the cetaceans common when Nathaniel Ransom and Scammon described them differ somewhat from terms in use today.

4. Samuel Colony, *A Private Journal of a Whaling Voyage to the Atlantic Pacific and Indian Ocean as kept by Samuel Colony of Dover, NH on board Barque Barnstable of New Bedford Massachusetts, Brownson Commander; May 22, 1860*. New Bedford Whaling Museum Research Library, ODHS Log #553. Apparently shipmate Gilman Clark took over keeping the journal as of May 24, 1861: "Remarks on board Bark Barnstable as kept by G. S. Clark." Like Colony and Nathaniel Ransom, Gilman Clark was just a seaman.

5. Robert Lloyd Webb, *On the Northwest; Commercial Whaling in the Pacific Northwest 1790–1967* (Vancouver, BC: University of British Columbia Press, 1988), p. 36.

6. For present day names of Arctic locations and their latitude and longitude I have relied upon John R. Bockstoce and Charles F. Batchelder, "A Gazetteer of Whalers' Place-Names for the Bering Strait Region and the Western Arctic," *Names: Journal of the American Name Society* 26, no. 3 (1975): 258–70.

7. Zephaniah W. Pease, ed. *History of New Bedford* 3 vols. (New York: Lewis Historical Publishing Company, 1918), 1: 40–41.

8. William M. Davis, *Nimrod of the Sea* (New York: Harper, 1874), p. 380–81.

9. From *John T. Perkins Journal at Sea, 1845.* Quoted in Mary Brewster, *"She Was A Sister Sailor": The Whaling Journals of Mary Brewster, 1845–1851,* ed. Joan Druett. (Mystic, CT: Mystic Seaport Museum, 1992), p. 60.

10. Scammon quotes other prices: sperm oil $1.78; whale oil $1.28 a gallon; bone $1.80 a pound. *Marine Mammals of the North-western Coast of North America,* p. 242. Scammon's figures result in a total value of sperm oil: $4485.60; whale oil: $83,260; and bone: $45,000. Total catch value: $132, 746, of which 1/200th = $664. Subtracting charges for slops chest, liberty money, etc. Ransom earned perhaps $600 for four years at sea.

11. Ebenezer Grinnell, Logbook of the *Clara Bell,* Providence, RI Public Library, Nicholson Whaling Collection, Reel Nr. 153.

12. These sparse details come from William A. Warden and Robert L. Dexter, *Genealogy of the Dexter Family in America; Descendants of Thomas Dexter* (Worcester, MA, 1905), p. 289, entry for Sarah A. Dexter.

Notes to Chapter II: "Who wouldn't sell a farm to go whaling?"

1. Information on the bowhead whale hunt and the decimation of that population comes from several sources by John R. Bockstoce and others. In particular I have drawn upon his "Preliminary Estimate of the Reduction of the Bowhead Whale Population by the Pelagic Whaling Industry 1848–1915." *Marine Fisheries Review* 42, nos. 9–10 (1980): 10–27 and John R. Bockstoce with John J. Burns, "Commercial Bowhead Whaling in the North Pacific Sector." *The Bowhead Whale* (Lawrence, KS: Society for Marine Mammology, 1993), p. 563–578.

2. Quoted in Peter Nichols, *Final Voyage; a Story of Arctic Disaster and One Fateful Whaling Season,* (New York: Putnam, 2009), p. 163.

3. The official logbook of the *Sea Breeze,* kept by various officers, is New Bedford Whaling Museum Research Library, ODHS #490A.

4. Charles Boardman Hawes. *Whaling* (Garden City, NY: Doubleday, Page & Company: 1924), p. 252.

5. *Mark Twain's Letters from Hawaii* (Letter dated Honolulu, April 1866), (Honolulu: University of Hawaii Press: 1966), p. 66.

6. Twain, 72.

7. Ransom clearly identifies his location as Ellis Island harbor, west arm of the northeast gulf in the Sea of Okhotsk. I have been unable to identify a modern name for this island or for Grampus and Crag Islands.

8. R. D. Wicks, Logbook of the *Sea Breeze,* Providence, RI Public Library, Nicholson Whaling Collection, Reel Nr. 242.

Notes to Chapter III: "This Three or Four Years Lot of Trash"

1. Laura Jernegan Spear and Marcus Wilson Jernegan, "A Child's Diary on a Whaling Voyage," *The New England Quarterly* 2, no. 1 (1929): 125–139.

2. Harold Williams, ed. *One Whaling Family* (Boston: Houghton Mifflin, 1964).

3. The journal kept by Susan Davis is identified as the Logbook of the *Navy*, New Bedford Whaling Museum Research Library, ODHS #0973. Some information about the lives of captains' wives in Honolulu is derived from Augusta Penniman, *Journal of a Whaling Voyage 1864–1868* (Eastham, MA: Eastern National Park and Monument Association, 1988). The author's husband, Edward Penniman, was captain of the whaling bark *Minerva*. See also Emma Mayhew Whiting and Henry Beetle Hough, *Whaling Wives* (Boston: Houghton Mifflin, 1953). Also useful is Mary Brewster, *"She Was A Sister Sailor": The Whaling Journals of Mary Brewster, 1845–1851.*

4. Captain Timothy Packard titled his journal of the voyage aboard the *Henry Taber* "His Book" and recorded events aboard ship from its departure on October 23, 1868 through June 29, 1870. (Providence, RI Public Library, Nicholson Whaling Collection, Reel Nr. 317.) Packard frequently included aphorisms and poetry in his journal.

5. These details come from Nathaniel Ransom's journal for the following year's voyage aboard the *John Wells*; the entry for June 12, 1870, notes that he came home a year ago, i.e., on June 12, 1869, when the *Navy* returned to New Bedford.

Notes to Chapter IV: "May God Have Mercy on This Whaling Fleet and Deliver Us from These Cold and icy Shores."

1. The Logbook of the *Seneca* kept by George Duffy covers the dates October 16, 1869 through September 14, 1871. New Bedford Whaling Museum Research Library, ODHS #7.

2. In addition to Captain Timothy Packard 's journal of his voyage as master of the *Henry Taber* information comes from the journal of boatsteerer Abram G. Briggs aboard the ship (New Bedford Whaling Museum Research Library Log #801). Briggs's account covers October 22, 1868, through the end of the voyage and the ice trap of 1871. Personal entries continue into November, 1871. Briggs illustrated his journal with pen and ink sketches of ships and the scenes surrounding them. First mate John R. Stivers kept the log of the *Henry Taber*'s last voyage from October 22, 1868, to September 13, 1871. New Bedford Whaling Museum Research Library, ODHS #282.

3. Captain Pease published his description of the 1870 bowhead season in New Bedford's *Whalemen's Shipping List and Merchant's Transcript* (November 29, 1870): 3.

4. Captain Valentine Lewis kept the log of the *Thomas Dickason's* voyage: November 2, 1869–September 14, 1871 (Providence, RI Public Library, Nicholson Whaling Collection, Reel Nr. 174.)

5. A. Howard Clark, "The Pacific Walrus Fishery," in G. B. Goode, *The Fisheries and Fishery Industries of the United States,* vol. 2, Section 5, Part 17 (Washington: GPO,1884), p. 77.

6. Verse written by journal keeper aboard *Eliza Adams* voyage 1852–1854. Quoted in Robert Lloyd Webb, *On the Northwest,* p. 67.

7. The log of the *Navy*, probably kept by Captain George F. Bauldry, covers October 8, 1869–August 2, 1871. (New Bedford Whaling Museum Research Library KWM #156).

8. Quoted in Julie Baker, "The Great Whaleship Disaster of 1871," *American History* (October 2005): 54.

9. The whaling industry's destruction of the Arctic walrus herd is detailed in John R. Bockstoce and Daniel B. Botkin, "The Harvest of Pacific Walruses by the Pelagic Whaling Industry 1848 to 1914," *Arctic and Alpine Research* 14, no. 3: 183–88.

10. Williams, ed. *One Whaling Family,* p. 236.

11. Whiting and Hough, *Whaling Wives,* p. 153.

12. The rescued captains' tribute to Captain Thomas Mellen was first published in Honolulu October 23, 1871, and reprinted in the *New York Times* on November 14, 1871. The shipwrecked captains' good wishes for Mellen's future success were fulfilled; he continued Arctic bowhead whaling for the next fifteen years.

13. Alexander Starbuck, *History of the American Whale Fishery* (reprint: Secaucus, N. J.: Castle Books, 1989), p. 109.

Notes to Chapter V: "Among the Wrecks"

1. A. Howard Clark in "The Pacific Walrus Fishery" estimates that the Pacific whaling fleet made 128,060 gallons of walrus oil and took 25,400 pounds of walrus ivory in 1875. See G. B. Goode, *The Fisheries and Fishery Industries of the United States,* vol. 2, Section 5, Part 17, p. 318.

2. Details of the collision with the *Europa* and damage to the *Illinois* come from the New Bedford Whaling Museum Library's account book of the Ivory Bartlett firm, item number 2003.97.11; p.2. Owners of the *Europa* brought suit against the firm for damage incurred in the collision on September 6, 1875.

3. Ivory Bartlett account book, p. 2.

4. Rates of pay to the crew of the *Illinois* appear in Ivory Bartlett account book, p. 19–20.

Note to Epilogue

1. Warden and Dexter. *Genealogy of the Dexter Family in America,* p. 108.

Sources

The physical description of Nathaniel Ransom and his journals of voyages aboard the *Barnstable*, *Sea Breeze*, the *Navy*, the *John Wells*, and the *Illinois* are in the Research Library of the New Bedford Whaling Museum. I am indebted to Nathaniel Ransom's great-grandson David R. Anderson for his transcript of Nathaniel Ransom's 1875 journal of his voyage on board the *Illinois*. Dates of whaling voyages and their yield come from the database *American Offshore Whaling Voyages*, from online issues of the *Whalemen's Shipping List and Merchants' Transcript* at www.nmdl.org, and from Alexander Starbuck's *History of the American Whale Fishery*, reprint. Secaucus, NJ: Castle Books, 1989.

Logbooks

The Research Library of the New Bedford Whaling Museum also holds logbooks of the final voyages and loss of the *Henry Taber* and the *Seneca*, and the journal kept by Samuel Colony and Gilman Clark of their voyage on the *Barnstable*. The official logbook of the *Barnstable* voyage belongs to the Providence, Rhode Island Public Library (Nicholson Whaling Collection), as does a logbook from the *Sea Breeze* kept by Rodolphus Delano Wicks, who came aboard the vessel in Hawaii as Nathaniel Ransom left it. The Providence Public Library's Nicholson Collection also owns logbooks of a voyage of the *Mary Wilder*, when Sidney Ransom was its boatsteerer, of the *Matilda Sears*, when Theodore Ransom served as third mate, and of the *Clara Bell*, when Joseph Ransom was a greenhand. While only the third logbook mentions a Ransom brother by name, all supply details of the places visited and the progress of the whale hunt. The Nicholson Collection's logbook of the *Europa* (1866–72) furnishes great detail about prices of "recruits" (food and other wares) in accounts kept by Captain Thomas Mellen. Digitized versions of most of these logbooks are now online.

The Loss of the Arctic Whaling Fleet in 1871

In addition to Nathaniel Ransom's journal of his voyage aboard the *John Wells*, six additional logbooks provided firsthand descriptions of the disaster. Three accounts cover the final voyage of the *Henry Taber*. The Nicholson Collection's logbook of the *Henry Taber*, kept by Captain Timothy C. Packard, ends in June 1870. Boatsteerer Abram Briggs wrote a handsome log of the voyage now in the Research Library of the New Bedford Whaling Museum (log #801). The same collection also contains the vessel's logbook kept by first mate John R. Stivers (ODHS # 282).

The New Bedford Whaling Museum's logbook of the *Thomas Dickason* covers the whaling bark's last voyage under Captain Valentine Lewis, ending with its abandonment in the ice on September 14, 1871. The log of the *Navy*, probably kept by Captain George Bauldry, covers its 1869–1871 voyage and is KWM #156 in the New Bedford Whaling Museum Research Library. The logbook of the *Seneca* kept by George Duffy covers the dates October 16, 1869 through September 14, 1871. New Bedford Whaling Museum Research Library, ODHS #7.

Everett S. Allen, *Children of the Light; the Rise and Fall of New Bedford Whaling and the Death of the Arctic Fleet* (Boston: Little, Brown, 1973) cites Ransom's 1871 journal as one of his sources. Other works which focus on the 1871 disaster include the following:

Harold Williams, ed. *One Whaling Family*. Boston: Houghton Mifflin, 1964. This history of the family of Captain Thomas William Williams includes recollections of the 1871 disaster by his son, William Fish Williams, who was twelve years old and aboard the *Monticello* with his parents and sister.

Julie Baker, "The Great Whaleship Disaster of 1871," *American History* (October 2005): 54–58.

John R. Bockstoce, *Whales, Ice, and Men; the History of Whaling in the Western Arctic*. Seattle: Univ. of Washington, 1986.

Peter Nichols, *Final Voyage; a story of Arctic disaster and one fateful whaling season*. New York: Putnam, 2009. Nichols draws upon *Children of the Light*, identifying it as an unpublished manuscript by Llewellyn Howland III. Nichols also makes use of Ransom's journal, identifying it as the logbook of the *John Wells*.

See also the *Whalemen's Shipping List and Merchants' Transcript* at www.nmdl.org, and Alexander Starbuck's *History of the American Whale Fishery*, pp. 103–109.

Useful for Other Aspects of Whaling:

Bockstoce, John R. with Charles Batchelder, "A Gazetteer of Whalers' Place-Names for the Bering Strait Region and the Western Arctic," *Names: Journal of the American Name Society*, 26:3: (1975): 258–270.

Bockstoce, John R. "A Preliminary Estimate of the Reduction of the Bowhead Whale Population by the Pelagic Whaling Industry 1848-1915," *Marine Fisheries Review* 42, nos. 9–10 (1980): 10–27.

_____, "Nineteenth Century Commercial Shipping Losses," *The Northern Mariner* 16 (April 2006): 62.

_____, and Daniel B. Botkin, "The Harvest of Pacific Walruses by the Pelagic Whaling Industry 1848 to 1914," *Arctic and Alpine Research* 14, no. 3: 183–88.

_____, et al. 'The Geographic Distribution of Bowhead Whales, Balaena mysticetus, in the Bering, Chukchi, and Beaufort Seas: Evidence from Whaleship Records, 1849–1914," *Marine Fisheries Review* 67, no. 3 (2005): 1–43.

_____, *Steam Whaling in the Western Arctic*. New Bedford, MA: Old Dartmouth Historical Society, 1977.

_____, "Alaska Whales and Whaling," *Alaska Geographic* 27: (2000): 36.

_____, "From New England to Bering Strait: The Arrival of the Commercial Whaling Fleet in North America's Western Arctic." *Arctic: The Journal of the Arctic Institute of North America* 37, no. 4 (1984): 528–532.

_____, with John Burns, "Commercial Bowhead Whaling in the North Pacific Sector." *The Bowhead Whale*, Chapter 14 special publication Nr. 2, Society for Marine Mammology, 1993, Lawrence, KS, 563–578.

_____, with John C. George et al. "Preliminary Estimates of Bowhead Whale Body Mass and Length from Yankee Commercial Oil Yield." Paper SC/59/BRG5 presented to International Whaling Commission Scientific Committee, Anchorage, AK, 2007.

Braham, Howard et al. "Spring Migration of the Western Arctic Population of Bowhead Whales," *Marine Fisheries Review* 42, nos. 9-10 (1980): 36–47.

Brewster, Mary. *"She Was A Sister Sailor": The Whaling Journals of Mary Brewster, 1845–1851*. Ed. by Joan Druett. Mystic, CT: Mystic Seaport Museum, 1992.

Busch, Briton Cooper. *Whaling Will Never Do For Me; the American Whaleman in the Nineteenth Century*. Lexington: University of Kentucky, 1994.

Clark, A. Howard. "The Pacific Walrus Fishery." Vol. 2, Section 5, Part 17 of G. B. Goode et al. *The Fisheries and Fishery Industries of the United States*. Washington: Government Printing Office, 1887: 313–318.

_____,"The Whale-fishery." Vol. 2, Section 5, Part 15 of G. B. Goode et al. *The Fisheries and Fishery Industries of the United States.* Washington: Government Printing Office, 1887: 3–218.

Darby, Andrew, *Harpoon, into the Heart of Whaling.* Cambridge, MA: Da Capo Press, 2008.

Dexter, Elisha. *Narrative of the Loss of the Whaling Brig William and Joseph, of Martha's Vineyard.* Boston: Charles C. Mead, 1848.

Dolin, Eric Jay, *Leviathan; the History of Whaling in America.* New York: Norton, 2007.

Gerlach, Craig. "Bowhead Whale (Balaena mysticetus) Length Estimations Based on Scapula Measurements." *Arctic* 46, no. 1 (1993): 55.

Haley, Nelson Cole. *Whale Hunt; the Narrative of a Voyage by NCH Harpooner in the Ship Charles W. Morgan 1849–1853.* New York: Ives Washburn, 1948.

Hawes, Charles Boardman. *Whaling.* Garden City, NY: Doubleday, Page & Company, 1924.

Hoare, Philip. *The Whale; in Search of the Giants of the Sea.* New York: Harper Collins, 2010.

Mahoney, Andrew R. et al. "Sea-Ice Distribution in the Bering and Chukchi Seas: Information from Historical Whaleships' Logbooks and Journals." *Arctic* 64, no. 4 (2011): 466–477.

Mawer, Allen, *Ahab's Trade; the Saga of South Seas Whaling.* New York: St. Martin's, 1999.

Melville, Herman. *Moby Dick.* Ed. Hershel Parker and Harrison Hayford. 2d edition. New York: Norton: 2002.

Pease, Zephaniah W. *History of New Bedford,* 3 vols. New York: Lewis Historical Publishing Company, 1918.

Scammon, Charles. *The Marine Mammals of the North-western Coast of North America together with an Account of the American Whale Fishery.* San Francisco: John Carmany, 1874.

Spear, Laura Jernegan and Marcus Wilson Jernegan. "A Child's Diary of a Whaling Voyage," *The New England Quarterly* 2, no. 1 (1929): 125–139.

Starbuck, Alexander. *History of the American Whale Fishery,* reprint. Secaucus, NJ: Castle Books, 1989.

Verrill, A. Hyatt. *The Real Story of the Whale.* New York: Appleton, 1923.

Webb, Robert Lloyd. *On the Northwest; Commercial Whaling in the Pacific Northwest 1790–1967.* Vancouver, BC: University of British Columbia Press, 1988.

Whiting, Emma Mayhew and Henry Beetle Hough. *Whaling Wives.* Boston: Houghton Mifflin, 1953.

Wood, Edward F. R. with Judith Navas Lund. *The Ports of Old Rochester;*
    Shipbuilding at Mattapoisett and Marion. New Bedford, MA: Quadequina
    Publishers, 2004.

Zerwick, S. A. "A Large Aggregation of Bowhead Whales (Balaena mysticetus)
    Feeding near Point Barrow, Alaska, in late October 1992." *Arctic* 47, no. 3
    (1994): 232.

Genealogy and Family History Sources:

Leonard, Mary Hall. *Mattapoisett and Old Rochester, Being a History of These Towns*
    and also in Part of Marion and a Portion of Wareham. New York: Grafton
    Press, 1907.

Warden, William A. and Robert L. Dexter. *Genealogy of the Dexter Family in*
    America; Descendants of Thomas Dexter. Worcester, MA: 1905.

Acknowledgments

I am most indebted to my cousin David R. Anderson for bringing to my attention Nathaniel Ransom's whaling journals. He also shared his transcription of the 1875 voyage aboard the *Illinois* as well as family photographs and some correspondence among the Ransom brothers. Cartographer Nicole Zachary Adams created the maps of the Arctic and Pacific Oceans to illustrate Nathaniel Ransom's peregrinations.

At the New Bedford Whaling Museum, where the journals are now kept, I wish to thank retired librarian Laura Pereira for her assistance. Mark Procknik handled the illustrations from the museum's collection. Arctic researcher John R. Bockstoce recommended his own work as background material.

Family members supported this project with enthusiasm and helpful suggestions. Naval architect Jonathan Leiby answered numerous questions about ship construction. My cousin Helen Hiller Hills supplied the Dexter family genealogy that solved the riddle of the ancestor who froze to death attempting to rescue others. My sister Eva Hathaway helped me locate Ransom family members on the ground in Mattapoisett and provided food, shelter, and encouragement. Our sister Sally Frink Ryder digitized family photographs. Annaliese Hiller Wolf furnished sources about Hawaii and about women who went whaling. Laura O'Shea Wolf applied her digital enhancement skills to several of the illustrations in this book.

Deepest thanks to Frederick James Wolf, who brought back maps and artifacts from his journey to Alaska. He never doubts my prospects for success. And finally, gratitude goes to his cousin Caroline Wolf, of Alaska, who gave me the handsomest piece of baleen in all New England.

About the Author

Helen Frink is descended from two families of Yankee whalers. When she left her family's farm in Newington, New Hampshire, and made her first voyage, her mother told her never to fear seasickness, for she had salt water instead of blood in her veins.

She studied at the German universities in Marburg an der Lahn and in Freiburg im Breisgau, earning a bachelor's degree in English from the University of New Hampshire, and master's and doctoral degrees in German from the University of Chicago. Her doctoral dissertation, *Animal Symbolism in Hormannsthal's Works*, was published in 1987. She has written numerous scholarly articles and is the author of two town histories: *These Acworth Hills* (1989) and *Alstead Through the Years* (1992). Her book *Women after Communism; the East German Experience* (University Press of America, 2001) examines the effects on women of the transition from socialism to capitalism.

Together with her husband and two daughters, she created a forest homestead in Acworth, New Hampshire, too far from the sea. After three decades teaching French, German, Women's Studies, and Holocaust Studies, she retired from Keene State College as Professor Emerita of Modern Languages. Leaving academia behind, she embarked on the exploration of family history and legend that brought her to the journeys of great-grandfather Nathaniel Ransom. She delights in using original journals, letters, newspapers, and documents to bring to life social and material history centered in New England.